Interactions 2

LISTENING/SPEAKING

Judith Tanka
Lida R. Baker

Jami Hanreddy
Listening/Speaking Strand Leader

McGraw Hill

Interactions 2 Listening/Speaking, Silver Edition

ISBN 13: 978-0-07-333741-8 (Student Book with Audio Highlights)
ISBN 10: 0-07-333741-2
15 VNH 15 14 13

Editorial director: Erik Gundersen
Series editor: Valerie Kelemen
Developmental editor: Mari Vargo
Production manager: Juanita Thompson
Production coordinator: Vanessa Nuttry
Cover designer: Robin Locke Monda
Interior designer: Nesbitt Graphics, Inc.
Artists: Johnathan Massie, NETS, Laura Nikiel, Kay McCabe
Photo researcher: Photoquick Research

The credits section for this book begins on page iv and is considered an extension of the copyright page.

Cover photo: Bob Krist/CORBIS

www.esl-elt.mcgraw-hill.com

The *McGraw-Hill* Companies

A Special Thank You

The Interactions/Mosaic Silver Edition team wishes to thank our extended team: teachers, students, administrators, and teacher trainers, all of whom contributed invaluably to the making of this edition.

Macarena Aguilar, **North Harris College**, Houston, Texas ■ Mohamad Al-Alam, **Imam Mohammad University**, Riyadh, Saudi Arabia ■ Faisal M. Al Mohanna Abaalkhail, **King Saud University**, Riyadh, Saudi Arabia; Amal Al-Toaimy, **Women's College, Prince Sultan University**, Riyadh, Saudi Arabia ■ Douglas Arroliga, **Ave Maria University**, Managua, Nicaragua ■ Fairlie Atkinson, **Sungkyunkwan University**, Seoul, Korea ■ Jose R. Bahamonde, **Miami-Dade Community College**, Miami, Florida ■ John Ball, **Universidad de las Americas**, Mexico City, Mexico ■ Steven Bell, **Universidad la Salle**, Mexico City, Mexico ■ Damian Benstead, **Sungkyunkwan University**, Seoul, Korea ■ Paul Cameron, **National Chengchi University**, Taipei, Taiwan R.O.C. ■ Sun Chang, **Soongsil University**, Seoul, Korea ■ Grace Chao, **Soochow University**, Taipei, Taiwan R.O.C. ■ Chien Ping Chen, **Hua Fan University**, Taipei, Taiwan R.O.C. ■ Selma Chen, **Chihlee Institute of Technology**, Taipei, Taiwan R.O.C. ■ Sylvia Chiu, **Soochow University**, Taipei, Taiwan R.O.C. ■ Mary Colonna, **Columbia University**, New York, New York ■ Lee Culver, **Miami-Dade Community College**, Miami, Florida ■ Joy Durighello, **City College of San Francisco**, San Francisco, California ■ Isabel Del Valle, **Ulatina**, San Jose, Costa Rica ■ Linda Emerson, **Sogang University**, Seoul, Korea ■ Esther Entin, **Miami-Dade Community College**, Miami, Florida ■ Glenn Farrier, **Gakushuin Women's College**, Tokyo, Japan ■ Su Wei Feng, **Taipei**, Taiwan R.O.C. ■ Judith Garcia, **Miami-Dade Community College**, Miami, Florida ■ Maxine Gillway, **United Arab Emirates University**, Al Ain, United Arab Emirates ■ Colin Gullberg, **Soochow University**, Taipei, Taiwan R.O.C. ■ Natasha Haugnes, **Academy of Art University**, San Francisco, California ■ Barbara Hockman, **City College of San Francisco**, San Francisco, California ■ Jinyoung Hong, **Sogang University**, Seoul, Korea ■ Sherry Hsieh, **Christ's College**, Taipei, Taiwan R.O.C. ■ Yu-shen Hsu, **Soochow University**, Taipei, Taiwan R.O.C. ■ Cheung Kai-Chong, **Shih-Shin University**, Taipei, Taiwan R.O.C. ■ Leslie Kanberg, **City College of San Francisco**, San Francisco, California ■ Gregory Keech, **City College of San Francisco**, San Francisco, California ■ Susan Kelly, **Sogang University**, Seoul, Korea ■ Myoungsuk Kim, **Soongsil University**, Seoul, Korea ■ Youngsuk Kim, **Soongsil University**, Seoul, Korea ■ Roy Langdon, **Sungkyunkwan University**, Seoul, Korea ■ Rocio Lara, **University of Costa Rica**, San Jose, Costa Rica ■ Insung Lee, **Soongsil University**, Seoul, Korea ■ Andy Leung, **National Tsing Hua University**, Taipei, Taiwan R.O.C. ■ Elisa Li Chan, **University of Costa Rica**, San Jose, Costa Rica ■ Elizabeth Lorenzo, **Universidad Internacional de las Americas**, San Jose, Costa Rica ■

Cheryl Magnant, **Sungkyunkwan University**, Seoul, Korea ■ Narciso Maldonado Iuit, **Escuela Tecnica Electricista**, Mexico City, Mexico ■ Shaun Manning, **Hankuk University of Foreign Studies**, Seoul, Korea ■ Yoshiko Matsubayashi, **Tokyo International University**, Saitama, Japan ■ Scott Miles, **Sogang University**, Seoul, Korea ■ William Mooney, **Chinese Culture University**, Taipei, Taiwan R.O.C. ■ Jeff Moore, **Sungkyunkwan University**, Seoul, Korea ■ Mavelin de Moreno, **Lehnsen Roosevelt School**, Guatemala City, Guatemala ■ Ahmed Motala, **University of Sharjah, Sharjah**, United Arab Emirates ■ Carlos Navarro, **University of Costa Rica**, San Jose, Costa Rica ■ Dan Neal, **Chih Chien University**, Taipei, Taiwan R.O.C. ■ Margarita Novo, **University of Costa Rica**, San Jose, Costa Rica ■ Karen O'Neill, **San Jose State University**, San Jose, California ■ Linda O'Roke, **City College of San Francisco**, San Francisco, California ■ Martha Padilla, **Colegio de Bachilleres de Sinaloa**, Culiacan, Mexico ■ Allen Quesada, **University of Costa Rica**, San Jose, Costa Rica ■ Jim Rogge, **Broward Community College**, Ft. Lauderdale, Florida ■ Marge Ryder, **City College of San Francisco**, San Francisco, California ■ Gerardo Salas, **University of Costa Rica**, San Jose, Costa Rica ■ Shigeo Sato, **Tamagawa University**, Tokyo, Japan ■ Lynn Schneider, **City College of San Francisco**, San Francisco, California ■ Devan Scoble, **Sungkyunkwan University**, Seoul, Korea ■ Maryjane Scott, **Soongsil University**, Seoul, Korea ■ Ghaida Shaban, **Makassed Philanthropic School**, Beirut, Lebanon ■ Maha Shalok, **Makassed Philanthropic School**, Beirut, Lebanon ■ John Shannon, **University of Sharjah**, Sharjah, United Arab Emirates ■ Elsa Sheng, **National Technology College of Taipei**, Taipei, Taiwan R.O.C. ■ Ye-Wei Sheng, **National Taipei College of Business**, Taipei, Taiwan R.O.C. ■ Emilia Sobaja, **University of Costa Rica**, San Jose, Costa Rica ■ You-Souk Yoon, **Sungkyunkwan University**, Seoul, Korea ■ Shanda Stromfield, **San Jose State University**, San Jose, California ■ Richard Swingle, **Kansai Gaidai College**, Osaka, Japan ■ Carol Sung, **Christ's College, Taipei**, Taiwan R.O.C. ■ Jeng-Yih Tim Hsu, **National Kaohsiung First University of Science and Technology**, Kaohsiung, Taiwan R.O.C. ■ Shinichiro Torikai, **Rikkyo University**, Tokyo, Japan ■ Sungsoon Wang, **Sogang University**, Seoul, Korea ■ Kathleen Wolf, **City College of San Francisco**, San Francisco, California ■ Sean Wray, **Waseda University International**, Tokyo, Japan ■ Belinda Yanda, **Academy of Art University**, San Francisco, California ■ Su Huei Yang, **National Taipei College of Business**, Taipei, Taiwan R.O.C. ■ Tzu Yun Yu, **Chungyu Institute of Technology**, Taipei, Taiwan R.O.C.

Author Acknowledgements

Dedicated to my family, friends and to my students around the world.
—Judith Tanka

This book is lovingly dedicated to my husband Paul and my daughter Galya, and to my dear mother-in-law Faye.
—Lida R. Baker

Photo Credits

Page 3: © Tom Stewart/CORBIS; 4: © The McGraw-Hill Companies, Inc./Mannic Media, photographer; 10: © Comstock Images/JupiterImages; 19 (both), 24: © BananaStock/ JupiterImages; 27: © Jonathan Nourok/Photo Edit; 28: © The McGraw-Hill Companies, Inc./Mannic Media, photographer; 36 (right): © S. Meltzer/PhotoLink /Getty Images; 37: © trbfoto/ Brand X Pictures/Jupiterimages; 38: © Ryan McVay/ Getty Images; 41: © Rob Melnychuk/Getty Images; 43: © John A. Rizzo/Getty Images; 51: © Reuters/CORBIS; 52 (left): © The McGraw-Hill Companies, Inc./Mannic Media, photographer; 52 (right): © Creatas Images/JupiterImages; 58: © Getty Images; 60: © Time & Life Pictures/Getty Images; 62 (top left): AP/Wide World Photos; 62 (top right): © Ted Thai//Time Life Pictures/Getty Images; 62 (bottom): © Reuters/ CORBIS; 65: © Rim Light/PhotoLink/Getty Images; 67 (left): © Kaz Chiba/Getty Images; 67 (right): © Dynamic Graphics/JupiterImages; 69: © C Squared Studios/Getty Images; 75: © Getty Images; 76 (left): © The McGraw-Hill Companies, Inc./Mannic Media, photographer; 76 (right): © Jack Star/PhotoLink/Getty Images; 89: © Digital Vision/Getty Images; 90 (top left): © Dave Thompson/Life File/Getty Images; 90 (top right): © Stockbyte/Punchstock Images; 90 (bottom left): © Royalty-Free/CORBIS; 90 (bottom right): © Keith Brofsky/ Getty Images; 97: © The McGraw-Hill Companies, Inc./Mannic Media, photographer; 98: © Royalty-Free/CORBIS; 101: © Digital Vision; 102: © Digital Vision/Getty Images; 108 (left): © SuperStock, Inc./SuperStock; 108 (right): © PhotoDisc/Getty Images; 110: © BananaStock/ PunchStock; 116: © Keith Thomas Productions/Brand X Pictures/ PictureQuest; 118 (left): © Goodshoot/ PictureQuest; 118 (right): © TRBfoto/Getty Images; 119 (top right): © Tom Grill/Age fotostock; 119 (middle left): © Royalty-Free/CORBIS; 119 (bottom right): © Geoff Manasse/Getty Images; 125: © Bill Bachman/PhotoEdit; 126: © The McGraw-Hill Companies, Inc./Mannic Media, photographer; 133 (top left): © Ryan McVay/Getty Images; 133 (top right): © David Young-Wolff/PhotoEdit; 133 (bottom left): © Royalty-Free/ CORBIS; 133 (bottom right): © Ryan McVay/Getty Images; 139: © Digital Vision/Punch Stock; 144: © Jeff Greenberg/ The Image Works; 146 (top left): © J. Griffin/The Image Works; 146 (top right, middle left and bottom both): © Royalty-Free/CORBIS; 146 (middle right): © Andrew Ward/ Life File/Getty Images; 149: © Getty Images; 150: © The McGraw-Hill Companies, Inc./Mannic Media, photographer; 155: © LaCoppola-Meier/Getty Images; 156: © BananaStock/JupiterImages; 162 (left): © Royalty-Free/CORBIS; 162 (right): © PhotoLink/Getty Images; 167: © Syracuse Newspapers/Jennifer Grimes/The Image Works; 169 (both), 170: © The McGraw-Hill Companies, Inc./Mannic Media, photographer; 173: © Brand X Pictures/PunchStock; 174: © The McGraw-Hill Companies, Inc./Mannic Media, photographer; 180 (top): © Ryan McVay/Getty Images; 180 (middle): © Amos Morgan/Getty Images; 180 (bottom) : © BananaStock/JupiterImages; 185: © Andy Gray; 190: © Digital Vision; 191: © BananaStock/ PunchStock; 197: © NASA; 198: © The McGraw-Hill Companies, Inc./Mannic Media, photographer; 203: © Creatas/PunchStock; 204: © NASA; 207: © Digital Vision/ PunchStock; 211: © C Squared Studios/Getty Images; 215 (top left): Chris Haston/© NBC/ Courtesy Everett Collection; 215 (top right): Everett Collection; 215 (bottom): © NBC/Courtesy Everett Collection; 221: © James Fossett/The Image Works; 222: © Royalty-Free/CORBIS; 227: © White Rock/Getty Images; 229 (top left): © Kevin R. Morris/CORBIS; 229 (bottom both): Courtesy of Wikipedia.org; 238 (left): © image100/PunchStock; 238 (right): © Suza Scalora/Getty Images; 241: © Stockbyte/SuperStock.

Table of Contents

v

Welcome to Interactions/Mosaic Silver Edition

Interactions/Mosaic Silver Edition is a fully-integrated, 18-book academic skills series. Language proficiencies are articulated from the beginning through advanced levels <u>within</u> each of the four language skill strands. Chapter themes articulate <u>across</u> the four skill strands to systematically recycle content, vocabulary, and grammar.

NEW to the Silver Edition:

- **World's most popular and comprehensive academic skills series**—thoroughly updated for today's global learners
- **Full-color design** showcases compelling instructional photos to strengthen the educational experience
- **Enhanced focus on vocabulary building, test taking, and critical thinking skills** promotes academic achievement
- **New strategies and activities for the TOEFL® iBT** build invaluable test taking skills
- **New "Best Practices" approach** promotes excellence in language teaching

NEW to Interactions 2 Listening/Speaking:

- **All new content:** Chapter 10 Ceremonies
- **Transparent chapter structure**—with consistent part headings, activity labeling, and clear guidance—strengthens the academic experience:
  - Part 1: Conversation
  - Part 2: Lecture
  - Part 3: Strategies for Better Listening and Speaking
  - Part 4: Real-World Task
- **New "Student Book with Audio Highlights"** editions allow students to personalize the learning process by listening to dialogs and pronunciation activities multiple times
- **All-new *Interactions* photo program** features a cast of engaging, multi-ethnic students participating in North American college life
- **New vocabulary index** offers students and instructors a chapter-by-chapter list of target words
- **Online Learning Center features MP3 files** from the Student Book audio program for students to download onto portable digital audio players

---

* TOEFL is a registered trademark of Education Testing Service (ETS). This publication is not endorsed or approved by ETS.

Interactions/Mosaic
Best Practices

Our Interactions/Mosaic Silver Edition team has produced an edition that focuses on Best Practices, principles that contribute to excellent language teaching and learning. Our team of writers, editors, and teacher consultants has identified the following six interconnected Best Practices:

Making Use of Academic Content

Materials and tasks based on academic content and experiences give learning real purpose. Students explore real world issues, discuss academic topics, and study content-based and thematic materials.

Organizing Information

Students learn to organize thoughts and notes through a variety of graphic organizers that accommodate diverse learning and thinking styles.

Scaffolding Instruction

A scaffold is a physical structure that facilitates construction of a building. Similarly, scaffolding instruction is a tool used to facilitate language learning in the form of predictable and flexible tasks. Some examples include oral or written modeling by the teacher or students, placing information in a larger framework, and reinterpretation.

Activating Prior Knowledge

Students can better understand new spoken or written material when they connect to the content. Activating prior knowledge allows students to tap into what they already know, building on this knowledge, and stirring a curiosity for more knowledge.

Interacting with Others

Activities that promote human interaction in pair work, small group work, and whole class activities present opportunities for real world contact and real world use of language.

Cultivating Critical Thinking

Strategies for critical thinking are taught explicitly. Students learn tools that promote critical thinking skills crucial to success in the academic world.

Highlights of Interactions 2
Listening/Speaking Silver Edition

Full-color design showcases compelling instructional photos to strengthen the educational experience

Interacting with Others
Questions and topical quotes stimulate interest, activate prior knowledge, and launch the topic of the unit.

Chapter 10

Ceremonies

Connecting to the Topic

1 Who are these people? Where are they from?

2 What are some reasons people have ceremonies?

3 Describe a ceremony that you know about.

In This Chapter

Conversation:	A Baby Shower
Lecture:	Water in Traditional Ceremonies
Using the Context:	Conversations About Ceremonies
Real-World Task:	Making Wedding Plans

❝ There is nothing like a ritual for making its participants think beyond their own appetites, and for making them feel that they belong to something greater, older and more important than themselves. ❞

—Tom Utley, British journalist (1921–1988)

Making Use of Academic Content
Lectures, academic discussions, and conversations among university students explore stimulating topics.

Cultivating Critical Thinking
Critical thinking strategies and activities equip students with the skills they need for academic achievement.

Part 2   Lecture: Exploring Mars

Before You Listen

1 **Prelistening Discussion** Discuss these questions in small groups.

▲ An illustration of the Mars Rover

1. Based on the picture, what does Mars look like? Describe it.
2. What do you think is the function of the rover in the picture?
3. What facts do you know about Mars (for example: distance from Earth, size, atmosphere, climate, etc.)?
4. What scientific news have you heard recently about Mars?

2 **Previewing Vocabulary** Listen to the following words from the lecture. Check (✓) the words you think you know. Discuss their meanings with a partner. Check the other words later as you learn them.

Nouns	Verbs	Adjectives
☐ disaster	☐ analyze	☐ critical
☐ evidence	☐ explore	☐ fascinating
☐ planet	☐ fascinate	
☐ resources		
☐ solar system		
☐ telescope		

Listen

Strategy

Recognizing Facts and Theories
When listening to lectures, especially about science, you need to recognize the difference between *facts* and *theories*.

Fact: proven, true information
Theory: unproven idea, may or may not be true

To hear the difference, listen for signal words and phrases like these:

FACT	THEORY
It's a well-known fact that . . .	(It) may/might /could + verb
(It) has been proven	(It's) possible that . . .
(Scientists) know . . .	(There's) a chance . . .
(There's) strong evidence . . .	possibly/probably

3 **Listening for Fact and Theory in the Lecture** Pay attention to signal words and phrases. Check (✓) Fact or Theory.

      Fact   Theory

1. _____   _____
2. _____   _____
3. _____   _____
4. _____   _____
5. _____   _____
6. _____   _____

Highlights of Interactions 2 Listening/Speaking Silver Edition

Activating Prior Knowledge
Pre-listening activities place the lecture, academic discussion, or conversation in context and allow the student to listen actively.

Enhanced focus on vocabulary building promotes academic achievement.

Part 1   Conversation: What Do You Like to Do for Fun?

Before You Listen

Jeff and his friend Dan play in a rock band. Last night Mari went to a club to hear them play. Today Dan has stopped by the house for a visit.

▲ Jeff, Mari, and Dan

 1 Prelisting Questions Discuss these questions with your classmates.

1. What do you think is happening in the photo?
2. Do you like to listen to music? What kind of music do you prefer? Do you like to go to clubs to listen to music?
3. In your opinion, is it important for two people to have the same tastes in order to be happy together?
4. What are some ways of asking about people's likes and dislikes in English?

2 Previewing Vocabulary Listen to the underlined words and phrases from the conversation. Then use the context to match them with their definitions.

Sentences

_____ **1. A:** Did you <u>have a good time</u> last night?
  B: Not really. The concert was boring.

_____ **2. A:** What do you think of this song?
  B: <u>I'm crazy about it!</u>
  A: I really like it, too.

_____ **3. A:** What is this delicious <u>dish</u>?
  B: It's vegetable lasagna. Carmen made it.

_____ **4. A:** I <u>can't stand</u> that old hat. When are you going to throw it out?
  B: Sorry, I like it.

_____ **5.** Harry and Renata don't <u>see eye to eye</u> on anything, but they are very happily married.

_____ **6.** Ahmed <u>doesn't care for</u> sports. He prefers to read and listen to music.

Definitions

a. to dislike a little

b. to dislike strongly; to hate

c. to enjoy oneself

d. to agree

e. "I love it!"

f. food cooked or prepared in a special way

Listen

3 Comprehension Questions Close your book as you listen to the conversation. Listen for the answers to these questions. After you listen, discuss your answers with a partner.

1. Do Mari and Dan like most of the same things?
2. At the end of the conversation, what do Dan and Mari agree to do together?
3. Fill in the chart with details about Dan's and Mari's tastes and preferences. If information is not given, fill in the box with an X.

	Dan Likes	Mari Likes
Music	rock	jazz
Food		
Art		
Sports		
Movies		

Scaffolding Instruction
Instruction and practice build gradually to support student in the listening tasks.

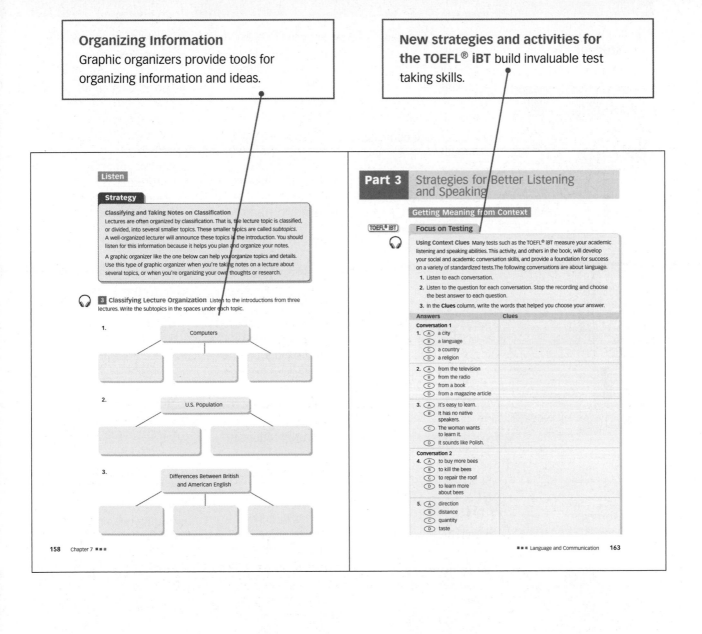

Listen

Strategy

Classifying and Taking Notes on Classification
Lectures are often organized by classification. That is, the lecture topic is classified, or divided, into several smaller topics. These smaller topics are called *subtopics*. A well-organized lecturer will announce these topics in the introduction. You should listen for this information because it helps you plan and organize your notes.

A graphic organizer like the one below can help you organize topics and details. Use this type of graphic organizer when you're taking notes on a lecture about several topics, or when you're organizing your own thoughts or research.

3 Classifying Lecture Organization Listen to the introductions from three lectures. Write the subtopics in the spaces under each topic.

1.

Computers

2.

U.S. Population

3.

Differences Between British and American English

Part 3 Strategies for Better Listening and Speaking

Getting Meaning from Context

TOEFL® IBT **Focus on Testing**

Using Context Clues Many tests such as the TOEFL® iBT measure your academic listening and speaking abilities. This activity, and others in the book, will develop your social and academic conversation skills, and provide a foundation for success on a variety of standardized tests. The following conversations are about language.

1. Listen to each conversation.
2. Listen to the question for each conversation. Stop the recording and choose the best answer to each question.
3. In the **Clues** column, write the words that helped you choose your answer.

Answers	Clues
Conversation 1	
1. Ⓐ a city	
Ⓑ a language	
Ⓒ a country	
Ⓓ a religion	
2. Ⓐ from the television	
Ⓑ from the radio	
Ⓒ from a book	
Ⓓ from a magazine article	
3. Ⓐ It's easy to learn.	
Ⓑ It has no native speakers.	
Ⓒ The woman wants to learn it.	
Ⓓ It sounds like Polish.	
Conversation 2	
4. Ⓐ to buy more bees	
Ⓑ to kill the bees	
Ⓒ to repair the roof	
Ⓓ to learn more about bees	
5. Ⓐ direction	
Ⓑ distance	
Ⓒ quantity	
Ⓓ taste	

Scope and Sequence

Chapter	Listening	Speaking	Critical Thinking
1 Education and Student Life page 2	▪ Listening for main ideas ▪ Listening for details ▪ Making inferences ▪ Getting meaning from intonation ▪ Recognizing compass directions ▪ Understanding expressions and statements of location ▪ Using the prepositions *in, on, at* in addresses and locations	▪ Showing interest ▪ Comparing university systems in different countries ▪ Talking about cheating ▪ Making, accepting, and refusing invitations ▪ Using expressions of location ▪ Describing map locations	▪ Interpreting a photo ▪ Getting meaning from context ▪ Speculating about hypothetical situations ▪ Using a lecture introduction to predict content ▪ Writing effective lecture notes ▪ Using a Venn diagram to compare and contrast
2 City Life page 26	▪ Listening for main ideas ▪ Listening for details ▪ Making inferences ▪ Listening for clues to relationships between people ▪ Following directions	▪ Using the phrase *by the way* ▪ Opening and closing phone conversations ▪ Talking about crime ▪ Expressing frustration ▪ Learning names of professions ▪ Requesting and giving directions ▪ Saying you don't understand	▪ Predicting questions speakers will ask ▪ Getting meaning from context ▪ Speculating about hypothetical situations ▪ Taking notes on statistics ▪ Using transitions as cues for note-taking ▪ Taking notes on an informal talk
3 Business and Money page 50	▪ Listening for main ideas ▪ Listening for details ▪ Making inferences ▪ Distinguishing between *can* and *can't* ▪ Distinguishing between teens and tens ▪ Recognizing expressions of advice	▪ Talking about managing money ▪ Talking about entrepreneurs ▪ Talking about abilities ▪ Using the words *borrow* and *lend* ▪ Asking for, giving, and refusing advice	▪ Outlining a lecture ▪ Getting meaning from context ▪ Taking notes on a process

Vocabulary Building	Pronunciation	Language Skills
■ Terms for academic life ■ Terms for showing interest ■ Terms used at an academic orientation ■ Expressions for making, accepting, and refusing invitations ■ Compass directions ■ Expressions of location ■ *In, on,* and *at* in addresses and locations	■ Identifying and practicing stressed words ■ Identifying and practicing reduced pronunciation	■ Using context clues to guess locations
■ Expressions for opening and closing conversations ■ Terms for expressing frustration ■ Expressions for requesting and giving directions ■ Names of professions ■ Terms for expressing lack of understanding ■ Using the phrase *by the way*	■ Identifying and practicing stressed words ■ Identifying and practicing reduced pronunciation	■ Using context clues to identify a speaker ■ Using context clues to guess a person's job
■ Terms for talking about money ■ *Borrow* vs. *lend* ■ Expressions for asking for, giving, accepting, and rejecting advice ■ Terms for talking about entrepreneurs and the entrepreneurial process ■ Terms related to banking	■ Identifying and practicing stressed words ■ Identifying and practicing reduced pronunciation ■ Pronouncing *can* and *can't* ■ Pronouncing teens and tens	■ Using context clues to identify banking services

Vocabulary Building	Pronunciation	Language Skills
■ Terms related to jobs and careers ■ Expressions for apologizing and reconciling ■ Idioms related to housework ■ Terms signaling cause and effect	■ Identifying and practicing stressed words ■ Identifying and practicing reduced pronunciation ■ Asking and answering negative tag questions	■ Using context clues to guess people's jobs
■ Two- and three-word verbs used in a conversation between neighbors ■ Expressions used to ask for help or a favor ■ Terms used to talk about changes in the American family ■ Expressions used to signal examples ■ Terms used for discussing lifestyles	■ Identifying and practicing stressed words ■ Identifying and practicing the dropped *h* in unstressed words ■ Pronouncing linked phrases	■ Using context clues to guess people's lifestyles
■ Computer terms ■ Expressions for interrupting ■ Expressions signaling similarity and difference ■ Adverbs used for generalizing ■ Correct use of "trip" vs. "travel"	■ Identifying and practicing stressed words ■ Identifying Intonation patterns ■ Saying names and sentences with blended consonants	■ Using context clues to guess about customs and body language

Vocabulary Building	Pronunciation	Language Skills
■ Terms used to talk about friendship vs. friendliness ■ Terms used for talking about languages and dialects ■ Examples of vocabulary differences between American and British English ■ Interjections ■ Expressions for guessing ■ Slang expressions	■ Identifying and practicing stressed words	■ Using context clues to guess about language and communication
■ Expressions for likes and dislikes ■ Expressions of approval and disapproval ■ Terms signaling paraphrases ■ Ways to say that something is popular	■ Identifying and practicing stressed words	■ Using context clues to identify people's tastes and preferences ■ Using intonation to identify feelings
■ Terms for talking about scientific progress ■ Terms for talking about space exploration ■ Terms for signaling facts and theories ■ Terms for solving a science problem ■ Terms for talking about inventions and discoveries ■ Expressions for signaling surprise	■ Identifying and practicing stressed words ■ Pronouncing the *th* sound ■ Pronouncing *-ed* endings	■ Recognizing signal words to guess the correct answer
■ Expressions to offer, accept, or decline help ■ Terms to express congratulations and sympathy ■ Expressions signaling digressions in a lecture ■ Terms related to ceremonies	■ Identifying and practicing stressed words ■ Using correct stress in compound phrases	■ Using context clues to identify ceremonies

Name: Dan
Nationality: American

Name: Yolanda
Nationality: American

Name: Mari
Nationality: Japanese

Name: Jeff
Nationality: American

Name: **Ali**
Nationality: **American**

Name: **Lee**
Nationality: **Korean**

Name: **Nancy**
Nationality: **American**

Name: **Andrew**
Nationality: **American**

Name: **Alicia**
Nationality: **Mexican**

Chapter 1

Education and Student Life

In This Chapter

Conversation:	On a College Campus
Lecture:	Undergraduate Courses in North America
Getting Meaning from Context:	Conversations About School; Invitations
Real-World Task:	Reading a Map

"Education's purpose is to replace an empty mind with an open one."

—Malcolm Forbes
U.S. art collector, author,
and publisher (1919–1990)

Connecting to the Topic

1 These college students live together in a dormitory. What do you see in the photo?

2 What is good about living like this? What is bad?

3 How and where do university students you know live?

Before You Listen

In the following conversation, an international student meets an American teacher on a college campus.

Culture Note

Colleges and Universities in the U.S.
In the United States, the words **college** and **university** both mean a four-year school after high school that gives academic degrees. However, a college can also be a two-year school where students take basic courses. Many two-year schools are public community colleges; they give associate degrees.

1 **Prelistening Questions** Discuss these questions in small groups.

1. Look at the picture. Describe what's happening. What are the women probably talking about?

2. What questions do you usually ask a person you are meeting for the first time?

3. When you are talking with people, how do you show that you are interested in what they are saying? For example, what do you say? What body language do you use?

4. What are some ways of asking for directions in English?

2 **Previewing Vocabulary** Listen to the underlined words and phrases from the conversation. Then use the context to match them with their definitions.

Sentences

_____ **1.** I'm going to sign up for an exercise class at the gym.

_____ **2.** She's planning to major in art at the University of Washington.

_____ **3.** I don't like classical music, but I am really into jazz.

_____ **4.** You have to get a good education if you want to get ahead in life.

_____ **5.** She has a successful career as a fashion designer.

Definitions

a. to succeed

b. to like or to love (*slang*[1])

c. to focus or specialize in a particular subject at a university

d. to register or to join

e. a profession or a job

Listen

3 **Comprehension Questions** Listen to the conversation. You don't need to understand all the words. Just listen for the answers to these questions. After you listen, discuss your answers with a partner.

1. Where are the women going? Why?

2. Who is Nancy? What does she do?

3. Who is Mari? Where is she from?

4. How did Mari learn to speak English?

5. Why does Mari need to take an English course?

6. What does Mari want to major in?

---

[1] *Slang* means very informal words and expressions that are used only in casual situations.

Stress

In spoken English, important words that carry information, such as nouns, verbs, and adjectives, are usually stressed. This means they are

■ higher   ■ louder   ■ spoken more clearly

than other (unstressed) words. Stress is an important part of correct pronunciation. Listen to this example:

Good **luck** on the **placement** exam.

In this example, the words *luck* and *placement* are stressed.

4 **Listening for Stressed Words** Listen to the conversation again. Some of the stressed words are missing. During each pause, repeat the phrase or sentence. Then fill in the missing stressed words.

Mari: _____ me. Could you _____ me where Kimbell Hall is?

Nancy: Oh, you mean _____ Hall?

Mari: Oh yeah, _____.

Nancy: Do you see that _____ building over there?

Mari: Uh, behind the _____?

Nancy: Yeah, that's it. Come on, _____ going there too. Are you here for the English _____ test?

Mari: Yes, I _____. How about _____?

Nancy: Actually, I'm one of the _____ teachers here.

Mari: Oh really? Maybe I'll be in your _____!

Nancy: It's _____. What's your _____?

Mari: Mariko Honda, but _____ people call me Mari. And you?

Nancy: I'm Nancy Anderson. So, where are you _____?

Mari: Japan.

Nancy: Aha. And, uh, how long have you _____ here?

Mari: Just _____ _____.

Nancy: Really? But your English sounds _____!

Mari: Thanks. That's because my _____ used to come here every summer to visit my grandmother when I was _____. I can _____ pretty well.

Nancy: Mmm-hmmm.

Mari: But now I want to go to _____ here, so I need to improve my skills, especially _____. Yeah, so, uh, that's why I signed up for this _____ program.

Nancy: I see. Uh, what do you want to _____ in?

Mari: International _____. My father has an _____-export company, and he does a _____ of business here in the States.

Nancy: Oh, I see.

Mari: And I _____ want to take _____ classes, because I'm _____ into art.

Nancy: Art and business. Wow. That's an interesting combination. But _____ you study those things in _____?

Mari: Well, sure, but you have to speak good _____ these days to get ahead in _____. It's _____ for my career if I go to college _____.

Nancy: Well, here's Campbell Hall. Good _____ on the _____ exam. It was nice _____ you, Mari.

Mari: Thanks. You too.

Nancy: See you later.

Mari: Bye-bye.

Check your answers using the listening script on page 263. Then read the conversation with a partner. Pronounce stressed words louder, higher, and more clearly than unstressed words.

Reductions

In spoken English, words that are not stressed are often shortened, or reduced. For example, we write: "Could you tell me where Campbell Hall is?" But we say, "Cudja tell me where Campbell Hall is?" Listen to the difference:

Unreduced Pronunciation	**Reduced Pronunciation**
could you	cudja

Reduced forms are a natural part of spoken English. They are not slang. However, reduced forms are not acceptable spellings in written English.

5 **Comparing Unreduced and Reduced Pronunciation** The following sentences are from the conversation. Listen for the difference between unreduced and reduced pronunciation. Repeat both forms after the speaker.

Unreduced Pronunciation	**Reduced Pronunciation**
1. Could you tell me where Kimbell Hall is?	Cudja tell me where Kimbell Hall is?
2. Oh, you mean Campbell Hall?	Oh, y'mean Campbell Hall?
3. How about you?	How boutchu?
4. What's your name?	Whatcher name?
5. My family used to come here every summer.	My family yoosta come here every summer.
6. I want to go to college here.	I wanna go ta college here.
7. What do you want to major in?	Whaddaya wanna major in?
8. You have to speak good English these days to get ahead in business.	You hafta speak good English these days ta get ahead in business.

6 **Listening for Reductions** Listen to the following conversation between an international student and a school office assistant. You'll hear the reduced pronunciation of some words. Write the unreduced forms of the missing words in the blanks.

A: Could you help me, please? I _____ _____ be a student at this school.

B: Oh yeah, I remember you. How are you?

A: Fine, thanks.

B: Can I help you with something?

A: Yes, I _____ _____ get an application for the TOEFL® test.

B: _____ _____ the international TOEFL® iBT? Let's see. They _____ _____ be here on this shelf. It looks like they're all gone. I'm sorry, you'll _____ _____ wait until they come in next week.

A: _____ _____ sending me one when they come in?

B: No problem. _____ _____ name and address?

Check your answers in the listening script on page 263. Then read the conversation with a partner. Try to use reduced forms.

7 Reviewing Vocabulary Discuss your answers to the following questions with a partner. Use the underlined vocabulary in your answers.

1. If you are a college or university student, what is your major, or what subject do you plan to <u>major in</u>?

2. If you are working, what is your <u>career</u>, or what career would you like to have in the future?

3. Is it important for you to know English if you want to <u>get ahead</u> in your career? Why or why not?

4. <u>Are</u> you <u>into</u> art, like Mari? What else <u>are</u> you <u>into</u>?

5. Why did you sign up for this English course? Are you going to <u>sign up</u> for another English course after this one?

Using Language Functions

SHOWING INTEREST

English speakers show that they are interested and paying attention by

- making eye contact,
- nodding their heads, and
- using specific words and expressions for showing interest. For example:

Really?	Oh?
Yeah?	Oh yeah?
I see.	Mmmm-hmm.
And?	Oh no!

8 Showing Interest Work in small groups. Take turns telling each other stories about important events in your lives. As each student speaks, show interest in different ways. You can use the sample topics below or choose your own topics.

- my favorite vacation
- a serious accident
- the best meal I have ever eaten
- the day I met my boyfriend/girlfriend/husband/wife
- my first day of high school/college/work

Part 2

Lecture: Undergraduate Courses in North America

Before You Listen

Mari goes to an orientation meeting given by the academic advisor in her English language program. At the meeting, the advisor gives some information about typical undergraduate courses in the United States and Canada.

▲ An academic advisor

Culture Note

Degrees in Most North American Universities
- B.A. or B.S. (Bachelor of Arts/Science): after four years of study
- M.A. or M.S. (Master of Arts/Science): after two additional years
- Ph.D. (Doctor of Philosophy): after two or more additional years

Students who are studying for a B.A. or B.S. are called undergraduates, or "undergrads." Those studying for an M.A. or a Ph.D. are called graduate, or "grad," students.

1 Prelistening Quiz How much do you know about typical university courses in the United States and Canada? Take this short quiz and find out. Write *T* if you think a statement is true and *F* if you think it is false. Then discuss your responses with your classmates. When you listen to the lecture, you will learn the correct answers.

1. _____ Some undergraduate lecture classes may have 300 students in them.

2. _____ Courses at American and Canadian universities are taught only by professors.

3. _____ The information in lectures is the same as the information in textbooks, so attending lectures is usually not necessary.

4. _____ Your homework will always be read and corrected by your professor.

5. _____ A discussion section is a class where students meet informally to help each other with their coursework.

6. _____ The ability to write well is not very important for undergraduates.

7. _____ Only graduate students are required to do research.

8. _____ If you cheat and you are caught, you might have to leave the university.

2 Previewing Vocabulary Listen to the following words and phrases from the lecture. Check (✓) the ones you think you know. Discuss their meanings with a partner. Check the other words and phrases later as you learn them.

Nouns
- ❑ cheating
- ❑ discussion section
- ❑ experiment
- ❑ laboratory ("lab")
- ❑ lecture
- ❑ midterm exam

- ❑ plagiarism
- ❑ quiz
- ❑ requirement
- ❑ teaching assistant
- ❑ term paper

Verbs
- ❑ attend
- ❑ fail a course
- ❑ get kicked out
- ❑ take notes

Listen

3 Note-Taking Pretest Listen to the first half of the lecture and take notes in any way you can. Don't worry about doing it the "right" way this first time. Just do your best. Use your own paper.

Using your notes, choose the best answers to the questions below:

1. Which two topics will the speaker talk about?
   - Ⓐ types of courses
   - Ⓑ academic advising
   - Ⓒ course requirements
   - Ⓓ student government

2. Which of the following is *not* a type of university course?
   - Ⓐ lecture
   - Ⓑ lab
   - Ⓒ advising
   - Ⓓ discussion section

3. Which two statements are true?

    (A) American students use their lecture notes to study for exams.

    (B) In undergraduate courses, the professors meet privately with every student.

    (C) Discussion sections can have 300 students.

    (D) The place where science majors do experiments is called a lab.

Work with one or more classmates and discuss your note-taking experience.

1. Were you able to listen to the lecture and take notes at the same time? If not, do you know why not?

2. Did you try to organize your notes in any way? For example, did you separate the main ideas from the details?

3. Did you write complete sentences? Why or why not?

4. Look at a classmate's notes. How are they similar to yours? Different?

Strategy

Using the Introduction to Predict Lecture Content

Like a composition, a lecture usually has three parts: the introduction, the body, and the conclusion. You should listen very carefully to the introduction because it will usually have two important pieces of information:

  1. the topic of the lecture

  2. a brief summary or list of the main ideas the speaker will talk about

Note: Lecturers often start their lectures with announcements, a review of the last lecture, or a story. It is usually not necessary to take notes on these things.

4 **Taking Notes on the Introduction** Listen to the lecture introduction again and fill in the blanks.

Topic of the lecture: _____

_____

_____

Main ideas that the speaker will discuss: _____

_____

_____

_____

Three Keys to Writing Effective Lecture Notes

Indentation *Indent* means "move your text to the right." Indent to show the relationship between main ideas and specific details. Write main ideas next to the left margin. Indent about one-half inch (about 1.5 cm) as information becomes more specific. Most of the time your notes will have three or four levels of indentation.

Example

Main Idea
    Detail
        More Specific Detail

Key Words When you take notes, do not write every word. Taking notes is not like writing a dictation. Write only the most important, or "key," words. Key words are usually nouns, verbs, adjectives, and adverbs.

Abbreviations and Symbols You can save time if you abbreviate (shorten) words and use symbols as much as possible. For example, write ↑ instead of "increase," or "go up." Look at the list of common abbreviations and symbols in the appendix on page 262. You can also create your own abbreviations and symbols as you take notes.

5 **Identifying the Three Keys to Taking Effective Lecture Notes**
Following are sample notes for the first part of the lecture. Look at the notes as you listen again. Notice how the writer used indentation, key words, abbreviations, and symbols.

Sept. 20, 2008

Topic: University System in U.S. & Canada

3 Types of Univ. Courses (undergrad.)

  1. Lecture course: Prof. talks. Sts. take notes.

    a. Important to take notes because

      —info in lec. ≠ info in books

      —exam q's. based on lecs.

    b. Sts. listen to lecs. 4–6 hrs./wk. per course

    c. Lecs. in large rooms cuz class size = 200+ students

---

2. Discussion section
   a. smaller: 20–30 sts.
   b meets 2–3 hrs./wk.
   c. ask q's, go over HW
   d. taught by TA (not prof.)
3. Lab
   a. for science majors
   b. do experiments

6 Indenting Following are notes for the second part of the lecture. However, the information is not indented correctly. Listen and rewrite the notes to show the relationship between main ideas and details. Use your own paper.

Course Requirements

tests or exams

midterm (in the middle of the course)

final (a big exam at the end of the course)

quizzes (small tests from time to time)

term paper = a large writing project

steps

choose a topic

do research in the library or on the Internet

use notes to write the paper in your own words

5-25 pgs. long

plagiarism

plag. = cheating

def.: copying

punishment

fail a course

get kicked out of univ.

After You Listen

7 Reviewing Vocabulary Work in small groups. Look back at the vocabulary list in Activity 2 on page 11. Quiz each other on the terms and their meanings.

in Activity 2 on page 11.

8 Discussing the Lecture Compare the U.S. university system with systems in other countries that you know about. Take notes in the following Venn diagram.

Topics to discuss:
- types of university courses
- who teaches university courses
- class sizes
- course requirements for different majors
- types of exams
- punishment for plagiarism

Example

At universities in Italy, all the classes are lectures. We don't have discussion sections like they do in the U.S. and we don't have TAs....

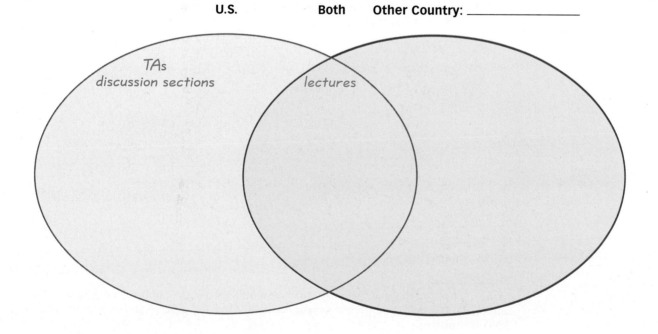

U.S.   **Both**   **Other Country:** _____

TAs
discussion sections   lectures

9 **What Would You Do?** Read the situation. Then discuss the questions below in small groups.

> **Situation**
>
> Last year you took a U.S. history course. One of the course requirements was a ten-page term paper. You worked hard on your paper and received an A.
>
> This year a close friend of yours is taking the same class. Your friend is a good student, but recently her mother has been sick, and she has been busy taking care of a younger brother and sister.
>
> Your friend comes to you and asks to copy your research paper from last year. She is sure the professor will not remember your paper because there are always so many students in the class.

1. Would you allow your friend to copy your paper in this situation? Why or why not?

2. Would your decision be different if your friend's mother were not sick?

3. Would your decision be different if you thought your friend might get caught?

4. Has a friend ever asked to copy from you? What did you do?

5. Have you ever asked a friend if you could copy a paper? Why? How did you feel about it?

6. If a person cheats in school, do you think this person will also cheat in other areas of life? Why or why not?

---

* When you're "on the spot," you have to make a difficult decision. In the On the Spot! activities in this book, you work with your classmates to solve difficult problems or discuss difficult situations.

Getting Meaning from Context

TOEFL® iBT

Focus on Testing

When you listen to people talking in English, it is probably hard to understand all the words. However, you can usually get a general idea of what they are saying. How? By using *clues* that help you to *guess*. These clues include:

- words
- synonyms and paraphrases
- transitions
- stressed words
- intonation
- a speaker's tone of voice
- your knowledge of the culture, speakers, or situation

Many tests such as the TOEFL® iBT measure your academic listening and speaking abilities. This activity, and others in the book, will develop your social and academic conversation skills, and provide a foundation for success on a variety of standardized tests.

Using Context Clues The following conversations take place on a college campus.

1. Listen to the beginning of each conversation.

2. Listen to the question for each conversation. Stop the recording and choose the best answer to each question.

3. In the **Clues** column, write the words that helped you choose your answer. Discuss them with your teacher and classmates.

4. Listen to the last part of each conversation to hear the correct answer.

Answers	Clues
1. Ⓐ in a bookstore 　 Ⓑ in a library 　 Ⓒ in a laboratory 　 Ⓓ in an English class	*term paper, books, checked out*

---

* TOEFL® and TOEIC® are registered trademarks of Educational Testing Service (ETS). This publication is not endorsed or approved by ETS.

Answers	Clues
2. (A) a chemist (B) a secretary (C) a roommate (D) a TA	
3. (A) chemistry (B) history (C) German (D) business	
4. (A) failed an exam (B) was late to class (C) plagiarized a term paper (D) forgot to do a homework assignment	

Focused Listening

GETTING MEANING FROM INTONATION

Meaning comes not only from words but also from the way English speakers use their voices. For example, listen to the sentence "I got 75 percent on the test" spoken in three different ways. Circle the speaker's feeling in each case:

1. a. sad b. happy c. angry d. disappointed

2. a. sad b. happy c. angry d. disappointed

3. a. sad b. happy c. angry d. disappointed

The *tone* (feeling) and direction of a speaker's voice (rising or falling *intonation*) can be important clues to meaning.

1 **Listening for Intonation Clues** In the items that follow, you will hear two conversations. Each of them is spoken in two ways. Use the differences in intonation and tone to decide what the speakers are feeling.

1A. (A) excited
(B) uninterested
(C) angry

1B. (A) excited
(B) uninterested
(C) angry

2A. (A) excited
(B) worried
(C) bored

2B. (A) happy
(B) worried
(C) bored

2 **Using Intonation to Express Feelings** Work with a partner. Choose one of the sentences below.

1. You left the groceries at the supermarket.

2. You put my car keys in the refrigerator.

Read your sentence to your partner in four different ways. Your partner will say which feeling you are trying to express each time.

- a. angry
- b. surprised
- c. amused
- d. bored

Now write your own sentence. Say it to your partner in different ways. Your partner will guess which feeling you are trying to express.

Using Language Functions

MAKING, ACCEPTING, AND REFUSING INVITATIONS

Read Ron and Kathy's conversation. How does Ron invite Kathy to the party? What does Kathy say to accept or refuse Ron's invitation?

Kathy: Hello?

Ron: Kathy? Uh, this is Ron, you know, from your history class?

Kathy: Oh, hi.

Ron: Listen, I was wondering . . . um, were you planning to go to Ali's party Sunday?

Kathy: Hmm. I haven't really thought about it yet.

Ron: Well, would you like to go?

Kathy: You mean, with you?

Ron: Yeah.

Kathy: Well, sure, Ron, I'd love to go.
OR: Well thanks, Ron, but I just remembered that I'm busy that night.

3 **Making, Accepting, and Refusing Invitations** Work with a partner. Complete this chart with expressions from the conversation. Add other expressions that you know.

Language Tip

To refuse the invitation, Kathy does not just say, "No, thank you." Instead, she gives a reason for refusing. This kind of reason (which may or may not be true) is called an **excuse,** and refusing an invitation this way is called **making (or giving) an excuse.**

Inviting	Accepting	Refusing (with an Excuse)

4 Role-Play: Making, Accepting, and Refusing Invitations Work with a partner. Write a short (2–3 minutes) conversation about one of the following situations. Practice your conversation several times. Then perform it for the class without reading.

1. Speaker A invites Speaker B to a foreign-language film. Speaker B accepts or refuses.

2. Speaker A invites Speaker B to a holiday party at Speaker A's parents' house. Speaker B accepts or refuses.

3. Speaker A invites Speaker B to dinner at an expensive restaurant to celebrate Speaker B's birthday. Speaker B accepts or refuses.

Now make a *real* invitation and see if your partner accepts or rejects it.

Part 4   Real-World Task: Reading a Map

Before You Listen

1 Reviewing Compass Points Study the picture of the compass. With your teacher, practice saying the names of the compass points: north, south, east, west, northeast, northwest, southeast, southwest.

Stand up and face north. The teacher will select one student to call out directions. As you hear each direction, turn and face that way. Repeat with other students calling out the directions.

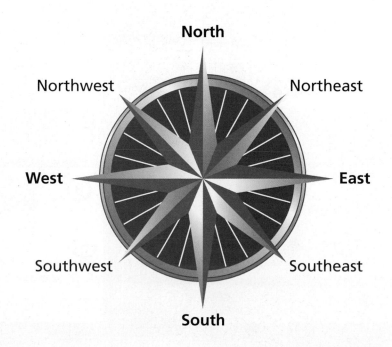

2 Expressions of Location Following are expressions for describing locations. Listen and repeat each expression after the speaker.

_____ a. on the (northwest, southeast, etc.) corner (of Central and Main)

_____ b. at the intersection (of Central and Main)

_____ c. beside/next to (the bank)

_____ d. across the street from/opposite (the camera shop)

_____ e. on both sides of the street

_____ f. in the middle of the block

_____ g. around the corner (from the camera shop, the supermarket, etc.)

_____ h. down the street (from the restaurant)

_____ i. in the middle of the street

_____ j. up the street (from the video store)

_____ k. between (the restaurant and the video store)

Write the numbers from the map next to the matching expressions on the list above.

The prepositions *in, on,* and *at* can be confusing. Look at these examples:

Examples	Hints
I live <u>on</u> Olympic Street.	*on* + street
The school is <u>at</u> 3204 Glendon Avenue.	*at* + address
Harvard University is <u>in</u> Cambridge.	*in* + city, state, country
It is <u>in</u> Massachusetts.	
It is <u>in</u> the United States.	

3 **Expressions of Location in Context** Study the following map of a college campus. Read the names of the buildings and streets. Then listen to statements about the map. Write *T* if a statement is true and *F* if it is false, based on the map. You will hear each statement twice.

1. _____   5. _____

2. _____   6. _____

3. _____   7. _____

4. _____   8. _____

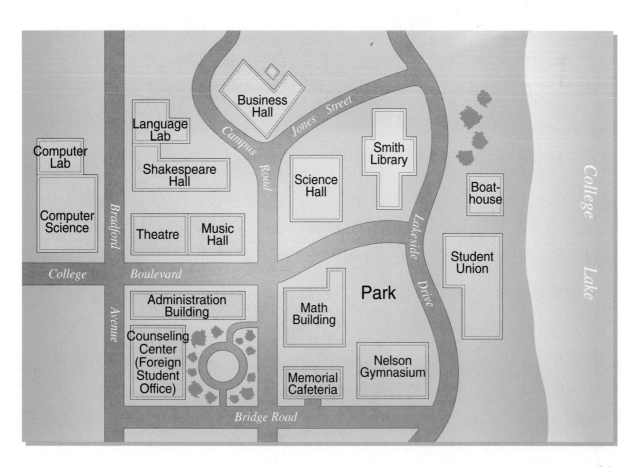

4 **Using Expressions of Location** Write five true or false statements about the map. Use a different expression from Activity 2 on page 22 in each statement. Then read your statements to one or more classmates. Your classmates will say if your statements are true or false.

1. _____

_____

2. _____

_____

3. _____

_____

4. _____

_____

5. _____

_____

 5 **Describing Map Locations** Work in pairs to ask and answer questions about locations. Student A should look at the map on page 244. Student B should look on page 252.

▲ College student using a campus map

Self-Assessment Log

Check the words you learned in this chapter.

Nouns

- ❏ career
- ❏ cheating
- ❏ discussion section
- ❏ experiment
- ❏ laboratory ("lab")
- ❏ lecture
- ❏ midterm exam
- ❏ plagiarism
- ❏ quiz
- ❏ requirement
- ❏ teaching assistant
- ❏ term paper

Verbs

- ❏ attend
- ❏ be into
- ❏ fail a course
- ❏ get ahead
- ❏ get kicked out
- ❏ major in
- ❏ sign up
- ❏ take notes

Check the things you did in this chapter. How well can you do each one?

	Very well	Fairly well	Not very well
I can hear and use stress and reductions.	❏	❏	❏
I can talk about university life in different countries.	❏	❏	❏
I can talk about important events in my life.	❏	❏	❏
I can take notes on a lecture.	❏	❏	❏
I can guess meanings from context.	❏	❏	❏
I can use intonation to express different feelings.	❏	❏	❏
I can make and respond to invitations.	❏	❏	❏
I can read a map and describe locations.	❏	❏	❏

Write what you learned and what you liked in this chapter.

In this chapter,

I learned _____

_____

I liked _____

_____

City Life

In This Chapter

Conversation:	Finding a Place to Live
Lecture:	Neighborhood Watch Meeting
Getting Meaning from Context:	Conversations in an Apartment Building
Real-World Task:	Following Directions

" I love cities. I love neighborhoods and the ways in
which they interact with each other . . .
I love the long gradual shifts in culture they contain.
I love the fact that they work at all. "

—Jason Sutter, U.S. blogger (1976–)

Connecting to the Topic

1. Describe the neighborhood you see in the foreground of the photo.

2. How is your neighborhood different from this neighborhood?

3. What are some different kinds of places to live? Name seven.

Before You Listen

The following telephone conversation is about an advertisement ("ad") for a roommate to share a house.

> Roommate wanted to share 5-bdr. house near campus w/3 working people. Furnished room, private bath, kitchen priv., backyard. $800/month + util. Call Nancy at 555-5949.

Culture Note

Student Housing Offices

In North America, most universities have housing offices. Students looking for places to live and people who are looking for **roommates** can advertise in these offices. It is quite common for students to move into a **dormitory**, house, or apartment with people they have not met before.

1 **Prelistening Questions** Discuss these questions in small groups.

1. Look at the picture. Where is Mari? Why do you think she is there?

2. If Mari calls about the ad, what questions will she probably ask? What questions will the owner of the house probably ask her?

3. Where are you living now? Do you have roommates? How did you find each other?

2 **Previewing Vocabulary** Listen to the underlined words and phrases from the conversation. Then use the context to match them with their definitions.

Sentences

1. _____ My roommate Sarah is a real slob.

2. _____ Sarah never lifts a finger to clean up after herself.

3. _____ It really bugs me that I have to do all the housework myself.

4. _____ **A:** Are you going to Nadia's party tonight?
   B: No, I can't make it. I have to study.

5. _____ **A:** Do you want to go out to dinner?
   B: Thanks, but I can't leave the house because my sister is going to come by around six o'clock.

6. _____ **A:** Where is the language lab?
   B: Go upstairs. It's the first door on your right. You can't miss it.

Definitions

a. to stop somewhere for a short visit

b. a messy person (*slang*)

c. to be able to see (something) easily

d. to irritate, annoy, bother (*slang*)

e. to help with work

f. to come or go (to a particular event)

Listen

3 **Comprehension Questions** Listen to the conversation. You don't need to understand all the words. Just listen for the answers to these questions. After you listen, discuss your answers with a partner.

1. Who are the speakers?

2. What is the student calling about?

3. Where does the student live now? What is the problem there?

4. Who lives in the house that the student is asking about?

5. How is the neighborhood?

6. At the end of the conversation, what do the speakers agree to do?

Stress

4 Listening for Stressed Words Listen to the conversation again. Some of the stressed words are missing. During each pause, repeat the phrase or sentence. Then fill in the missing stressed words.

Nancy: Hello?

Mari: May I speak to Nancy, please?

Nancy: _____.

Mari: Uh hi, uh, my name is Mari, and I'm calling about the _____ for rent. I saw your _____ at the campus _____ office.

Nancy: Oh, right. OK, uh, are you a _____?

Mari: Well, right now I'm just studying _____, but I'm planning to start _____ full-time in _____.

Nancy: I see. _____ are you living _____?

Mari: I've been living in a _____ with some other students, but I _____ _____ it there.

Nancy: Why? What's the _____?

Mari: Well, _____ of all, it's really _____, and it's not very clean. The other people in the house are real _____. I mean they never lift a _____ to clean _____ after themselves. It really _____ me! I need a place that's cleaner and more _____.

Nancy: Well, it's really _____ here. We're not _____ very much.

Mari: What do you _____?

Nancy: I teach _____ at the college.

Mari: _____ a minute! Didn't we meet yesterday at the _____ exam?

Nancy: Oh . . . _____ the girl from _____! What was your name again?

Mari: Mari.

Nancy: Right. What a _____ _____!

Mari: It really is. By the way, who _____ lives in the house? The ad said there are _____ people.

Nancy: Well, besides me there's my _____, Andrew, and my _____, Jeff. He's a musician and a part-time _____. Uh, are you OK with having _____ roommates?

Mari: Sure, as long as they're clean and not too _____.

Nancy: _____ worry. They're both _____ to live with.

Mari: OK. Um, is the _____ safe?

Nancy: Oh sure. We haven't had _____ problems, and you can _____ to school from here.

Mari: Well, it sounds really _____. When can I come by and _____ it?

Nancy: Can you make it this _____ around _____? Then you can meet the _____ too.

Mari: Yeah, five o'clock is _____. What's the _____?

Nancy: It's 3475 Hayworth Avenue. Do you know where _____ is?

Mari: No, I don't.

Nancy: OK. From University Village you go seven blocks _____ on Olympic Avenue. At the intersection of Olympic and Alfred, there's a _____. Turn _____ and go _____ one and a half blocks. Our house is in the _____ of the block on the _____.

Mari: That sounds _____.

Nancy: Yeah, you _____ _____ it. Listen, I've got to go. Someone's at the door. See you this _____.

Mari: OK, see you _____. Bye.

Nancy: Bye-bye.

Check your answers in the listening script on page 267. Then read the conversation with a partner. Pronounce stressed words louder, higher, and more clearly than unstressed words.

Many students of English have difficulty with the phrase *by the way*. Speakers use this phrase to introduce a new topic in a discussion or conversation. For example, in the conversation you heard:

Nancy: Oh . . . you're the girl from Japan! What was your name again?
Mari: Mari.
Nancy: Right. What a small world!
Mari: It really is. <u>By the way</u>, who else lives in the house? The ad said there are three people.

At first, Mari and Nancy are speaking about their meeting at the placement test the day before. Mari says "by the way" because she wants to interrupt this topic to introduce another topic.

Reductions

5 **Comparing Unreduced and Reduced Pronunciation** The following sentences are from the conversation. Listen for the difference between unreduced and reduced pronunciation. Repeat both forms after the speaker.

Unreduced Pronunciation	Reduced Pronunciation
1. Where are you living now?	<u>Where're</u> <u>ya</u> living now?
2. What do you do?	<u>Whaddaya</u> do?
3. You can walk to school from here.	<u>Ya</u> <u>kin</u> walk <u>ta</u> school from here.
4. When can I come by and see it?	When <u>kin</u> I come by <u>'n</u> see it?
5. Can you make it this evening around five?	<u>Kinya</u> make it this evening around five?
6. Do you know where that is?	<u>D'ya</u> know where that is?
7. I've got to go.[1]	I've <u>gotta</u> go.

---

[1] *I've got to* means "I must" or "I have to."

6 Listening for Reductions Listen to the following conversations. You'll hear the reduced pronunciation of some words. Write the unreduced forms of the missing words in the blanks.

Conversation 1

Mari: Hey Jeff, _____ _____ _____ going?

Jeff: I _____ _____ get a present for Nancy. It's her birthday, _____ know.

Mari: Yeah, I know. _____ _____ _____ think I should get her?

Jeff: Well, she likes music. _____ _____ a CD?

Conversation 2

Nancy: _____ _____ _____ like my new haircut, Mari?

Mari: It's great! Who's your hairstylist?

Nancy: His name's José.

Mari: _____ _____ give me his phone number?

Nancy: Sure, but he's always very busy. _____ _____ try calling him, but he might not be able _____ see _____ until next month.

Conversation 3

Andrew: _____ _____ _____ _____ _____ do tonight, Nancy?

Nancy: Nothing special. I've _____ _____ stay home _____ correct my students' compositions.

Check your answers in the listening script on page 267. Then read the conversation with a partner. Try to use reduced forms.

7 **Reviewing Vocabulary** With a partner, read the beginning of the following phone conversation. Then complete the conversation. Try to use all the words and phrases in the box. Perform your conversation in front of the class.

Noun	Verbs	Expressions
slob	come by	can't miss
	bug	make it
		never lifts a finger

Speaker 1: Hello?

Speaker 2: Hi _____ [name of partner]. This is _____ [your name].

Speaker 1: Oh hi! How are you?

Speaker 2: Well, I got a new roommate last week.

Speaker 1: Really? How is [he or she]?

Speaker 2: Terrible! . . .

Using Language Functions

OPENING A PHONE CONVERSATION

Reread the beginning of the phone conversation between Mari and Nancy in Activity 4 on page 30. Phone conversations between strangers often begin similarly. Typically, they contain these functions and expressions:

Function	Expressions
■ A caller asks to speak to a person	Can/Could/May I please speak to _____? Is _____ there? I'd like to speak to _____.
■ The person that the caller asked for identifies himself or herself.	Speaking. This is he/she. This is _____.
■ The caller identifies himself or herself.	My name is _____. [used by strangers talking for the first time] This is _____. [used when people know each other]
■ The caller gives a reason for calling.	I'm calling about . . . I'm calling because . . . Let me tell you why I called.

CLOSING A PHONE CONVERSATION

Reread the end of the phone conversation between Mari and Nancy. It has these typical elements:

Functions	Expressions
▪ One speaker signals that the conversation is finished.	I've got to go.
▪ The other speaker uses a closing expression	See you later. Bye.
▪ The first speaker uses a closing expression.	Bye.
▪ Here are some other expressions that signal that you want to end the conversation:	Well, thanks for the information. It was nice talking to you. Thanks for calling. I'll be in touch (with you).

8 Role-Play Work with a partner. Role-play phone conversations. Be sure to use the expressions for opening and closing a phone conversation. Student A should look at page 245. Student B should look at page 253.

9 Telephone Game For this activity your teacher will divide you into groups of five or six. Each person in the group will receive a number from 1 to 5 (or 6).

1. Exchange phone numbers with the people in your group.

2. Your teacher will give a "secret" message to each person who got number 1.

3. This evening, person 1 will call person 2 in your group and give him or her the message. Person 2 will call person 3, and so on until everyone is called.

4. The next day, person 5 (or 6) from each group will repeat the message in class. See if the message changed as it passed from person to person.

Remember: When you call your classmate,

- ask for your classmate by name,
- identify yourself,
- say why you are calling,
- give the message,
- use correct expressions for ending the conversation.

Before You Listen

Last week there was a burglary in Nancy's neighborhood. The people on her street decided to form a Neighborhood Watch. This is their first meeting. A police officer is speaking about ways to prevent crime.

Culture Note

In many American cities, neighbors join together to form a **Neighborhood Watch.** They agree to work together to stop crimes in their area. They watch out for unusual activity in their neighborhood. If they see anything suspicious, they call the police.

At the first Neighborhood Watch meeting, a police officer usually comes to speak to the neighbors about crime prevention.

▲ Neighborhood Watch signs

1 Prelistening Discussion Discuss these questions in small groups.

1. Look up the meaning of the following word pairs: neighbor/neighborhood; burglar/burglary; robber/robbery; crime (uncountable)/crimes (countable); thief/theft.

2. Is there much crime in the area where you live? What kind? Do you feel safe in your area?

3. Does your area have something like a Neighborhood Watch? Do you think it would be a good idea? Why or why not?

4. What are some things you can do to protect yourself and your home against crime?

2 **Previewing Vocabulary** Listen to these words and phrases from the lecture. Check (✓) the ones you think you know. Discuss their meanings with a partner. Check the other words and phrases later as you learn them.

Nouns	Verbs	Adjective	Expression
❑ alarm	❑ break into	❑ violent	❑ get into the habit
❑ break-in	❑ prevent		
❑ deadbolt			
❑ decal			
❑ device			
❑ front/back (of)			
❑ license			
❑ right			
❑ (car) theft			
❑ timer			
❑ valuables			

▲ A deadbolt lock

Listen

Strategy

Taking Notes on Statistics

Statistics are numbers that give facts about a situation. Often, statistics are expressed as a percentage or fraction; for example, "Thirty percent of the students in our class are men" or "People spend about one-fourth of their salaries on rent." Statistics are very common in lectures. When people talk about statistics, the following terms appear frequently:

Nouns

___%___ percent

_____ number

_____ half

_____ third

_____ quarter

Other phrases

_____ less than

_____ more than

_____ equal to or the same as

Verbs

_____ increase, go up, rise

_____ decrease, decline, go down

_____ double

▲ About 66 percent of the people in this photo are women.

3 Abbreviating Statistics Write abbreviations or symbols next to the items in the chart above. If you don't know the abbreviation or symbol for an item, create one.

4 Taking Notes on Statistics Listen to sentences from the lecture. Use abbreviations and symbols from the chart to take notes. You will hear each sentence twice.

1. _____

2. _____

3. _____

Exchange notes with a partner. Try to repeat the sentences you heard by using your partner's notes.

Transitions (Connecting Words)

Transitions are words and phrases that connect the parts of a speech or composition. There are usually transitions *between* the major sections of a talk. In addition, we also use transitions to connect details *within* each main section. If you listen for transitions, you can tell when a new idea or topic is starting.

Example

"Tonight I'd like to give you some simple suggestions to make your homes and cars safer. OK? So <u>first of all</u>, let's talk about lights."

"<u>Next</u>, let's talk about lights inside the house."

5 **Listening for Transitions** Following is a list of transitions from the lecture. Listen to the lecture. When you hear each transition, write the topic or suggestion that follows it.

PART 1

First of all, _____

Next, _____

All right then. The next topic I want to discuss is _____

    First of all, _____

    Also, _____

PART 2

OK, now let's move on and talk about _____

    First, _____

    The most important thing is _____

Now my last point is _____

    The main thing is _____

    Also, _____

    And one more thing: _____

Answer these questions with your classmates.

1. How many main ideas did the speaker discuss? Which transitions introduced them?

2. Why are some of the transitions indented in the outline on page 39?

3. When you take notes, should you write transitions in your notes? Why or why not?

 6 Taking Notes Following are sample notes on the police officer's suggestions. Notice that they do not contain transitions; instead, the relationship among main ideas and details is shown by underlining, indenting, and listing.

Use your notes from Activities 4 and 5 to fill in the missing information. Remember to use abbreviations and symbols. If necessary, listen to the lecture again.

Date: _____

Ways to Prevent Crime

PART 1

<u>Intro:</u>

Very little violent crime in neigh'hood. But:

Burglaries ↑:

   –Last yr: _____

   –This yr: _____

Car theft ↑: _____

<u>How to keep home & auto safe:</u>

1. House lights

   –need lights in front and _____

   –turn on at _____

2. _____

   –bright lights in garage, hallway, apt. door

   –fix broken lights

   –house or apt: use automatic _____

---

3. _____

   –_____ not safe

   –every door needs _____

   –get special locks for _____

     –50% _____

PART 2

4. _____

   –use _____

   –put _____

   –alarms don't _____

   –better to have _____

5. _____

   –Go on vacation, _____

   –See someth. unusual, _____

   –Put _____

▲ Is this home safe from burglers?

7 **Discussing the Lecture** Discuss the following questions about the lecture and your own experience. Refer to your notes as necessary.

PART 1

1. Has anyone ever broken into your home or your car? If yes, what did the burglars steal?

2. What advice did the police officer give about lights? Do you do these things in your house or apartment?

3. How does an automatic timer work? Do you use timers in your home?

4. What types of locks did the officer recommend? Do you use locks like that?

PART 2

5. According to the officer, how can you prevent car theft? Do you follow these suggestions?

6. What is the officer's opinion about car alarms? What do you think?

7. What is a decal? Where do people often put them? Do you have any?

8. How do people in a Neighborhood Watch help each other? Do you help your neighbors this way?

8 **Reviewing Vocabulary** Work in small groups. Look back at the vocabulary list in Activity 2 on page 37. Quiz each other on the terms and their meanings.

On the Spot!

9 **What Would You Do?** Read the situation and discuss the following questions.

> **Situation**
> You have come to the United States to study at a university. You have rented a room in the home of a very nice American family. The neighborhood is quiet and pretty, and the house is near your school. You are comfortable and happy in your new home.
>
> One day, while preparing food in the kitchen, you discover a gun inside a cabinet.

Discuss the following questions in small groups.

1. Imagine that you have just discovered the gun. How do you feel?

2. What will you do next? Will you speak to the homeowners about the gun? What will you say?

3. Will you look for another place to live?

4. Imagine that the family with the gun lives next door to you. You have a young child, and this family also has a young child. The two children want to play together. Would you allow your child to play at this house?

5. Do you believe that people have the right to own guns, or should guns be illegal?

6. If a person illegally owns a gun, what should the punishment be?

▲ According to a Police Foundation report, over 35% of American households contain at least one firearm (gun).

Getting Meaning from Context

TOEFL® iBT

Focus on Testing

Using Context Clues Many tests such as the TOEFL® iBT measure your academic listening and speaking abilities. This activity, and others in the book, will develop your social and academic conversation skills, and provide a foundation for success on a variety of standardized tests. The following conversations take place in an apartment building.

1. Listen to the beginning of each conversation.

2. Listen to the question for each conversation. Stop the recording and choose the best answer.

3. In the **Clues** column, write the words that helped you choose your answer. Discuss them with your teacher and classmates.

4. Listen to the last part of each conversation to hear the correct answer.

Answers	Clues
Questions 1 through 3 are based on a conversation between a man and a woman.	
1. (A) a neighbor (B) the apartment manager (C) Donna's father (D) a repairman	
2. (A) a repairperson (B) a painter (C) an exterminator[1] (D) a plumber[2]	
3. (A) It's on the third floor. (B) It's in bad condition. (C) It's in a good neighborhood. (D) It's cheap.	

---

[1] An exterminator is a professional who uses poison to kill insects.
[2] A plumber is a person who installs and repairs water pipes, sinks, toilets, and so on.

Questions 4 and 5 are based on a conversation between two neighbors.	
4. (A) He thinks it's very funny. (B) He's surprised to see Donna. (C) He's a little angry. (D) He is happy to help Donna.	
5. (A) He is happy to help Donna. (B) He's surprised to see Donna. (C) He's annoyed with Donna. (D) He's very worried.	

Focused Listening

GUESSING RELATIONSHIPS BETWEEN PEOPLE

The way people address each other in North America can give clues about their relationships. For example:

- In very formal situations, it is polite to use the titles "Sir" or "Ma'am" when you are talking to an older person or someone important. With adults you do not know well, it is correct to use a title with the person's last name. For example, "Ms. Adams" or "Dr. Snow."

- On the other hand, two people who are equal in age or position, or who are meeting in a casual situation, usually use each other's first names.

- People in close personal relationships often use "pet" names to address each other. For example:
  - Married people, people in romantic relationships, or relatives speaking to children: *honey, dear, sweetheart, darling*
  - Children to parents: *Mom, Mommy, Mama, Dad, Daddy, Papa*
  - Children to grandparents: *Grandma, Granny, Grammy, Grandpa*
  - Friends: *pal, buddy, brother, sister, girl*

1 Listening for Clues to Relationships Between People

1. Work in groups of four, divided into two pairs. Pair A, turn to page 245. Pair B, turn to page 253. Look only at your box and follow the instructions. Study the information in your box for a few minutes before you begin.

Using Language Functions

EXPRESSING FRUSTRATION

Frustration is what people feel when they cannot get what they want, even after many tries. For example, imagine that your neighbor's dog wakes you up every night. You complain to your neighbor many times, but the situation does not improve.

In this situation you would feel *frustrated*.

The underlined idioms in the following sentences mean that a speaker is frustrated. Notice the grammar in each sentence.

- My roommate is a total slob! She never cleans up after herself! <u>I am fed up with</u> her mess!

- Mother (to fighting children): <u>I've had it with</u> your fighting! Go outside right now. I want some quiet in here!

- Student: I've been working on this physics problem for three hours. <u>I'm sick of it</u>!

2 Role-Play Work in pairs to role-play situations in an apartment building. Student A should look at page 246. Student B should look at page 254.

3 Follow-up Discussion Discuss the following questions with your classmates.

1. Do you live in an apartment? If yes, does your building have a manager? What responsibilities does he or she have?

2. In Activity 1, you learned that a person who kills insects is called an exterminator. Below is a list of other professionals who work in houses and apartments. Use a dictionary to find out what each person does. Then tell your group if you have ever called this person to fix a problem in your home. Describe the problem.

architect	electrician	phone technician
cable installer	gardener	plumber
carpenter	painter	roofer
carpet cleaner		

3. Tell your classmates about any other problems you have had in your home or with your neighbors. Also, explain what you did to solve the problem(s).

Before You Listen

1 Prelistening Questions Look at the map. Imagine that two people are standing at the spot marked with a red X. Speaker A wants to go to the Chinese restaurant.

1. What expressions can Speaker A use to ask for directions?

2. Imagine that you are Speaker B. How would you answer Speaker A?

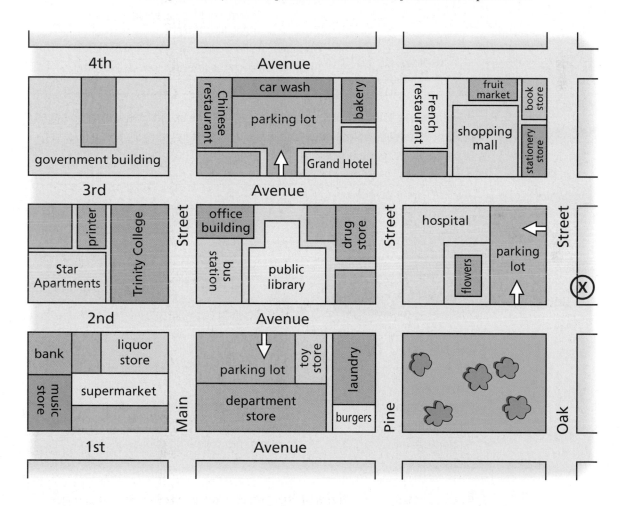

REQUESTING AND GIVING DIRECTIONS

Function	Expressions
Use these expressions to *request* directions.	Excuse me, where is _____? Can/could you tell me where _____ is? How do I get to _____? Do you know where _____ is?
Use these expressions to *give* directions.	**Verbs:** go, walk, drive, turn **Directions:** up/down the street; north, south, east, west; right, left; straight **Distance:** half a block, one mile, two kilometers **Prepositions:** on the left/right; on _____ Street;

2 Following Directions You will hear directions based on the map on page 47. Follow the directions on the map. At the end of each item you will hear a question. Write the answer to the question in the space. You will hear each item twice.

1. _____

2. _____

3. _____

4. _____

SAYING YOU DON'T UNDERSTAND

If you don't understand directions that someone gives you, use one of these expressions.

I don't understand.   I'm in the dark.

I'm confused.   I didn't catch that.

I don't get it.   I'm not following you.

I'm lost.

3 Requesting and Giving Directions Work in pairs to request and give directions using maps. Student A should look at page 246. Student B should look at page 254.

Self-Assessment Log

Check the words you learned in this chapter.

Nouns	**Verbs**	**Adjectives**	**Expressions**
❑ alarm	❑ break into	❑ violent	❑ can't miss
❑ break-in	❑ bug		❑ get into the habit
❑ deadbolt	❑ come by		❑ make it
❑ decal	❑ prevent		❑ never lift a finger
❑ device			
❑ front/back (of)			
❑ license			
❑ right			
❑ slob			
❑ (car) theft			
❑ timer			
❑ valuables			

Check the things you did in this chapter. How well can you do each one?

	Very well	**Fairly well**	**Not very well**
I can hear and use stress and reductions.	❑	❑	❑
I can make telephone calls.	❑	❑	❑
I can talk about crime and crime prevention.	❑	❑	❑
I can take notes on statistics and transitions.	❑	❑	❑
I can guess meanings from context.	❑	❑	❑
I can use phrases to express frustration.	❑	❑	❑
I can ask for and give directions.	❑	❑	❑

Write what you learned and what you liked in this chapter.

In this chapter,

I learned _____

_____

I liked _____

_____

3

Business and Money

> **"** If you work just for money, you'll never make it, but if you love what you're doing and you always put the customer first, success will be yours. **"**
>
> —Ray Kroc
> U.S. businessman, founder of McDonald's Corp. (1902–1984)

Connecting to the Topic

1. Why is the woman in this photo happy?

2. What would you do with the money?

3. Imagine you were to start a business with this money. What kind of business would you start? Describe it.

Part 1 Conversation: Borrowing Money

Before You Listen

In the next conversation, Jeff talks with his father about borrowing money.

▲ Jeff

▲ Jeff's father

1 **Prelistening Questions** Discuss these questions in small groups.

1. Look at the photos. Jeff is asking his father for money. Do you think his father will give it to him? Why or why not?

2. In your community, who usually pays for a person's education after high school?

3. Is it easy or difficult for you to manage your money?

4. What do you do when you need more money?

5. Do you know anyone who works and goes to school at the same time?

2 **Previewing Vocabulary** Listen to the underlined words and phrases from the conversation. Then use the context to match them with their definitions.

Sentences

_____ **1.** It's hard to live alone in the United States because everything costs an arm and a leg.

_____ **2.** Serena can't make ends meet because she doesn't earn enough money.

_____ **3.** We didn't go away on vacation last summer because we were broke.

_____ **4.** I can't buy everything I want, because I am living on a budget.

_____ **5.** With his two jobs, Tom has an income of $3,200 a month.

_____ **6.** You don't earn much money as a server at a fast-food restaurant.

Definitions

a. a lot of money

b. a plan for how to spend one's money each month

c. without any money

d. to pay all one's bills

e. to receive money for work

f. all the money you receive for work or any other reason

Listen

3 **Comprehension Questions** Listen to the conversation. You don't need to understand all the words. Just listen for the answers to these questions. After you listen, discuss your answers with a partner.

1. What is Jeff's problem?

2. What solutions does his father suggest?

3. Why can't Jeff work more hours?

4. How does Jeff feel at the end of the conversation?

Stress

4 Listening for Stressed Words Listen to the conversation again. Some of the stressed words are missing. During each pause, repeat the phrase or sentence. Then fill in the missing stressed words.

Dad: Hello?

Jeff: Hi, Dad.

Dad: Jeff! How _____ you?

Jeff: I'm fine Dad. How's Mom? Did she get over her _____?

Dad: Yes, she's _____ now. She went back to _____ yesterday.

Jeff: That's good. Um, Dad, I need to _____ you something.

Dad: Sure, son, what _____ it?

Jeff: Well, uh, the truth is, I'm _____ again. Could you _____ me $200 just till the end of the month?

Dad: Broke again? Jeff, when you moved _____ with Nancy and Andrew, you said you could _____ ends _____. But this is the _____ time you've asked me for help!

Jeff: I know, I know, I'm sorry. But, see, my old guitar broke, and I had to buy a _____ one. I _____ _____ on a broken guitar, right?

Dad: Look Jeff, if you want to play in a _____, that's OK with me. But you _____ keep asking _____ to pay for it!

Jeff: OK, OK, you're right. But what do you think I ought to _____? Everything costs an _____ and a _____ around here.

Dad: Well, first of all, I think you'd better go on a _____. Make a list of all your _____ and all your expenses. And then it's simple. Don't _____ more than you _____.

Jeff: But that's _____ the problem! My expenses are _____ larger than my income. That's why I need to borrow money from _____.

Dad: Then maybe you should work more hours at the _____ store.

Jeff: Dad! I _____ work 15 hours a week! How can I _____ and _____ and find time to play with my band?

Dad: Come _____, Jeff, when _____ was your age . . .

Jeff: I know, I know. When _____ were my age you were already

_____ and working and going to school.

Dad: That's right. And if I could do it, why can't _____?

Jeff: Because _____ not _____, Dad, that's why!

Dad: All right, Jeff, calm down. I don't _____ you to be like me.

But I _____ _____ you any more money. Your

mother and I are on a budget _____, you know.

Jeff: Maybe I should just drop _____ of school, _____

full-time, and play in the band in the evenings. I can go back to school

_____.

Dad: I wouldn't do that if I were you.

Jeff: Yeah, but you're _____ me, remember? It's my life!

Dad: All right, Jeff. Let's not _____. Why don't you _____

about this very carefully and call me _____ in a few days.

And in the meantime, you'd _____ find a way to

_____ for that new guitar.

Jeff: Yes, Dad.

Dad: All right. Good-bye, son.

Jeff: Bye.

Check your answers in the listening script on pages 270–271. Then read the
conversation with a partner. Remember that stressed words are louder, higher,
and pronounced more clearly than unstressed words.

Language Tip

The words *borrow* and *lend* can be confusing. Look at this example:

Jeff wants to *borrow* money from his father, but his father doesn't want to
lend money to him.

An easy way to remember the difference is like this:

borrow = take

lend = give

Also notice the grammar:

to borrow (something) from (someone)

to lend (something) to (someone)

Reductions

5 **Comparing Unreduced and Reduced Pronunciation** The following sentences are from the conversation. Listen for the difference between unreduced and reduced pronunciation. Repeat both forms after the speaker.

Unreduced Pronunciation	**Reduced Pronunciation**
1. I need to ask you something.	I need ta ask you something.
2. This is the third time you've asked me for help.	This is the third time you've ast me for help.
3. My old guitar broke, and I had to buy a new one.	My old guitar broke, 'n I hadta buy a new one.
4. What do you think I ought to do?	Whaddaya think I oughta do?
5. If I could do it, why can't you?	If I could do it, why cantchu?
6. Why don't you think about this very carefully and call me back in a few days?	Why dontchu think about this very carefully 'n call me back in a few days?

6 **Listening for Reductions** Listen to the following conversation between a bank teller and a customer. You'll hear reduced forms from Chapters 1, 2, and 3. Write the unreduced forms of the missing words in the blanks.

Customer: Hi, my name is Chang Lee.

Teller: How _____ I help you?

Customer: I _____ _____ check my balance.

Teller: OK. _____ I have your account number, please?

Customer: 381335.

Teller: Your balance is $201.

Customer: OK. _____ I _____ my father _____ wire me some money. I'd like _____ know if it's arrived.

Teller: I'm sorry. Your account doesn't show any deposits.

Customer: Oh, no. I need _____ pay my rent tomorrow. _____ _____ _____ think I _____ _____ do?

Teller: Well, we're having some computer problems today. So, why _____ _____ call us later to check again? Or _____ _____ come back. We're open till 5:00.

Customer: OK, thanks.

Teller: You're welcome.

Check your answers in the listening script on page 271. Then read the conversation with a partner. Try to use reduced forms.

After You Listen

7 Using Vocabulary Write a question using each of these words. Then use your questions to interview a classmate.

1. borrow _____

2. lend _____

3. earn _____

4. income _____

5. budget _____

In pairs, practice the words and idioms from this section. Student A should look at page 247. Student B should look at page 255.

Pronunciation

CAN VERSUS *CAN'T*

To hear the difference between *can* and *can't,* you must listen to the differences in vowel quality and stress.

Examples

1. You can **buy** a cheap house these days. (Pronounce: kin buy)
2. You **can't buy** a cheap house these days. (Pronounce: kant buy)

Remember: *Can't* is always stressed.
            Can is normally reduced and the main verb is stressed.

8 Pronouncing *Can* and *Can't* Listen and repeat the following pairs of sentences. Place an accent mark over the stressed words *can't* and the main verb. The first one is done for you.

Affirmative	**Negative**
1. Jeff can pláy on a broken guitar.	**1.** Jeff cán't pláy on a broken guitar.
2. Jeff's father can pay for his new guitar.	**2.** Jeff's father can't pay for his new guitar.
3. Jeff can work more hours at the computer store.	**3.** Jeff can't work more hours at the computer store.
4. I can lend you more money.	**4.** I can't lend you more money.
5. Jeff can go back to school later.	**5.** Jeff can't go back to school later.

9 **Distinguishing Between *Can* and *Can't*** Listen to the sentences. Decide if they are affirmative or negative. Circle *can* or *can't*.

1. can	can't		**6.** can	can't
2. can	can't		**7.** can	can't
3. can	can't		**8.** can	can't
4. can	can't		**9.** can	can't
5. can	can't		**10.** can	can't

 10 **Talking About Abilities** Look at the following list of activities. Which ones can you do? With a partner, take turns making true sentences with *can* and *can't*. As you listen to your partner, put a check in the *Can* or *Can't* column.

Example

Student A says, "I can sew a button on a shirt."

▲ I can stand on my head.

My Partner Can . . .	My Partner Can't . . .	
✓	_____	a. sew a button on a shirt
_____	_____	b. bake a cake
_____	_____	c. stand on his or her head
_____	_____	d. do a handstand
_____	_____	e. water-ski
_____	_____	f. snowboard
_____	_____	g. sing
_____	_____	h. dance
_____	_____	i. drive a stick-shift car
_____	_____	j. pilot a plane
_____	_____	k. understand our teacher
_____	_____	l. understand TV news in English
_____	_____	m. run a mile (1.6 kilometers)
_____	_____	n. run a marathon
_____	_____	o. speak Latin
_____	_____	p. play a musical instrument

Check with your partner to make sure you understood his or her sentences correctly. Ask your partner about additional skills or abilities that are not on the list. Tell the class three things your partner can and can't do.

Using Language Functions

11 **Recognizing Expressions of Advice** Reread the conversation from Activity 4 in the listening script on pages 270–271. Find one place where Jeff asks his father for advice. Find four places where his father gives him advice. Fill in the chart with the language they use.

Asking for Advice	Giving Advice
Jeff: _____ _____ _____ _____	Jeff's father: 1. _____ _____ 2. _____ _____ 3. _____ _____ 4. _____ _____ 5. _____ _____

 12 **Role-Play** With a partner, role-play one of the following situations. Use expressions from the chart. Your teacher may ask you to perform your role-play in front of the class.

USEFUL EXPRESSIONS OF ADVICE			
Asking	**Giving**	**Accepting**	**Rejecting**
Can you give me any/some advice? What should I do? What do you suggest/recommend/advise? What do you think I should/ought to do?	You should + *verb*. I advise you to + *verb*. I suggest that you + *verb*. You can/could + *verb*. Why don't you + *verb*? Verb/Don't + *verb*.	Thanks for the advice. That sounds like a good idea. Thanks. I'll do that.	Thanks, but I don't think that's a good idea. Thanks. I'll think about it. Thanks, but I'm not so sure.

Situation 1

Person A is spending more money each month than he or she is earning. Person B gives suggestions for managing money.

Situation 2

Person A bought a radio and paid cash for it. Unfortunately, he or she didn't keep the receipt. Two days later the radio broke. Person A asks Person B for advice on how to get his or her money back.

Situation 3

Person A doesn't trust banks and keeps all his or her money in a box under the bed. Person B explains why this is a bad idea and gives Person A advice about safer places to keep money.

Situation 4

Person A, a foreign student, is planning a vacation to Person B's home city. Person A asks Person B for advice on ways to have a good time without spending a lot of money. (Example: Person A asks about inexpensive places to stay and eat.)

Part 2 Lecture: Entrepreneurs

Before You Listen

The following lecture is about people who start new businesses or industries—they are called entrepreneurs—and about the process they follow in creating their businesses.

▲ Jeff Bezos, founder of Amazon.com

1 **Prelistening Discussion** Discuss these questions in small groups.

1. Have you ever seen or heard the word *entrepreneur*? Tell what you know about this word.

2. What makes a business leader successful? Knowledge? Skill? Personal characteristics? Make a list on the board. Write both the noun and adjective forms of the words.

   Example
   creativity/creative

3. Give examples of people you know about who have started their own businesses. Which of these characteristics did they have?

4. Which of these characteristics do *you* have? Do you think you would be a good entrepreneur? Why or why not?

2 **Previewing Vocabulary** Listen to these words and phrases from the lecture. Check (✓) the ones you think you know. Discuss their meanings with a partner. Check the other words and phrases later as you learn them.

Nouns	**Verbs**
❏ brilliant idea	❏ found
❏ quality	❏ have (something) in common
❏ solution	❏ hire
❏ team	❏ identify
❏ vision	❏ raise capital
	❏ solve
	❏ surf the Internet
	❏ take risks

Listen

3 **Taking Notes** Listen to the first part of the lecture and take notes in the best way you can. Use your own paper. Listen specifically for the following information:

- What are entrepreneurs?
- What characteristics do they have?

Outlining

In Chapters 1 and 2 you learned how to indent to show the relationship between main ideas and specific details. You can also show this relationship by using an outline. An outline looks like this:

I. First main topic

  A. First subtopic

    1. First detail about subtopic A

    2. Second detail

  B. Second subtopic

II. Second main topic

(Etc.)

You can see that outlines use indentation together with letters and numbers to organize information. Outlining is a very common way of taking notes in English.

▲ Frederick Smith, founder of FedEx

▲ Anita Roddick, founder of The Body Shop

▲ Jerry Yang, founder of Yahoo!

 4 **Outlining the Lecture** Here is a sample outline of the first part of the lecture. Use your notes from Activity 3 to fill in as much information as you can. Remember to use abbreviations and symbols and write key words only. Listen again if necessary.

Date: _____

Topic: Entrepreneurs

I. Intro
   A. Example: _____
   B. Def. of entrep.: _____
II. Characteristics (similar)
   A. _____
      1. Ex.: _____
   B. _____
      1. Ex.: _____
III. Background (diff.)
   A. _____
      1. Ex.: _____
      2. Ex.: _____
   B. Rich and poor
      1. Ex.: _____
   C. Many ent. are _____
      1. Ex.: _____
   D. _____
   E. _____
      1. Ex.: _____

5 **Taking Notes on a Process** Listen to the second part of the lecture. Continue taking notes on your own paper. After listening, use your notes to fill in the missing information below.

IV. Entrepreneurial process

A. Identify a problem

B. _____

C. _____

D. _____

E. _____

F. _____

After You Listen

 6 **Discussing the Lecture** Discuss the following questions about the lecture and your own experience. Refer to your notes as necessary.

1. Match each person with the company he or she founded. Have you ever used any of these companies' products?

   _____ **1.** Jeff Bezos   a. Microsoft Corporation

   _____ **2.** Bill Gates   b. FedEx

   _____ **3.** Jerry Yang   c. The Body Shop

   _____ **4.** Anita Roddick   d. Yahoo!

   _____ **5.** Frederick Smith   e. Amazon

2. What qualities do all entrepreneurs have in common? Do you have these qualities?

3. In what ways can entrepreneurs be different from each other?

4. What are the six steps in the entrepreneurial process?

5. Why are entrepreneurs cultural heroes in the United States?

6. Would you like to be an entrepreneur? Why or why not?

 7 **Reviewing Vocabulary** Work in small groups. Look back at the vocabulary list in Activity 2 on page 61. Quiz each other on the terms and their meanings.

8 **Become an Entrepreneur!** Work in small groups. Pretend that you are an entrepreneurial team. Design a product or service together. Don't worry if your idea seems impossible. Use your imagination. Use the following questions to guide you. When you are finished, make a presentation to your classmates. Use pictures, posters, or PowerPoint to make your presentation more interesting.

1. Think of a problem, need, or opportunity on which you would like to focus.

2. Invent a solution to the problem. It can be a product or a service.

3. Design a business plan. Make decisions about the following items:
   a. Will you need any special equipment?
   b. Where will your business be located?
   c. What special people will you need to hire in order to produce your product or provide your service?
   d. Where or how will you get the money to create and market your product or service?
   e. Where, when, and how will you test-market it?
   f. How will you raise capital to make and sell your product?

Part 3 | Strategies for Better Listening and Speaking

Getting Meaning from Context

1 **Prelistening Questions** Discuss these questions with your classmates.

1. Most American banks offer many different services. Look at the lettered list of banking services in the Focus on Testing box on page 66. Define the unfamiliar items with the help of your teacher.

2. Which of these services are offered by your bank? Which ones have you used?

3. Have you ever tried banking by phone, by mail, or online?

▲ Getting money from an ATM

Focus on Testing

Using Context Clues Many tests such as the TOEFL® iBT measure your academic listening and speaking abilities. This activity, and others in the book, will develop your social and academic conversation skills, and provide a foundation for success on a variety of standardized tests. You are going to hear some advertisements about banking services.

1. Listen to the beginning of each advertisement.

2. Listen to the question for each ad. Stop the recording and write the letter of the best answer on the line next to each question.

3. In the **Clues** column, write the words that helped you choose your answer.

4. Listen to the last part of each advertisement to hear the correct answer.

Banking Services

a. a safe deposit box	d. an automated teller machine (ATM)
b. a savings account	e. a credit card
c. a home improvement loan	f. a car loan

Questions	Clues
_____ 1. What is the speaker talking about?	_____ _____
_____ 2. What is the speaker talking about?	_____ _____
_____ 3. What is the speaker talking about?	_____ _____
_____ 4. What is the speaker talking about?	_____ _____

Pronunciation

TEENS AND TENS

In American English it is hard to hear the difference between the "teens," 13 to 19—and the "tens," every tenth number from 30 to 90. To hear the difference, pay attention to the following:

1. In the *teen* numbers, the *t* sounds like "*t.*"
   Example   seventeen

2. In the *ten* numbers, the *t* sounds similar to "*d.*"
   Example   seventy

3. Speakers usually stress the *ten* numbers on the first syllable and the *teen* numbers on the last.
   Example   thírty   thirtéen

2 **Pronouncing Teens and Tens** Listen and then repeat the pairs of numbers after the speaker.

1. thirteen	thirty
2. fourteen	forty
3. fifteen	fifty
4. sixteen	sixty
5. seventeen	seventy
6. eighteen	eighty
7. nineteen	ninety

3 **Distinguishing Between Teens and Tens** Listen and then circle the numbers you hear.

1. $40.10	$14.10
2. $16.99	$60.99
3. 18%	80%
4. 90	19
5. 230	213
6. 216	260
7. 40.5	14.5
8. $2,250	$2,215
9. 7064	1764
10. 8090	1890

4 **Pair Practice with Teens and Tens** Work in pairs to practice teens and tens. Student A should look at page 247. Student B should look at page 255.

▲ "They're eighteen."

▲ "They're eighty."

On the Spot!

5 What Would You Do? Read the following situations. Decide what to do in each case. Choose the best answer to each question, or write your own answer in the space provided.

1. While walking down the street, you find a wallet. It contains $100 (or the equivalent) and an identification card with the owner's name, address, and phone number. What would you do?
   - (A) Call the owner and return the wallet with the money.
   - (B) Keep the money and mail the empty wallet to the owner.
   - (C) Keep the money and throw away the wallet.
   - (D) Take the wallet with the money to a police station.
   - (E) Other: _____

2. It's the same situation as No. 1, but the wallet contains only $5. What would you do?
   - (A) Call the owner and return the wallet with the money.
   - (B) Keep the money and mail the empty wallet to the owner.
   - (C) Keep the money and throw away the wallet.
   - (D) Take the wallet with the money to a police station.
   - (E) Other: _____

3. You went to the bank to take money out of your account. By mistake, the bank teller gave you more money than you requested. What would you do?
   - (A) Return the extra money immediately. The amount doesn't matter.
   - (B) Keep the extra money.
   - (C) It depends on the amount.
   - (D) Other: _____

4. You went to your favorite department store and bought four items. When you got home, you noticed that the clerk only charged you for three items. What would you do?
   - (A) Keep the extra item and use it.
   - (B) Keep the extra item but give it to a friend or to charity.
   - (C) Return the extra item to the store.
   - (D) Other: _____

6 Discussing the Situations Discuss the following questions in small groups.

1. What answers did you select for the situations? Explain your choices.

2. Have any of these situations ever happened to you? What did you do with the money or items?

3. Do you think you are an honest person?

Real-World Task: Balancing a Checkbook

Most adults in the United States have a checking account. Once a month they receive a *statement* from the bank, which lists all their *deposits* and *withdrawals* for the month. At that time they must *balance their checkbook.* This means they check to make sure that they, or the bank, did not make a mistake in adding or subtracting. Some people do online banking and balance their checking account on line.

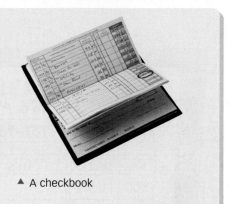

▲ A checkbook

Before You Listen

1 **Prelistening Questions** Answer these questions with a small group.

1. Do you have a checking account at a bank?

2. How often do you write checks?

3. How often do you balance your checkbook?

4. In Activity 3 on page 70 you can see a sample page from a couple's checkbook record. It has six columns. What kind of information is in each column?

2 **Previewing Vocabulary** Listen to these words and expressions from the conversation. Match them with their definitions.

Vocabulary

_____ **1.** balance (noun)

_____ **2.** balance a checkbook (verb)

_____ **3.** pay off (a credit card) (verb)

_____ **4.** interest (noun)

_____ **5.** enter (an amount) (verb)

Definitions

a. a monthly percentage that is paid on borrowed money

b. to write an amount on a check or in a checkbook record

c. the amount of money in an account

d. to pay all of a bill with one payment

e. to check all payments and deposits in a checking account

3 **Balancing a Checkbook** George and Martha Spendthrift have a joint checking account; that is, they share one checking account and both of them can write checks from it. Here is one page from their checkbook record. Listen as they try to balance their checkbook. Fill in the missing information.

CHECKBOOK RECORD

NAME: _George & Martha Spendthrift_

ACCOUNT: _132-98804_

NO.	DATE	DESCRIPTION	PAYMENT	DEPOSIT	BALANCE
200	10/25		30.21		490.31
201	10/27	Electric Company	57.82		
202	10/27	Time magazine			
203	10/30		70.00		327.49
204	11/1	Compu-Tech	125.00		202.49
205		Dr. Painless	40.00		162.49
	11/1	Deposit		1234.69	
206	11/2				985.18
207	11/4	Visa Payment	155.00		830.18
208	11/8		305.00		525.18
209	11/10	Traffic ticket			

After You Listen

4 **Discussion** Discuss the following questions in small groups.

1. Look at the checkbook record. What could the couple do to spend less money?

2. Do you think a joint checking account is a good idea? Why or why not?

3. Who manages the money in your family?

5 Find Someone Who . . . Walk around the room and find one person who fits each of the following descriptions. Write that person's name in the blank space. Then move on and talk to a different person. Collect as many names as possible.

Example

> You read: "Find someone who . . . has used an ATM this week."
>
> You ask a classmate: "Excuse me, can I ask you something? Have you used an ATM this week?"

Language Tip

Question Openers

Before asking someone a question, especially a personal question, it is polite to use one of the following conversation openers:

- Excuse me, can/could/may I ask you a question?
- Can/could/may I ask you something?
- Do you mind if I ask you a (personal) question?

Find Someone Who . . .	Name
is not carrying any money today	
works or has worked in a bank	
has a checking account	
pays bills online	
has her or his own business	
has borrowed money to buy a car	
has a credit card	
has used an ATM this week	
knows how to read the stock market numbers in the newspaper	
owns a house or an apartment	
bought something and returned it to the store the next day	
has shopped at a second-hand store	
wants to start a new business in the future	

Talk It Over

6 **Interview** Attitudes about money vary from culture to culture, family to family, and person to person. Interview someone outside your class about his or her attitude about money. Use the following questions. Take notes in the spaces provided. When you return to class, share what you've learned in small groups.

Name of the person you interviewed: _____

Questions	Answers
1. Would you normally ask a friend how much money he or she makes?	
2. Would you feel comfortable borrowing money from your relatives? In what situation? How much?	
3. If you borrowed a dollar from a classmate, how soon would you return the money?	
4. Ask a man: How would you feel if your wife earned more money than you? Ask a woman: How would you feel if you earned more money than your husband?	
5. When you want to buy an expensive item like a car, do you pay the listed price or do you bargain for a lower price?	
6. When you buy something expensive, do you pay for the whole thing at one time or do you prefer to make payments (pay a little each month)?	
7. Do you think children should receive money (an allowance) from their parents to spend as they like? At what age should they begin receiving it?	

Self-Assessment Log

Check the words you learned in this chapter.

Nouns
- ❏ balance
- ❏ brilliant idea
- ❏ budget
- ❏ income
- ❏ interest
- ❏ quality
- ❏ solution
- ❏ team
- ❏ tightwad
- ❏ vision

Verbs
- ❏ balance a checkbook
- ❏ earn
- ❏ enter
- ❏ found
- ❏ have (something) in common
- ❏ hire
- ❏ identify
- ❏ pay off
- ❏ raise capital
- ❏ solve
- ❏ surf the Internet
- ❏ take risks

Adjectives
- ❏ broke

Expressions
- ❏ an arm and a leg
- ❏ make ends meet

Check the things you did in this chapter. How well can you do each one?

	Very well	Fairly well	Not very well
I can hear and use stress and reductions.	❏	❏	❏
I can distinguish between *can* and *can't.*	❏	❏	❏
I can talk about abilities.	❏	❏	❏
I can ask for and give advice.	❏	❏	❏
I can take notes on a process, using an outline.	❏	❏	❏
I can guess meanings from context.	❏	❏	❏
I can talk about starting a business.	❏	❏	❏
I can distinguish between tens and teens.	❏	❏	❏
I can talk about money and banking.	❏	❏	❏

Write about what you learned and liked in this chapter.

In this chapter,

I learned _____

_____

I liked _____

_____

Jobs and Professions

❝ Work and play are words used to describe the same thing under differing conditions. ❞

—Mark Twain
U.S. author and humorist (1835–1910)

Connecting to the Topic

1 Describe this man's job. What does he do every day?

2 What is your ideal job? Why?

3 What do you need to do to get your ideal job?

Before You Listen

In the next conversation, Jeff, Mari, and Nancy talk about jobs.

▲ Jeff looks for a job in the classified ads.

▲ The classified ads list job openings.

1 Prelistening Questions Discuss these questions with your classmates.

1. Nancy is a teacher; Jeff plays guitar in a rock band; Mari is an international student. What job-related problems might each of them have?

2. Look at the picture. What are classified ads? Why do you think Jeff is reading them?

3. How do people in your home country find jobs?

4. Have you ever had a job? What was your first job?

2 Previewing Vocabulary Listen to the underlined words and phrases from the conversation. Then use the context to match them with their definitions.

Sentences

_____ 1. I'm not in the mood to go to a movie tonight.

_____ 2. He has two jobs because he is supporting his mother.

_____ 3. He spends a lot of time playing his guitar.

_____ 4. A: How was your day today?
B: It was the worst.

_____ 5. The students complained about the bad food in the cafeteria.

Definitions

a. to say that you are unhappy or angry with someone or something

b. terrible (*slang*)

c. to pay for (someone's) expenses

d. (not) to want to do or to have something

e. to use time (doing something)

Listen

3 Comprehension Questions Listen to the conversation. You don't need to understand all the words. Just listen for the answers to these questions. After you listen, discuss your answers with a partner.

1. Why is Jeff reading the classified ads?

2. What kind of job would Jeff prefer?

3. What was Jeff's first job?

4. What was the problem with Jeff's first job?

5. Why is Nancy unhappy with her job?

6. Why can't Mari work in the United States?

7. What does Jeff suggest at the end of the conversation?

Stress

4 **Listening for Stressed Words** Listen to the conversation again. Some of the stressed words are missing. During each pause, repeat the phrase or sentence. Then fill in the missing stressed words.

Mari: Hey, Jeff, what's going _____?

Jeff: Oh, I'm looking at the _____ ads. It looks like I have to get a _____.

Mari: I thought you _____ a job, at a computer store or something.

Jeff: Yeah, but that's _____-time. I need something _____-time.

Mari: Really? But what about _____? What about your _____? How can you work full-time?

Jeff: Well, to tell you the _____, I'm probably going to drop _____ of school for a while. I'm just not in the _____ for _____ these days. I'd rather spend my time _____ with my band. But my father won't _____ me if I'm not in school.

Mari: I see . . . Well, what kind of job do you want to _____?

Jeff: Well ideally, something involving _____, like in a record store. But if _____ not possible . . . I don't know. But whatever I do, it'll be better than my _____ job.

Mari: Oh yeah? What was _____?

Jeff: Believe it or not, the summer after I finished _____ school I worked at Burger Ranch.

Mari: You? In a _____-food place? What did you _____ there?

Jeff: I was a _____ flipper. You know, I made hamburgers all day long.

Mari: That sounds like a pretty _____ job!

Jeff: It was the _____. And I haven't gone inside a Burger Ranch since I _____ that job.

Nancy: Hi, what's so _____?

Jeff: Do you remember my _____ at the Burger Ranch?

Nancy: Oh yeah. That was pretty _____. But actually, it doesn't sound so bad to me right now.

Mari: Why, Nancy? What's _____?

Nancy: Oh, I'm just really, really _____. I'm teaching four different _____ this term, and _____ of them are really _____. Sometimes I think I've been _____ too long.

Mari: How long have you been _____?

Nancy: Twelve years. Maybe it's time to try something _____.

Mari: Like _____?

Nancy: Well, I've always wanted to be a _____. I could work at home . . .

Jeff: Oh, _____ listen to her, Mari. She _____ talks this way when she's had a bad day at school. At least you _____ a good _____, Nancy. Look at me: I'm _____, and Dad won't _____ me any more money . . .

Nancy: Oh, stop _____. If you're so poor, why don't you go _____ to the Burger Ranch?

Mari: Listen you two, stop _____. Look at me! I _____ work at _____ because I'm an international student.

Jeff: OK, OK. I'm _____, Nancy. Tell you what. Let's go out to _____. _____ pay.

Nancy: But you're _____!

Jeff: All right, _____ pay!

Check your answers in the listening script on pages 274–275. Then read the conversation with two classmates. Remember that stressed words are louder, higher, and pronounced more clearly than unstressed words.

Reductions

5 Comparing Unreduced and Reduced Pronunciation The following sentences are from the conversation. Listen for the difference between unreduced and reduced pronunciation. Repeat both forms after the speaker.

Unreduced Pronunciation	**Reduced Pronunciation**
1. What's going on?	What's <u>goin'</u> on?
2. I'm probably going to drop out of school for a while.	I'm probably <u>gonna</u> drop <u>outa</u> school for a while.
3. What did you do there?	What <u>didja</u> do there?
4. What kind of job do you want to get?	What <u>kinda</u> job <u>dya wanna</u> get?
5. Oh, I don't know.	Oh, I <u>dunno</u>.
6. If you're so poor, why don't you go back to the Burger Ranch?	If you're so poor, why <u>doncha</u> go back <u>ta</u> the Burger Ranch?

6 Listening for Reductions Listen to the following conversation. It contains reduced forms. Write the unreduced forms of the missing words in the blanks.

Manager: I'm _____ _____ ask you some questions, OK? What _____ _____ jobs have you had?

Applicant: Mostly factory jobs. The last five years I worked in a plastics factory.

Manager: _____ _____ _____ do there?

Applicant: I _____ _____ cut sheets of plastic.

Manager: _____ _____ _____

_____ _____ do here?

Applicant: I _____ _____. I'll do anything. I'm good with my hands and I'm a hard worker.

Manager: Why _____ _____ fill out an application in the office. It looks like we're _____ _____ have an opening next week. I'll call you.

Applicant: Thanks.

Check your answers in the listening script on page 275. Then read the conversation with a partner. Try to use reduced forms.

After You Listen

7 Reviewing Vocabulary Work in pairs to practice the new vocabulary. Student A should look at page 248. Student B should look at page 256.

Using Language Functions

To **reconcile** with someone after a disagreement, people in the U.S. have the following customs:
- They can do something nice for the person. ("I'll wash the dishes tonight.")
- They can buy the person a gift.
- They can say that they will change their behavior in some way. ("Next time I'll be more polite to your brother.")

APOLOGIZING AND RECONCILING

At the end of the conversation, Jeff and Nancy have a short argument. It ends like this:

Mari: Listen you two, stop arguing. Look at me! I can't work at all because I'm an international student.

Jeff: OK, OK. I'm sorry, Nancy. Tell you what. Let's go out to dinner. I'll pay.

Notice that Jeff does two things. First he *apologizes* to Nancy. He says, "I'm sorry." Then he *reconciles* with her. This means that he offers to do something nice for her—to take her out to dinner—so that she will not be angry anymore. Here are some expressions you can use to apologize:

- I'm sorry.
- I apologize.
- (Please) Forgive me.

8 Role-Play Prepare short conversations with a partner for the following situations. Take turns apologizing and reconciling. Then role-play one of the situations for the class.

1. You forgot your boyfriend's/girlfriend's birthday.

2. You came to work late. As you came in, your boss was standing by the door waiting for you. Your boss is angry.

3. You had a loud party in your apartment, and your neighbor is very upset with you.

4. While arguing with your roommate, you called him or her "stupid" and slammed the door on your way out of the room.

9 Discussion Work in groups of three or four and discuss the following questions.

1. In the conversation, Mari complains that she can't work because she is an international student. This is the law in the United States.
   - Do you think this law is fair? What might be the reasons for this law?
   - If you were a student in the United States and needed money, what would you do?

2. After twelve years of teaching, Nancy is thinking about changing careers. This is not unusual in the United States and Canada.
   - Is it easy for people to change careers in other countries?
   - Why do you think it is more common in the United States than in other places?
   - If, after working for several years, you discovered that you hated your career, what would you do?

3. In North America, it is very common for people to go to college and have jobs at the same time.
   - Do you think this is common in other countries?
   - Do you or any of your friends have jobs right now? What kind?

In the following lecture, a job counselor is speaking to a group of students about changes in the U.S. job market and future job possibilities.

 1 **Prelistening Discussion** Study the table and answer the questions that follow.

Fastest Growing Occupations, 2002–2012

Job	Percent Change	Salary Rank[1]	Training Needed Post-High School[2]
1. Medical assistants	59%	3	On the job
2. Network systems and data communications analysts	57%	1	B.A.
3. Physician's assistants	49%	1	B.A.
4. Home health aides	48%	4	On the job
5. Computer software engineers, applications	46%	1	B.A.
6. Computer software engineers, systems software	45%	1	B.A.
7. Fitness trainers and aerobics instructors	44%	3	Vocational
8. Database administrators	44%	1	B.A.
9. Veterinary technologists and technicians	44%	3	Associate degree
10. Hazardous materials removal workers	43%	2	On the job
11. Dental hygienists	43%	1	Associate degree
12. Personal and home care aides	40%	4	On the job
13. Computer systems analysts	39%	1	B.A.
14. Environmental engineers	38%	1	B.A.
15. Postsecondary teachers	38%	1	M.A. or Ph.D.

---

[1] Jobs are divided into four groups according to salary. Number 1 means a salary in the top 25 percent, and so on.

[2] *Associate degree* means a diploma from a two-year community college. *On the job* means no previous training or education is needed. *Vocational* refers to schools that offer training in nonacademic fields.

Job	Percent Change	Salary Rank	Training Needed Post-High School
16. Network and computer systems administrators	37%	1	B.A.
17. Preschool teachers, except special education	36%	4	Vocational
18. Computer and information systems managers	36%	1	B.A. or higher
19. Physical therapists	35%	1	M.A.
20. Occupational therapists	35%	1	B.A.

Source: "Fastest Growing Occupations, 2002–2012," U.S. Department of Labor

1. What information is given in this table?

2. What years are covered?

3. The table has four columns. What information is given in each one?

4. What job do you hope to have in the future? Is it on this list?

5. Which jobs require a college education?

6. Which jobs have the highest salaries?

2 **Previewing Vocabulary** Listen to these words and phrases from the lecture. Check (✓) the ones you think you know. Discuss their meanings with a partner. Check the other words and phrases later as you learn them.

Nouns
- ❏ automation
- ❏ bottom line
- ❏ category
- ❏ competition
- ❏ economy
- ❏ health care
- ❏ illness
- ❏ job market
- ❏ labor costs
- ❏ manufacturing
- ❏ rank
- ❏ salary
- ❏ service
- ❏ trend

Verb
- ❏ grow by X%

Strategy

Taking Notes on Causes and Effects

To understand the main points in the lecture, you need to recognize the relationship between *causes* (reasons) and *effects* (results). Study the examples below. Notice that sometimes the cause is mentioned first, and other times the effect is first. In some sentences the order can be switched.

Many people use arrows in notes to indicate cause and effect. For example, X → Y means that X causes Y. In other words, X is the cause and Y is the effect.

Examples with Cause First

Because of/due to robots, the number of factory jobs has decreased.

Because/since robots are cheaper than human workers, factories are using more robots.

Human workers cannot work 24 hours a day; **as a result,/therefore,** more and more factories are using robots.

Labor costs are cheaper in Asia, **so** many American factories are moving there.

Examples with Effect First

The number of factory jobs decreased **because of/due to** robots.

Factories are using more robots **because/since** they are cheaper than human workers.

The (first, second, main, etc.) **cause of/reason for** unemployment is automation.

3 **Taking Notes on Cause-and-Effect Statements** Take notes on each sentence from the Strategy Box above. Remember to abbreviate, use symbols, and write key words only. Compare notes with a classmate.

1. _____
2. _____
3. _____
4. _____
5. _____
6. _____
7. _____

4 Creating Abbreviations Following are key words from the lecture. Create abbreviations or symbols for them before you listen.

Words	Abbreviations
economy	
manufacturing	
service	
technology	
approximately	
number	
million	
medical	
computer	
percent	
Bachelor of Arts	

5 Listening and Taking Notes on Causes and Effects Listen to cause-and-effect statements from the lecture and take notes. You will hear each statement twice.

Example

You hear: "In many cases, automation causes unemployment."

You write: *automation → unemp.*

1. _____
2. _____
3. _____
4. _____
5. _____

6 Taking Notes on Statistics Review "Taking Notes on Statistics" on page 38. Listen to sentences from the lecture and take notes. You will hear each sentence twice.

1. _____
2. _____
3. _____
4. _____
5. _____

Exchange notes with a partner. Try to repeat the sentences by using your partner's notes.

7 Taking Notes Listen to the lecture and take notes in the best way you can. Use your own paper. Listen specifically for the following information:

Part 1
- How has the U.S. job market changed?
- Why?

Part 2
- What are three categories of fast-growing occupations between 2002 and 2012?
- What should people do in order to get high-paying jobs?

 8 Outlining the Lecture Complete the outline with the information from Activities 3 through 7. Listen again if necessary.

The Changing U.S. Job Market

Part 1

I. 2 questions this lec. will answer:

   A. _____

   B. _____

II. History: Last 100 yrs., change in U.S. labor market: from _____ to _____ economy

   A. Definitions

      1. _____

        e.g.: _____

      2. _____

        e.g.: _____

III. Reasons for ↓ in manuf. jobs

   A. _____

   B. _____

      1. stat: _____ since 2001

      2. _____

IV. _____

_____

   A. Stat: _____

Part 2

V. Fastest growing service jobs

   A. _____

      1. e.g.: _____

      2. Reasons

        – _____

        – _____

   B. _____

      1. e.g.: _____

      2. Stat: _____

   C. _____

      1. e.g.: _____

      2. Reason: _____

VI. Educ. requirement for good jobs: _____

After You Listen

9 **Discussing the Lecture** Use your notes and experience to discuss the
following questions.

   1. What is the difference between a service economy and a manufacturing
economy? Give examples of jobs in each category.

   2. How has the American job market changed? What are two reasons for this
change?

   3. Why will there be more health care jobs in the future?

   4. How much will the computer industry grow in the next ten years? What kind of
jobs will there be?

   5. What are examples of jobs in the category of personal care services? Why is the
number of these jobs increasing?

   7. Look at the list of Fastest Growing Occupations, 2002–2012 on pages 82–83.
Which of these jobs would you like to have? What do you need to do to prepare
yourself for this job?

10 Reviewing Vocabulary Use vocabulary from the box to complete the summary of the lecture.

automation	economy	salary
bottom line	health care	service
categories	labor costs	trend
competition	manufacturing	

One hundred years ago, the United States had a _____ economy. This meant that most people made things by hand or machine. In contrast, today the United States has a _____ economy, in which workers provide services instead of making products. The United States has lost a lot of manufacturing jobs, and it is certain that this _____ will continue in the future.

There are several reasons for this important change in the U.S. _____. The first is _____. It is cheaper to use machines than human workers in factories. Another reason is _____ from foreign countries where _____ are lower than in the United States. Therefore, many products that used to be manufactured in the United States are now made overseas.

What will the good jobs of the future be? Over the next ten years, the fastest growing occupations will be in three _____: _____, computers, and personal care and services. Many of these jobs will not pay very well, however. If you want to get a good job with a high _____, the _____ is this: Get a good education.

11 **What Would You Do?** Read the situation and follow the instructions.

Situation

A new supermarket is opening in your neighborhood. The company needs to hire four people for job openings immediately. The jobs are: manager, checker,[1] stock clerk,[2] and butcher.[3] You are going to role-play job interviews for these people.

1. Choose four people to be interviewers. Each interviewer will interview the applicants for one of the jobs available.

2. All other students will play the role of job applicants. The teacher will tell you which position you are applying for.

3. Go to page 260 to find the information you need for your role. Learn it well so that you don't have to read it during your interview. You can add information during your interview if you want to.

4. Your teacher will divide the class into four groups. Each group will consist of an interviewer and all the interviewees for that job. The interviewers will interview each interviewee for five minutes. The four groups should have their interviews at the same time. (You can listen to other groups while you wait to be interviewed. Don't listen to your own group's interviews.)

5. After all the interviews are finished, the interviewers will report to the class. They will tell which applicant they picked for the job and why they chose that person.

▲ A checker and shoppers at a supermarket

---

[1] A checker is the same thing as a cashier or a checkout clerk.
[2] Stock clerks put new merchandise on the shelves of a supermarket. They often work at night.
[3] A butcher cuts and prepares meat.

Getting Meaning from Context

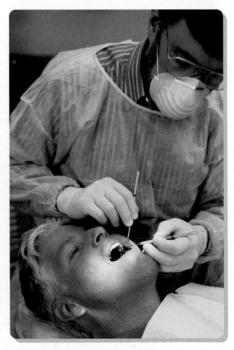

1 **Prelistening Questions** Look at the pictures on page 90 and the list of occupations in the Focus on Testing box below. For each job, answer these questions:

1. What does this person do?

2. What education or training is needed for this job?

3. Would you enjoy doing this job? Why or why not?

Focus on Testing

Using Context Clues Many tests such as the TOEFL® iBT measure your academic listening and speaking abilities. This activity, and others in the book, will develop your social and academic conversation skills, and provide a foundation for success on a variety of standardized tests. The following conversations take place at work.

1. Listen to the first part of each conversation.

2. After each conversation, stop the recording. Write the letter of each speaker's job in the blank.

3. In the **Clues** column, write the words that helped you choose your answer.

4. Listen to the next part of the conversation to hear the correct answer.

Occupation

a. architect	d. restaurant host	g. receptionist
b. computer programmer	e. dentist	h. tailor
c. accountant	f. police officer	i. electrician

Questions	Clues
_____ 1. What's the woman's job?	_____
_____ 2. What's the woman's job?	_____
_____ 3. What's the man's job?	_____
_____ 4. What's the man's job?	_____
_____ 5. What's the man's job?	_____

2 **Game: Twenty Questions** In this game, one person thinks of a job but does not tell the class what it is. The class tries to guess by asking a maximum of 20 *Yes* or *No* questions.

Examples

"Can you do this job outdoors?"
"Is a college education necessary for this job?"
"Is this job normally done by women?"

The student who correctly guesses the occupation wins. If no one guesses after 20 questions, the same person leads another round.

Focused Listening

UNDERSTANDING THE INTONATION OF TAG QUESTIONS

When people need information or don't know something, they normally ask a question. For example, "Are you from China?" However, when English speakers *think* they know the answer to a question, but they *aren't sure,* they often form tag questions with *rising intonation:*

You're from China, aren't you?   You speak Chinese, don't you?

The rising intonation means that the person is asking for information.

In contrast, it is also possible to form tag questions with *falling intonation,* like this:

It's nice weather, today, isn't it?   That test was hard, wasn't it?

Tag questions with falling intonation are not real questions. When people ask these kinds of questions, they expect agreement. The tag is a way of making conversation or small talk.

3 **Recognizing the Intonation of Tag Questions** Listen to these ten tag questions. Decide if they are real questions (if the speaker is really asking for information) or if the speaker is just looking for agreement. Put a check (✓) in the correct column.

Question	Real Question	Expecting Agreement
1.		
2.		
3.		
4.		
5.		
6.		
7.		
8.		
9.		
10.		

Using Language Functions

ANSWERING NEGATIVE TAG QUESTIONS

In Activity 3, the main verb in each sentence was affirmative, and the verb in the tag question was negative.* Here is the proper way to *answer* such questions:

Tag with rising intonation:

A: You're from China, aren't you?

B: Yes, I am.

Meaning of answer:

Speaker A is correct. Speaker B *is* from China.

A: We have homework tonight, don't we?

B: No, we don't.

Meaning of answer:

Speaker A is mistaken, so Speaker B corrects him.

Tag with falling intonation:

A: It's really cold today, isn't it?

B: Yes, and I don't have a jacket.

Meaning of answer:

Speaker B agrees with Speaker A.

* You will practice tag questions with affirmative verbs ("You're not a student, are you?") in Chapter 10.

 4 **Asking and Answering Negative Tag Questions** Work in pairs. Student A should look at page 248. Student B should look at page 256. Complete the statements in your box and add negative tag questions. Decide if the intonation should rise or fall. Then, ask your partner the questions and listen for your partner's answers.

Example

> **A:** This is your cell phone, isn't it? [rising intonation]
> **B:** No, it's Kathy's.

Part 4 | Real-World Task: A Homemaker's Typical Day

Before You Listen

 1 **Prelistening Discussion** Answer the questions with a small group.

1. Do you think managing a house and children is a job? Why or why not?

2. It is estimated that homemakers work as many as 60 hours a week. Is (or was) your mother or father a full-time homemaker? How many hours does/did she or he work each week?

3. Make a list of skills that a homemaker needs to have, such as cooking and financial planning.

2 **Previewing Vocabulary** Listen to these idioms related to work in the home. Discuss their meanings. Write the meaning of each item. (The words *make* and *do* are often used in these kinds of idioms.)

Idiom	Meaning
to make (breakfast, lunch, dinner)	
to do the dishes	
to make the beds	
to balance the family budget	
to do the laundry	
to water the lawn (garden)	
to shop for groceries	

3 **Predicting** The pictures in Activity 4 on page 95 show a typical day in the life of an American "househusband." The pictures are not in the correct order. With a partner, look at each picture and use the vocabulary from Activity 2 to describe what is happening. Then try to predict the order of the pictures.

4 **Sequencing Events** Listen to the man describe his day. Write numbers under the pictures to show the order in which each activity occurred. If two things happened at the same time, give them the same number. Pay attention to time words (*before*, *after, during,* etc.) and verb tenses. (Note: Only *some* of the activities are shown in the pictures.) Then compare answers with a partner.

After You Listen

5 **Discussion** Discuss the following questions in small groups.

1. Which tasks does the man do? Who does or did these things in your family?

2. Which tasks does the man's wife do? How does this compare to your family?

3. Would you like to have this man's life? Why or why not?

Strategy

Graphic Organizer: Matrix Diagram
A matrix diagram organizes information about two or more characteristics of two or more topics. You can use a matrix diagram to compare these characteristics or to show them clearly so that you can study or discuss them easily. You will use a matrix diagram in Activity 6.

6 **Talking About "Men's" and "Women's" Jobs**

1. Following is a list of jobs. Put a check (✓) in the column that describes the *traditional* thinking of people from your culture. Put an X in the column that describes *your* thinking.

Job	Men	Women	Both
computer programmer			
nurse			
architect			
college professor			
bus driver			
film director			
police officer			
computer software salesperson			
mail carrier			
lawyer			
pilot			
administrative assistant			
manager of a company			
telephone repairperson			

Job	Men	Women	Both
firefighter			
diplomat			
farmer			

2. Work in small groups and compare your charts. Discuss the differences between attitudes in different countries. Also, explain differences between your opinion and the traditional opinion of people from your culture.

3. While traveling or living in new countries, have you been surprised to see women doing what were traditionally men's jobs or vice versa? Where? What kinds of jobs?

▲ Is being a chef traditionally a man's job or a woman's job?

7 Interview Interview someone outside of class about his or her work experience. Work in small groups. Add to the list of the following interview questions.

1. What do you do?

2. How long have you been working at your present job?

3. How many jobs have you had in your life?

4. What was the worst or strangest job you've ever had?

5. _____

6. _____

7. _____

8. _____

9. _____

Prepare a short oral report about your interview. Tell about the person you interviewed and the most interesting things you learned about him or her.

You may begin your report like this:

"I interviewed Mr. Richard Baldwin. He works as the student advisor at the English Language Center. He has worked in this job for eight years. Mr. Baldwin had many other jobs before this one. The worst job was in college, when he worked as a dishwasher in the cafeteria . . ."

▲ "Here's a photo of Mr. Richard Baldwin."

Self-Assessment Log

Check the words you learned in this chapter.

Nouns

- ❑ automation
- ❑ bottom line
- ❑ category
- ❑ competition
- ❑ economy
- ❑ health care
- ❑ illness
- ❑ job market
- ❑ labor costs
- ❑ manufacturing
- ❑ rank
- ❑ salary
- ❑ service
- ❑ trend

Verbs

- ❑ complain
- ❑ grow by X%
- ❑ spend time
- ❑ support

Expressions

- ❑ in the mood
- ❑ the worst

Check the things you did in this chapter. How well can you do each one?

	Very well	Fairly well	Not very well
I can hear and use stress and reductions.	❑	❑	❑
I can use phrases for apologizing.	❑	❑	❑
I can talk about jobs and careers.	❑	❑	❑
I can read and understand a table.	❑	❑	❑
I can ask for and give advice.	❑	❑	❑
I can take notes on causes and effects using an outline.	❑	❑	❑
I can guess meanings from context.	❑	❑	❑
I can participate in interviews.	❑	❑	❑
I can use tag questions.	❑	❑	❑

Write what you liked and what you learned in this chapter.

In this chapter,

I learned _____

_____

I liked _____

_____

Lifestyles Around the World

" It takes a village to raise a child. **"**

—African proverb

1. Describe the relationship of the man and the boy.

2. Where are they? What is the man doing? What is the boy doing?

3. Imagine a typical day for this man. How is it different from a typical day for your parents when you were a child?

Before You Listen

In the following conversation, a neighbor comes over to ask Jeff for a favor.

▲ Sharon

1 **Prelistening Questions** Discuss these questions with your classmates.

1. What does it mean to "ask someone for a favor"? Give an example.

2. What is a single mother or a single father?

3. What kinds of challenges do you think single parents face?

2 **Previewing Vocabulary** Listen to the underlined expressions from the conversation. Then use the context to match them with their definitions.

Sentences

_c_ **1.** I will <u>look into</u> your problem as soon as I have time.

_e_ **2.** If I don't <u>take off</u> right this minute, I'm going to miss my bus.

_b_ **3.** My mother is very <u>old-fashioned</u>. She doesn't like new ideas.

_d_ **4.** Time is <u>running out</u> for me to finish this paper. It's due tomorrow!

_a_ **5.** My mother is sick. I want to <u>check up on</u> her on my way home from work.

Definitions

a. to see if someone is OK

b. not modern

c. to find information about something

d. to end

e. to leave

Listen

3 **Comprehension Questions** Close your book as you listen to the conversation. Listen for the answers to these questions. After you listen, discuss your answers with a partner.

1. What does Sharon want from Jeff? Why?

2. What surprised Mari about Sharon?

3. What was Nancy thinking about doing before she got married?

4. How does Mari feel about what Nancy says? Why?

Stress

TWO- AND THREE-WORD VERBS

Many verbs in English consist of two or three words. The first word is a verb and the second and third words are usually prepositions. In most of these verbs, the second word receives the stress. Listen to these examples:

The plane **took óff** at seven o'clock.

John **checked úp on** his mother.

Please **drop** me **óff** at the corner.

🎧 **4 Listening for Stressed Words (Part I)** Listen to the following sentences from the conversation. They contain two- and three-word verbs. During each pause, repeat the sentence; then fill in the missing stressed words.

1. Come on _____.

2. They want me to look _____ a computer problem right away.

3. If he wakes _____, just give him a bottle.

4. Listen, I've got to take _____.

5. Thanks so much, Jeff, for helping me _____.

6. I take _____ of him from time to time when Sharon's busy.

7. I worried that time was running _____.

8. I could never bring _____ a baby by myself.

9. I'd better check _____ on Joey.

Compare answers and discuss the meaning of the two- and three-word verbs with a partner. Then take turns reading the sentences using the correct stress.

🎧 **5 Listening for Stressed Words (Part II)** Now listen to part of the conversation again. Some of the stressed words are missing. During each pause, repeat the phrase or sentence. Then fill in the missing stressed words.

Mari: Hey, Jeff, I didn't know you liked ___babies___.

Jeff: Well, Joey is ___special___. I take care of him from time to time when Sharon's ___busy___. And then ___she___ does favors for _____ in return. Like last week she lent me her ___car___.

Mari: And her ___husband___? Is he . . .

Jeff: She's not ___married___. I don't think she _____ was, actually.

Mari: Never?

Jeff: ___no___, ___Never___. I think she's _____ being a _____ mother.

Mari: Oh. Is that pretty ___common___ in America?

Jeff: Well, it's ___sortley___ becoming more and more common. Even _____ used to talk about it. You know, before she got ___married___.

Nancy: Hi, guys.

Mari/Jeff: Hi.

Nancy: Uh, _what_ were you saying about me?

Jeff: That you _____ to talk about having a _____ by yourself before you _self_ Andrew.

Nancy: Oh yeah, I _____ that _____ was running out. You know, like, what if I _were_ got married?

Mari: Maybe I'm _____-_____, but I could _____ bring up a baby by _myself_. I think it would be so difficult . . .

Nancy: Yeah, raising a _____ is tough. I'm really _look_ I met Andrew.

Mari: And, if you have a baby, you'll have _____ here to help you with _City_.

Jeff: We'll see. Speaking of babysitting, I'd _better_ check up on Joey.

Check your answers using the listening script on pages 278–279. Then read the conversation with two classmates. Pronounce stressed words louder, higher, and more clearly than unstressed words.

Reductions

Sometimes the letter *h* is not pronounced at the beginning of English words.

> **Example** give him ⟶ give <u>im</u>
> Where has he been? ⟶ Where <u>as e</u> been?

The letter *h* is often <u>not</u> pronounced when

- a word is unstressed (such as **h**im, **h**er, **h**as) **and**
- it doesn't come at the beginning of a phrase or sentence.

Compare:
1. Unreduced: Is he asleep?
   Reduced: Is <u>e</u> asleep?

2. Unreduced: The children have gone.
   Reduced: The children <u>uv</u> gone.

3. Unreduced: Here's the newspaper.
   The *h* is not dropped because it is at the beginning of the sentence.

In a few words, like *honest* and *hour,* the *h* is never pronounced.

6 **Listening for Reductions** Listen to the following sentences from the conversation. Repeat them after the speaker. Draw a slash (/) through any *h* sounds that are dropped.

Example:

Is H̸e asleep?

1. If he wakes up, just give him a bottle.

2. Thanks so much, Jeff, for helping me out.

3. I take care of him from time to time when Sharon's busy.

4. And her husband?

5. Hi, guys.

6. You'll have Jeff here to help you with babysitting.

After You Listen

7 **Using Vocabulary** Work in pairs to practice the new vocabulary. Student A should look at page 248. Student B should look at page 256.

Discuss your answers to the following questions with a partner.

1. Do you sometimes argue with your parents because you think their ideas are <u>old-fashioned</u>? Give examples.

2. At what age does a woman's time to have a baby <u>run out</u>?

3. Would you <u>look into</u> raising a baby by yourself? Why or why not?

Using Language Functions

ASKING FOR HELP OR A FAVOR

In the conversation, Sharon asks Jeff for a favor, and Jeff agrees.

Sharon: Can you do me a big favor? Would you mind watching Joey until
I get back?

Jeff: Sure, no problem.

Sometimes it is necessary to say no when someone asks for help or a favor.
In that case, we usually apologize and give a reason why we cannot help.
For example, Jeff might have said, "I'm really sorry, Sharon, but I have to go to
work now."

The following expressions are used for talking about favors.

Asking for a Favor	Responding	
	Yes	**No**
Can/could you do me a (small/big) favor? Can/could I ask you for a favor? Will/can/could you + verb? Could you give me a hand (with something)? Can/could you help me with (something)? Would you mind verb + *-ing*?	Sure./Yes./OK./ Yeah./Of course. Sure, what do you need? I'd be glad to. No, not at all.*	I'm sorry, but . . . I'd like to, but . . . I wish I could, but . . . Let me think about it. I really can't.

* The answer "No, not at all" means that the speaker *doesn't mind doing* something. In other words, the speaker agrees to do it.

---

8 **Asking for a Favor** Work in pairs to practice asking for help and responding. Student A should look at page 249. Student B should look at page 257.

9 **Role-Play** Work in pairs to practice asking for help and responding. Take turns, using the situations below. Then role-play one of the situations for the class.

1. Ask a classmate if you can copy his or her lecture notes because you were absent.

2. You want to ask out a girl or guy from your biology class. Ask his or her best friend to introduce you.

3. Ask your neighbor if she can feed your cat for three days while you are out of town.

4. Ask a co-worker if you can borrow five dollars until you have a chance to get some cash.

5. Ask your brother if you can live with him and his wife for the next three months so that you can save some money to go on vacation with your friends.

6. Ask a friend if you can borrow his or her favorite sweater to wear on a very special date.

7. In a crowded movie theater, ask the person sitting next to you if he or she will change seats with you because the person sitting in front of you is very tall.

In groups, discuss whether you would feel comfortable asking for favors in these situations.

Before You Listen

This lecture is about changes in the American family and how some businesses are responding to those changes.

 1 **Prelistening Discussion** Discuss these questions in small groups.

1. Look at the photos of the two families. Describe the family members and their lifestyles. When do you think each photo was taken?

2. Based on the photos, how do you think the "typical" American family has changed since the 1950s?

3. How are families changing in your community? Why?

2 **Previewing Vocabulary** Listen to these words and phrases from the lecture. Check (✓) the ones you think you know. Discuss their meanings with a partner. Check the other words and phrases later as you learn them.

Nouns		Verbs	Adjective
❏ cost of living	❏ maternity leave	❏ benefit	❏ flexible
❏ day care center	❏ opportunity	❏ can/can't afford	
❏ flexibility	❏ policy	❏ transfer	
❏ homemaker		❏ volunteer	

Listen

Strategy

Taking Notes on Examples

In English there are many expressions to signal examples. Here are a few:

> For example, . . .
> For instance, . . .
> As an example, . . .
> . . . such as . . .
> To give (one) example, . . .

In notes, people often use the abbreviation *e.g.* to indicate an example.

3 **Taking Notes on Examples** You will hear statements supported by examples. Notes for the statements are below. Listen and take notes on the missing examples. Be sure to indent the examples and use abbreviations, symbols, and key words. You will hear each item twice.

1. Today women are wrking. in profs. not open 30–40 yrs. ago

_____

2. Now most Am. homes no full-time homemaker → new probs

_____

_____

3. Some co's. give new parents pd. vacation

_____

_____

Exchange notes with a classmate. Use your partner's notes to try to restate the information you heard.

4 Taking Notes (Part I) Listen to the first part of the lecture and take notes in the best way you can. Use your own paper. Listen specifically for this information:

1. How has the American family changed? What is the biggest change?

2. What's the main reason for this change?

5 Outlining the Lecture

Here is a sample outline of the first part of the lecture. Use your notes from Activities 3 and 4 to fill in the missing information. Remember to use abbreviations and symbols. Listen again if necessary.

▲ Children having lunch at a day care center

Topic: Changes in the American Family

I. "Typical" Am. fam

A. 1950s: _____

_____

_____

B. Changes today:

1. _____

_____

2. _____

_____

3. _____

Stats: _____

_____

Reasons: _____

_____

New problems: _____

_____

6 **Taking Notes (Part II)** Listen to the second part of the lecture. Continue taking notes on your own paper. After listening, use your notes to fill in the missing information below.

II. Company policies/programs:

A. _____

_____

B. If co. transfers worker, co. finds job for husb/wife

C. _____

_____

D. _____

_____

E. _____

_____

_____

Concl.: _____

After You Listen

7 **Discussing the Lecture** Discuss the following questions about the lecture and your own experiences. Refer to your notes as necessary.

1. In the U.S., why are more and more mothers in two-parent families working these days? (Give two reasons.) How does this compare with what is happening in your home country?

2. With both mothers and fathers working, what new problems do families in the U.S. have?

3. Review the five programs and policies that some U.S. businesses have introduced to help working parents. For each program or policy, talk about the advantages and disadvantages (a) to workers, (b) to employers.

4. Why don't *all* U.S. companies offer these programs to their employees?

5. Of the five programs and policies, which one would be the most useful for you and your family?

8 **Reviewing Vocabulary** Work in small groups. Look back at the vocabulary list in Activity 2 on page 109. Quiz each other on the terms and their meanings.

9 **What Would You Do?** Read the following story from the *Los Angeles Times* newspaper. In small groups, discuss the questions that follow.

Husband Sues Wife over Housework

Tokyo—A 33-year-old Japanese woman divorced her husband after he demanded that every day she cook him breakfast, iron his pants, and clean the house. The woman worked full time, but the husband said it was the wife's job to do all the housework.

The husband, a 35-year-old public servant, filed a lawsuit demanding that the wife pay him about $38,000 because she did not live up to her end of the marriage arrangement.[1]

1. If you were the judge in this case, what would you decide? Do you agree with the wife or the husband? Why? (To find out what really happened, turn to page 261.)

The newspaper article continues:

Increasingly, young [Japanese] women delay marriage or even refuse to get married because of the long-established expectations that women alone should raise the children and take care of the housework. Surveys show the average age at which Japanese women marry has risen to 27, with an increasing number now deciding not to tie the knot[2] at all.

Source: *Los Angeles Times*
[1] She did not do the things that her husband expected her to do.
[2] to get married

2. Compare the situation of Japanese women and women in other countries. Are women in other countries getting married later? Do some women refuse to get married? Why?

3. In your opinion, whose job is it to take care of children and do housework? Why?

Average age to tie the knot

1900		2005	
22	26	26	27
Women	Men	Women	Men

Source: U.S. Census Bureau

Focused Listening

LINKING

In writing, words are separated by spaces. In speech, words are usually separated by pauses. However, sometimes words don't have pauses between them. The words are *linked,* or connected.

Example Please put it in a box. ⟶ Please **pudidinabox.**

Words are linked according to the following rules:

1. In a phrase, when a word ends in a consonant sound and the next word starts with a vowel sound, the two words are linked. For example:

   an͜ eye   where͜ are   run͜ out͜ of   put͜ it͜ in͜ a box

2. If a word ends in the vowel sounds /iy/ as in *me*, /ey/ as in *say*, /ay/ as in *eye*, or /oy/ as in *boy*, and the next word starts with a vowel, the words are linked with the sound /y/. For example:

   the͜ end of   say͜ it   my͜ aunt   enjoy͜ it

3. If a word ends in the vowel sounds /uw/ as in *you*, /ow/ as in *show*, or /aw/ as in *how*, and the next word starts with a vowel, the words are linked with the sound /w/. For example:

   you͜ are late   show͜ us   how͜ are you

Note: Don't try to memorize these rules. If you practice listening to English a lot, you will learn the rules naturally.

1 **Pronouncing Linked Phrases** Listen and repeat the linked phrases.

Rule 1: Consonant sound + vowel

1. fifty dollars a month
2. the check is late
3. care about
4. in an apartment
5. get a job

Rule 2: Vowel + vowel

6. the end of (the month)
7. people my own age
8. come see us
9. no way out
10. the toy is broken

Rule 3: Vowel /uw/, /ow/, or /aw/ + vowel

11. grow up
12. go on
13. who is it
14. now it's ready
15. new art

2 **Pronouncing Sentences** Listen and repeat these sentences. Notice the stress, intonation, linking, reductions, and pauses.

1. I usually get up at 7 A.M., but today my alarm clock didn't go off.
2. At 8 A.M., I woke up in a panic. My first class was at 8:30! I couldn't be absent because we were having a test.
3. I jumped out of bed and got dressed in two minutes.
4. Then I ran out of the house, jumped in my car, and drove off.
5. Luckily, I found a parking spot and made it to class by 8:40.
6. I was out of breath and sweating.
7. A few people looked at me curiously.
8. Luckily, no one noticed that I wasn't wearing any shoes.

With a partner, take turns reading the sentences again. Pay attention to stress, intonation, linking, reductions, and pauses.

Getting Meaning from Context

TOEFL® iBT

Focus on Testing

Using Context Clues Many tests such as the TOEFL® iBT measure your academic listening and speaking abilities. This activity, and others in the book, will develop your social and academic conversation skills, and provide a foundation for success on a variety of standardized tests. You're going to hear several people talking about their lifestyles.

1. Listen to the beginning of each passage.

2. Listen to an incomplete statement. Stop the recording and choose the best way to complete the statement.

3. In the **Clues** column, write the words that helped you choose your answer.

4. Listen to the last part of each passage to hear the correct answer.

Answers	Clues
1. (A) a factory worker (B) a retired person (C) a landlord (D) a fashion model	
2. (A) the police (B) her teachers (C) her friends (D) her parents	
3. (A) is a day care worker (B) has never been married (C) is divorced (D) is married now	
4. (A) with his parents (B) in a college dormitory (C) alone (D) with roommates	
5. (A) a retirement home (B) a house with friends (C) an apartment (D) her son's house	

3 Discussing Lifestyles Do you know any people like those in the recording? If yes, tell about their lifestyles and their problems or difficulties. Tell about the following and answer the questions below.

- a retired man living on Social Security (money that retired people receive each month from the U.S. government)
- a teenage girl who feels that her parents treat her like a baby
- a divorced parent raising his or her children alone
- a young man who lost his job and moved back into his parents' house
- an elderly person living in a retirement home

1. As a teenager, how is/was your relationship with your parents? Do/Did you ever feel that your parents treat/treated you like a baby?

2. In your opinion, is it the government's responsibility to take care of people when they retire? If not, whose responsibility is it?

▲ Senior citizens in a retirement home

Real-World Task: Using Numbers, Percentages, Graphs

In this section you are going to compare lifestyles in different countries. In Chapter 2, page 38, you practiced taking notes on statistics. Review the vocabulary from that page. In this section you will continue learning how to talk about numbers and percentages.

Before You Listen

NUMBERS AND PERCENTAGES

Read the following sentences with numbers and percentages. Pay close attention to prepositions.

1. Seventy-five percent **of** U.S. women are married by age 30.

2. By age 30, 75 percent **of** women in the United States have been married.

3. By 2020, the percentage **of** elderly people in Japan will grow **from** 19 percent **to** 25 percent.

4. The number **of** unmarried Korean women in their 30s rose **from** 0.5 percent **to** 10.7 percent.

5. China's divorce rate went up **by** 21.2 percent in 2004.

6. The number **of** children declined **to** 1.6 (pronounced "one point six") **per** family.

1 **Prelistening Discussion** Discuss the following questions about *your* community.

1. In the last 50 years, has the number of working women increased, decreased, or stayed the same?

2. Is the divorce rate increasing or decreasing?

3. With whom do older people usually live?

Strategy

Graphic Organizer: Line Graph

A line graph can help you understand change or growth. For example, it can show changes in things like divorce rates or salaries over a period of time.

2 Completing Line Graphs

1. Here are three incomplete line graphs. Listen to the information and complete the graphs. The first item is done for you.

2. Work with a partner and compare graphs.

Population of Working Women in the U.S.

%

65
60 · 57.6
55 · 51.1
50
45
40 · 37.8
35
30
25
20

1960   1980   1990   2003

Year

61

U.S Divorce Rate, 1960–2003
(per 1,000 people)

Rate

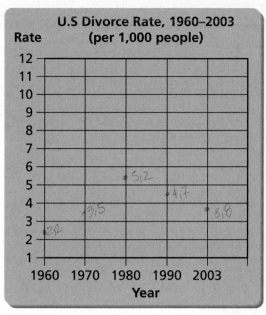

2,2 (1960)
3,5 (1970)
5,2 (1980)
4,7 (1990)
3,8 (2003)

Year

People in the U.S. over Age 65
Living Alone,1970–2000

%

Year

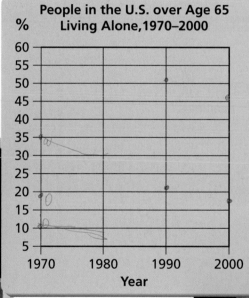

3 **Talking About Statistics** Write five true or false statements based on the information in the graphs. Then take turns saying your statements to one or more partners. If a statement is false, your classmate(s) should correct it.

Example

   A: In 2000, 20 percent of elderly women lived alone.

   B: That's false. In 2000, 40 percent of elderly women lived alone.

Discuss your answers to the following questions with a partner.

   1. Are you surprised by the information you learned from the graphs? Why or why not?

   2. What are some possible reasons for the decrease in divorce rates since the 1990s?

   3. Why do you think more elderly women than men live alone?

Talk It Over

4 **Comparing Lifestyles in Different Countries** The charts on page 121 and 122 are from *The World Factbook.* They contain information about lifestyles in different countries. However, the charts are not complete. Work in groups of three. Each student should look at one chart. Take turns asking and answering questions about the information in your chart. Fill in the missing information as your group members answer your questions.

Examples

   Q: What was the average life expectancy in France?

   A: The life expectancy in France was 79.44 years. (or "almost 80 years.")

   Q: What was the GDP in Russia?

   A: The GDP in Russia was $8,900.

   Q: How many children did the average woman have in Mexico?

   A: The average woman had 2.49 children (or "between 2 and 3 children").

Chart A

Country	# Children per Woman	Life Expectancy	TV Sets per Person	Per Capita GDP[1]
Korea	1.5	75.5	.4	$17,800
United States	2.07	77.43		37,800
Argentina	2.24	75.7	.3	11,200
France	1.84	79.44	.6	27,600
Senegal		56.56	.08	1,600
Thailand	1.89	71.41	.5	7,400
Mexico	2.49	74.94	.3	9,000
Italy	1.27	79.54	.5	26,700
Saudi Arabia	4.11	75.23	.3	11,800
China (PRC)	1.69	71.96	.3	5,000
Egypt	2.95	70.71	.2	4,000
Iran	1.93	69.66	.1	7,000
Russia		66.39	.5	8,900
Japan	1.38		.8	28,200
Turkey	1.98	72.08	.4	

Chart B

Country	# Children per Woman	Life Expectancy	TV Sets per Person	Per Capita GDP[1]
Korea	1.5	75.5	.4	
United States	2.07		1.00	$37,800
Argentina	2.24	75.7	.3	11,200
France	1.84	79.44	.6	27,600
Senegal	4.84		.08	1,600
Thailand	1.89	71.41	.5	7,400
Mexico	2.49	74.94	.3	9,000
Italy	1.27	79.54	.5	26,700
Saudi Arabia	4.11	75.23	.3	11,800
China (PRC)		71.96	.3	5,000
Egypt	2.95	70.71	.2	4,000
Iran	1.93	69.66		7,000
Russia	1.26	65.12	.5	8,900
Japan	1.38	81.04	.8	28,200
Turkey	1.98	72.08	.4	6,700

[1] *GDP* means "gross domestic product." This number refers to the total value of goods and services produced by a country over a certain period of time. *Per capita GDP* is this number divided by the number of people living in the country.

Chart C				
Country	# Children per Woman	Life Expectancy	TV Sets per Person	Per Capita GDP
Korea	1.5	75.5	.4	$17,800
United States	2.07	77.43	1.00	37,800
Argentina	2.24	75.7	.3	
France	1.84	79.44	.6	27,600
Senegal	4.84	56.56	.08	1,600
Thailand	1.89		.5	7,400
Mexico	2.49	74.94	.3	9,000
Italy	1.27	79.54	.5	
Saudi Arabia	4.11	75.23	.3	11,800
China (PRC)	1.69	71.96	.3	5,000
Egypt		70.71	.2	4,000
Iran	1.93	69.66	.1	7,000
Russia	1.26	65.12		8,900
Japan	1.38	81.04	.8	28,200
Turkey	1.98	72.08	.4	6,700

Source: *The World Factbook*

 5 Discussion Discuss the questions below with your group.

1. Based on the information in the charts, which five countries have the highest GDP?

2. Which five countries have the lowest GDP?

3. Compare the number of the children per woman, the life expectancy, and the TV sets per person for the countries you named in questions 1 and 2. What general statements can you make, based on this information? Make complete sentences.

Example

The countries with the lowest GDPs usually have the largest number of children per woman, and the countries with the highest GDPs have the smallest number. For example, in Japan, the average woman has 1.38 children, but in Senegal, the average woman has more than 4 children.

Self-Assessment Log

Check the words you learned in this chapter.

Nouns	**Verbs**	**Adjectives**
❑ cost of living	❑ benefit	❑ flexible
❑ day care center	❑ can/can't afford	❑ old-fashioned
❑ flexibility	❑ check up on	
❑ homemaker	❑ look into	
❑ maternity leave	❑ run out	
❑ opportunity	❑ take off	
❑ policy	❑ transfer	
	❑ volunteer	

Check the things you did in this chapter. How well can you do each one?

	Very well	Fairly well	Not very well
I can hear and use stress and reductions.	❑	❑	❑
I can ask for and respond to requests for favors.	❑	❑	❑
I can take notes on examples using an outline.	❑	❑	❑
I can talk about lifestyles and company policies.	❑	❑	❑
I can guess meanings from context.	❑	❑	❑
I can complete graphs.	❑	❑	❑
I can talk about statistics.	❑	❑	❑

Write what you learned and what you liked in this chapter.

In this chapter,

I learned _____

_____

I liked _____

_____

Global Connections

❝ No culture can live if it attempts to be exclusive. **❞**

—Mahatma Gandhi
Indian nationalist and spiritual leader (1869–1948)

Connecting to the Topic

1. Where is the person in the photo? What is the person doing?

2. Why do you think this person needs a computer?

3. List the types of technology that you use. How do you use each type?

Part 1

Conversation: Using Technology to Stay in Touch

Before You Listen

In the following conversation, Mari and Jeff talk about using technology to stay in touch with family and friends.

▲ Jeff, making a telephone call over the Internet

1 Prelistening Questions Discuss these questions with your classmates.

1. In the photo, Jeff is using special software to make a telephone call over the Internet. What do you know about this technology? Have you used it?

2. How often do you use a computer and for what purposes?

3. What technology do you use to stay in touch with your family and friends in other countries?

2 Previewing Vocabulary

1. Listen to these computer terms from the conversation. Define them with your classmates. Check the terms you know. If you are not sure about a term, look it up in a dictionary.

Nouns	Verbs
❑ blog	❑ download
❑ headset	❑ install (software)
❑ sound card	❑ post (a message or comment)

2. Listen to the underlined words and expressions from the conversation. Then use the context to match them with their definitions.

Sentences

_____ **1.** I need to <u>catch up on</u> the reading for my economics course. I was sick for two weeks, and I'm really behind.

_____ **2.** My teacher wrote several <u>comments</u> and questions on my paper and asked me to rewrite it.

_____ **3.** Fatima <u>stays in touch</u> with her family by phone and email.

_____ **4.** **A:** Could you give me a ride to school tomorrow?
B: <u>No sweat</u>.

_____ **5.** There's a $3.00 <u>charge</u> for ordering concert tickets over the phone.

Definitions

a. an opinion or statement about something or someone

b. to do something necessary that you didn't have time to do in the past

c. "No problem" or "That's easy."

d. a cost or fee

e. to communicate with someone regularly

3 **Comprehension Questions** Listen to the conversation. You don't need to understand all the words. Just listen for the answers to these questions. After you listen, discuss your answers with a partner.

1. Where does this conversation probably take place? *blog*
2. What is Jeff doing?
3. Who is Hasan?
4. How much was Mari's cell phone bill?
5. What does Mari want to know about?
6. What equipment will Mari need to buy?
7. How much does VoIP software cost?

Stress

4 **Listening for Stressed Words** Listen to the conversation again. Some of the stressed words are missing. During each pause, repeat the phrase or sentence. Then fill in the missing stressed words.

Jeff: Come in!

Mari: Am I _____?

Jeff: It's OK, I was just catching up on my _____.

Mari: Oh yeah? What's it _____?

Jeff: Mostly it's about _____. Like, here's a _____ from a guy named Hasan talking about, let's see . . . hip-hop in Istanbul.

Mari: In Turkey? _____ hip-hop?

Jeff: Sure. And _____ one from my friend Hiroshi, the _____ in Tokyo.

Mari: Hmm. Maybe _____ should start a blog about learning _____.

Jeff: Well, it's a great way to meet _____ people, that's for sure. And all you need is an _____ connection.

Mari: Well, _____ of the Internet, I wanted to ask your _____ about something.

Jeff: OK. What's up?

Mari: Well, I just got my _____ phone bill for last month, and it was $160!

Jeff: Ouch.

Mari: Yeah, I can't _____ it. Cell phone calls are so

_____ here.

Jeff: Are they _____ in Japan?

Mari: _____ cheaper. And we use our cell phones for

_____, too. A lot of people don't even _____

a computer.

Jeff: It's _____ what you can do with cell phones these days.

Talk, take _____, send email . . .

Mari: Yeah. But _____ Jeff, I need to find a cheaper way to stay

in _____ with my parents and my friends in Japan. And

I _____ there's a way you can call overseas for

_____ using your computer. Do you know anything

about that?

Jeff: Of course, it's a _____ called Voice over Internet. I use it all

the _____.

Mari: How does it _____?

Jeff: Well, you need a computer with a _____ card, if you've

got that.

Mari: Yeah, I do . . .

Jeff: And you also need a microphone and a _____.

Mari: Hmm. I don't have those.

Jeff: No sweat, you can buy them at any _____ store.

Mari: OK. What else?

Jeff: Well, then you'll need to _____ the software, which is

_____, and then if the person you're calling installs the

_____ software, there's no _____ for calling.

Mari: But what if they _____? Can I call from my

_____ to someone's _____?

Jeff: Yes. There's a _____ for that, but it's a lot cheaper than

using your _____ _____, believe me.

Mari: Could you show me how it works on _____ computer?

Jeff: Right now?

Mari: No, it's _____ in Japan now. Can we do it in about three

_____?

Jeff: No problem. I'll be here.

Mari: Great. See you later.

Check your answers using the listening script on page 282. Then read the conversation with a partner. Remember that stressed words are louder, higher, and pronounced more clearly than unstressed words.

Intonation

 INTONATION IN QUESTIONS AND REQUESTS

Information questions have a rising-falling intonation pattern:

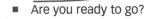

- Where do you live?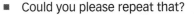

- What's your name?

Yes/No questions and requests have a rising intonation pattern:

- Are you ready to go?

- Could you please repeat that?

 5 Practicing Intonation of Questions Listen to the following items from the conversation and repeat them after the speaker.

Yes/No questions

1. Am I interrupting?

2. Are they cheaper in Japan?

Request for help or permission

3. Could you show me how it works on your computer?

4. Can we do it in about three hours?

Information questions

5. What's it about?

6. How does it work?

 6 Identifying Intonation Patterns Listen to the following sentences. Repeat each sentence after the speaker; then circle the up arrow for rising intonation, or the down arrow for rising-falling intonation.

1.   **4.**

2.   **5.**

3.   **6.**

7 **Reviewing Vocabulary** Discuss the following with a partner. Use the underlined vocabulary in your answers.

1. Do you read email every day, or do you wait until the weekend to catch up on all your messages?

2. How do you stay in touch with your family and friends when you're traveling?

3. Before you buy an expensive product, such as a camera or computer, do you read the comments posted on the Internet by other people who have used it? Why or why not?

4. (Complete the following conversation with a request for help or permission.)

   A: _____

   B: No sweat.

5. How much is the monthly charge on your cell phone? Would you like to find a cheaper monthly fee?

Using Language Functions

INTERRUPTING POLITELY

At the beginning of the conversation, Mari enters Jeff's room and asks, "Am I interrupting?" In many cultures it is impolite to interrupt a person who is speaking or working. However, most Americans are accustomed to interruptions and don't mind them. Here are some expressions that English speakers use to interrupt politely.

Expressions for Interrupting Politely

Am I interrupting?	I'm sorry to interrupt, but . . .
Can/May I interrupt?	Pardon me, but . . .
Excuse me (for interrupting), but . . .	Sorry, but . . .
I'd like to say something.	Wait (a minute). (I have a question.)

8 **Role-Play** Work in groups of three. In each of the situations, two people are talking and a third person interrupts. Take turns playing the role of speakers and interrupter.

1. Two colleagues are talking about a computer problem in their department. An assistant enters, interrupts, and tells one of them that their boss is on the phone and wants to talk to him or her right away.

2. It is time for class to start, and several students are talking on their cell phones. The teacher interrupts and asks them to put away their phones and take out their homework.

3. Two friends are having coffee together. They are talking about travel plans. A third friend interrupts and asks if he or she can join them.

9 **The Interrupting Game** Work in groups of four to five students. Your teacher will give each student in the group a topic to discuss.

1. When it is your turn, start speaking about your topic.

2. Your classmates will interrupt you often, using the expressions in the explanation box.

3. When you are interrupted, answer the person who interrupted you, but then return to your topic. Follow the example.

Example

Speaker: Last night I went to a baseball game . . .
Student 1: Excuse me for interrupting, but which one?
Speaker: The Red Sox and the Yankees. Anyway, I went to the game and got to my seat . . .
Student 2: Sorry, but where was your seat?

And so on.

4. The game ends when the speaker finishes the story.

10 **Survey: Find Someone Who . . .** Ask your classmates about the ways that they stay in touch with family and friends. Find one person who fits each description below. Write the person's name in the space.

Example Have you ever used Voice over Internet Protocol?

Find someone who . . .	Name
has used Voice over Internet Protocol	
uses Instant Messenger regularly	
receives more than 10 emails a day	
enjoys writing letters	
has a PDA (personal digital assistant)	
does not have a cell phone	
has a cell phone, but no landline	
sends text messages regularly	

Before You Listen

The lecture in this chapter is about misunderstandings that can occur if people from different countries do not know about each other's customs.

 1 Prelistening Discussion Discuss these questions in small groups.

1. What are the people in each photo doing? Can you guess which countries they are from?

2. Have you ever invited guests from another country to your home? If so, did their behavior surprise you? How did you react?

3. When visiting another country, have you ever insulted someone or embarrassed yourself because you didn't know the local customs? What happened?

2 Previewing Vocabulary Listen to these words and phrases from the lecture. Check (✓) the ones you think you know. Discuss their meanings with a partner. Check the other items later as you learn them.

Nouns	Verbs	Adjectives
❏ chopsticks	❏ bow	❏ appropriate
❏ hug	❏ illustrate	❏ embarrassing
❏ misunderstanding		❏ insulted
❏ title (of a person)		
❏ utensils		
❏ variation		

Listen

Strategy

Taking Notes on Similarities and Differences

Taking Notes on Differences
The following sentence is from the lecture:

"In the United States, greetings often involve some sort of touching . . . On the other hand, people from most Asian countries don't usually feel as comfortable touching in public."

Here are sample notes for this sentence. Notice the use of indenting, key words, and abbreviations:

Greetings

   U.S.: involve touching

   Asia: not comf. touching

Taking Notes on Similarities

"The Japanese, like many other people in Asia, give gifts often."

Jap. + other Asians give gifts often

Expressions Signaling Similarity and Difference
The following expressions are used in the lecture.

Differences	Similarities
on the other hand	(be) similar to
in contrast	also
however	like
while	

3 Taking Notes on Similarities and Differences Listen to sentences with similarities and differences. Complete the notes. You will hear each sentence twice.

1. *Ams = comf. using 1st names*

_____

_____

Other cultures:

_____

_____

2. *Egypt: leave food on plate*

_____

_____

_____

3. _____: *eat everyth. on plate*

_____

_____

_____

4. *Many Jap. bow when they greet*

bow   taylant Hollow the he.

_____

_____

5. *U.S. + West. countries:*

greeting hand shake if Know very well

_____

_____

Now, exchange notes with a classmate. Use your partner's notes to try to restate the information you heard.

4 Taking Notes (Part I) Listen to the first part of the lecture and take notes in the best way you can. Use your own paper. Listen for similarities and differences in two areas of cultural behavior.

5 Outlining the Lecture Here is a sample outline of the first part of the lecture. Use your notes from Activities 3 and 4 to fill in the missing information. Remember to use abbreviations and symbols. Listen again if necessary.

Part 1

　　　　Topic: _____

Intro: _____

_____

_____

　I. Greetings

　　A. U.S. + West. countries: _____

　　　_____

　　B. France: _____

　　　_____

　　C. Asia: _____

　　　_____

　　　1. _____

　　　　_____

　　　2. _____

　　　　_____

　II. _____

　　　_____

　　A. Americans: _____

　　　_____

　　B. _____

　　　_____

　　　E.g. _____

　　C. Korea: _____

　　　_____

6 Taking Notes (Part II) Listen to the second part of the lecture. Continue taking notes on your own paper. After listening, use your notes to fill in the missing information below.

III. _____

   A. Utensils _____

      1. _____

      2. _____

      3. _____

   B. _____

      1. Egypt: _____

      2. _____

      3. _____

IV. _____

   A. _____

      1. for dinner: bring flowers, wine, small gift from your country

      2. business: _____

   B. Japanese + other Asians: _____

      _____

      _____

   C. _____

      E.g.: _____

V. _____

   _____

 7 Discussing the Lecture Discuss the following questions about the lecture and your own experiences. Refer to your notes as necessary.

   1. Explain the "rules" for greeting people in the U.S., Japan, Thailand, and France. How do the customs of these countries compare with the customs of your home country or culture?

   2. Compare the use of names and titles in the United States and other countries. What advice would you give an American visiting your culture about the proper way to address people?

3. Name one or more countries where people do the following:

   - eat with a knife and fork

   - eat with chopsticks

   - eat with their hands

   - leave food on their plate to be polite

   - finish all the food on their plate to be polite.

4. Restate the examples of gift-giving customs from the lecture. Does your culture have any "rules" for types of gifts to give and to avoid?

 8 **Reviewing Vocabulary** Work in small groups. Look back at the vocabulary list in Activity 2 on page 134. Quiz each other on the terms and their meanings.

On the Spot!

Strategy

Graphic Organizer: T-chart
T-charts can help you organize and compare two different sides of a topic.
For example,

- you can compare the advantages and disadvantages of an idea to help you make a decision;

- you can compare facts and opinions;

- or you can list the strengths and weaknesses of an idea or of something you read or listen to.

9 **What Would You Do?** Read the situation and discuss the questions.

Situation

At a party, a friend introduces you to a young man or woman. You begin talking and discover that the two of you have many opinions and ideas in common. You have such a good time talking that you agree to meet for coffee the following day.

In the following weeks you meet many more times. As you get to know each other better, you begin to fall in love and talk about the future. However, there is a serious problem. Your parents expect you to date people from the same background (race, religion, education, or social class) as you. Your new boyfriend/girlfriend comes from a very different background. You know that your parents will be angry if you decide to keep seeing this person. You must make a decision. Will you continue going out together, knowing that your parents will disapprove, or will you end the relationship now, before it becomes more serious?

▲ A couple from different backgrounds

1. What would you do in the situation described on page 138? Why?

2. Could you ever fall in love with or marry a person from a different background than you? What would your parents say if you wanted to do this?

3. What are the advantages and disadvantages of two people from different backgrounds getting married? Use the following T-chart.

Advantages	Disadvantages

Focused Listening

BLENDING CONSONANTS

When one word ends in a consonant sound and the next word begins with the same consonant sound, the two sounds are *blended,* or pronounced as one sound. There is no pause between the two words.

Example

black + cat = **blakat**

big + girl = **bigirl**

famous + singer = **famousinger**

1 **Pronouncing Names with Blended Consonants** Here are some typical English names. Listen and repeat them after the speaker. Blend the consonants so that each name sounds like one word.

1. Alan Norton
2. Pat Thompson
3. Philip Pearson
4. Dick Cantor
5. Brad Davis
6. Meg Gray

7. Tom Madison
8. Peter Ramsey
9. Val Lewis
10. Trish Sherman
11. Cass Saxon
12. Seth Thayer

2 **Listening for Blended Consonants** Listen to the sentences and circle the blended sounds.

Example Harris saw a fat tiger at the zoo.

1. Yesterday Yolanda had a really bad day.
2. June ninth is the date of Valerie's last test.
3. Let's save money to buy a car radio.
4. Ron needs a tall ladder to reach that high window.
5. Please bring me some hot tea.
6. Camille lives in a dangerous city.
7. Malik called his mother eight times.

Listen again. Stop the recording after each sentence and repeat.

3 **Pronouncing Sentences** Circle the blended consonants and mark the linked sounds in the sentences below. Then practice saying these sentences with correct blending, linking, stress, reductions, and intonation. Finally, listen to the tape to check your pronunciation.

Example The air was full of fall leaves.

1. We need to cancel our dinner reservations.

2. I live with three roommates.

3. Have a good day.

4. I don't know her phone number.

5. This song is so sad.

6. We're ready to take a walk.

7. Did he put his black coat away?

8. She bought an expensive vase.

Getting Meaning from Context

Focus on Testing

Using Context Clues Many tests such as the TOEFL® IBT measure your academic listening and speaking abilities. This activity, and others in the book, will develop your social and academic conversation skills, and provide a foundation for success on a variety of standardized tests. You are going to hear short passages about customs in different countries.

1. Listen to each passage.

2. Listen to the question for each passage. Stop the recording and choose the best answer to each question.

3. In the **Clues** column, write the words that helped you choose your answer.

Answers	Clues
1. (A) They wanted to help the professor get ready for the party. (B) They forgot to check their watches. (C) Koreans and Americans have different ideas about arriving on time. (D) Parties in the U.S. always start early.	

Answers	Clues
2. (A) Take off your shoes when you enter the house. (B) Keep your feet on the floor. (C) Stand up when your host enters the room. (D) Don't give shoes as a gift in the Middle East.	
3. (A) Japanese people are friendlier than Americans. (B) Americans smile more than people from other cultures. (C) A smile can have different meanings in different cultures. (D) A smile has the same meaning in the United States and Puerto Rico.	
4. (A) an old tradition (B) a way to make trees healthier (C) how to use old shoes (D) couples who have many children	
5. (A) The officer will disapprove of you. (B) You will get special treatment. (C) It could help your business. (D) You could be arrested.	

Using Language Functions

GENERALIZING

To speak about your daily routine or typical activities, use the present tense with any of these expressions.

generally	typically	most of the time	as a rule
in general	normally	usually	ordinarily

Examples

I wear sandals most of the time, even in winter.

I usually drink French or Colombian coffee for breakfast.

Typically, I leave for work at 7:30 A.M.

4 **Discussing a Reading** In the following passage, a resident of Brooklyn describes a typical Sunday in her neighborhood. Read the passage and discuss the questions that follow.

Brooklyn, New York is a very large, vibrant village. Its streets are full of world music, its buildings built by the hands of every culture. On a typical Saturday afternoon, as I walk through my neighborhood in search of lunch, I'm aware of the beautiful small world I inhabit. A group of Puerto Rican children play baseball in the street, making way for cars as they pass—first, a German car with sounds of Dominican bachata music flowing from its windows, followed by a Japanese truck whose driver enjoys Afro-Caribbean calypso. I stop inside the corner store to say hello to the Korean owner who sells me fresh flowers. My quest for food continues as I wander past many different types of restaurants. Should I eat a gyro from the Greek diner? Maybe a sugar bun from the Jamaican bakery or some minestrone soup from the Italian cafe will cure my hunger. Finally, I'm lured by the smell of curried chicken and decide to have my meal at an Indian restaurant. My stomach full, I continue my walk through the neighborhood, this time listening to the variety of different languages I hear on the street and I realize that language *is* music. Between Farsi and French, Swahili and Polish, each language has a unique rhythm and melody. Surrounded by so many international feasts and sounds, I am proud to call the global village of Brooklyn my home.

1. How many types of music does the writer hear, and where do they come from?

2. What does the writer see around her on the street?

3. What languages does the writer hear on the street?

4. Which foods does the writer mention, and where do they come from?

Prepare a short presentation about *your* typical day as an international citizen. Follow these instructions:

1. Use the questions above to guide you. For example: Which imported products do you use every day?

2. Make a list of other activities and products that are part of your daily routine.

3. Organize your presentation in chronological order, from the time you get up in the morning until you go to bed at night. Do not include every detail of your day; include only those activities and products that have an international aspect.

4. Remember to use expressions for generalizing from the instruction box on page 142.

5. Speak for two to three minutes. If possible, use one or more visual aids in your presentation.

FYI

trivia
(noun, plural)
things that are
very unimportant:
unimportant or
useless details;
little-known facts

A popular party game in the United States is called Trivial Pursuit. This game tests people's knowledge of detailed facts ("trivia") in many subjects such as world geography, movies, computers, and many more. Many Americans enjoy playing trivia games or taking trivia quizzes in magazines and newspapers.

▲ Playing TRIVIAL PURSUIT

Before You Listen

1 **Prelistening Discussion** Answer the questions with a small group.

1. Have you ever played a trivia game? With whom did you play? Did you enjoy the game? Why or why not? Did you win?

2. Do you know anyone who is a trivia expert? Describe this person.

3. Are you an expert in any topic? How did you get your knowledge or skill?

2 **Taking a Trivia Quiz** In the following conversation, Joyce reads a trivia quiz to her friend Kevin. As she asks the questions, circle *your* answers in the chart. Then listen to the next part of the conversation, and you will hear the correct answer.

1. (A) the United States
   (B) Canada
   (C) Russia
   (D) China

2. (A) France
   (B) the United States
   (C) Italy
   (D) China

3. (A) North America
   (B) Europe
   (C) Latin America
   (D) Middle East

4. (A) China
   (B) United States
   (C) Russia
   (D) Canada

5. (A) 5 hours
   (B) 8 hours
   (C) 11 hours
   (D) 15 hours

6. (A) Mexico
   (B) Russia
   (C) England
   (D) Greece

7. (A) German
   (B) Spanish
   (C) Japanese
   (D) Chinese

8. (A) Moscow
   (B) New York
   (C) Tokyo
   (D) London

What score did *you* get on the quiz? Compare with your classmates.

After You Listen

3 **Designing a Trivia Game** Write five trivia questions about your community and give them to your teacher. He or she will select questions to use in a class trivia game. You can write questions about:

- geography
- history
- customs
- products
- cities
- people
- natural resources
- tourist attractions

Talk It Over

4 Choosing Your Dream Vacation Work in small groups. Look at the photos and answer the questions that follow on page 147.

1. Can you guess where each photo was taken? What do you know about each place? For example,
   - the weather
   - the attractions
   - places to stay
   - dangers

2. Have you ever visited any of these places or similar ones? If so, tell your group about your trip.

3. If you could choose *one* of these places to take an all-expenses-paid vacation, which one would you choose? Why?

Self-Assessment Log

Check the words you learned in this chapter.

Nouns
- ❑ blog
- ❑ charge
- ❑ chopsticks
- ❑ comment
- ❑ headset
- ❑ hug
- ❑ misunderstanding
- ❑ sound card
- ❑ title (of a person)
- ❑ universal
- ❑ utensils
- ❑ variation

Verbs
- ❑ bow
- ❑ catch up on
- ❑ download
- ❑ illustrate
- ❑ install (software)
- ❑ post (a message or comment)
- ❑ stay in touch

Adjectives
- ❑ appropriate
- ❑ embarrassing
- ❑ insulted

Expressions
- ❑ No sweat.

Check the things you did in this chapter. How well can you do each one?

	Very well	Fairly well	Not very well
I can hear and use stress.	❑	❑	❑
I can use intonation in questions and requests.	❑	❑	❑
I can use phrases for interrupting politely.	❑	❑	❑
I can take notes on similarities and differences using an outline.	❑	❑	❑
I can talk about customs in different countries.	❑	❑	❑
I can guess meanings from context.	❑	❑	❑
I can design and play a trivia game.	❑	❑	❑

Write what you learned and what you liked in this chapter.

In this chapter,

I learned _____

_____

I liked _____

_____

Language and Communication

" To have another language is to possess a second soul. "

—Charlemagne
King of the Franks, Emperor of the West, (742?–814)

Connecting to the Topic

1 Where are the man and woman? What is their relationship?

2 What do you think he is saying? How do you think he feels? How do you think she feels?

3 What do you think will happen next?

Before You Listen

In the following conversation, Nancy and Mari talk about friendliness and friendship in the United States.

▲ Yolanda, Nancy, and Mari

1 Prelistening Questions Discuss these questions with your classmates.

1. What do you think is happening in the photo on page 150?

2. What is the difference between "friendliness" and "friendship"?

2. Have you ever had a friend from another culture? Was it difficult to communicate with this person at first? In what way?

2 Previewing Vocabulary Listen to the underlined words and expressions from the conversation. Then use the context to match them with their definitions.

Sentences

_B_ **1.** Nobody is using this chair. Have a seat and rest.

_h_ **2.** A: I don't like Kathleen. She's so two-faced!

B: Yeah, she's nice when she's with you, but she says bad things about you behind your back.

_F_ **3.** The student from Brazil was popular because of her friendliness.

_A_ **4.** If a good friend lied to me, I would end my friendship with her.

_G_ **5.** It's hard to make friends with people if you don't speak their language well.

_D_ **6.** After the teacher explained the math problem five times, the students finally began to catch on.

_C_ **7.** I don't understand what our teacher wants us to do. I am completely in the dark.

_E_ **8.** It's hard to say if he likes me because he never talks about his feelings.

Definitions

a. a close, trusting relationship

b. "Sit down."

c. understanding or knowing nothing about a particular thing

d. to begin to understand

e. "I can't be sure."

f. a warm and open way of behaving with people

g. to become friendly with someone

h. dishonest

3 Comprehension Questions Listen to the conversation. You don't need to understand all the words. Just listen for the answers to these questions. After you listen, discuss your answers with a partner.

1. What is the relationship between Yolanda and Mari?

2. Why is Mari confused?

3. What does Nancy say about friendship and friendliness in the United States?

4. Do Yolanda and Mari go to the movies together often?

5. According to Nancy, what does "How are you?" mean?

Stress

4 Listening for Stressed Words Now listen to part of the conversation again. Some of the stressed words are missing. During each pause, repeat the phrase or sentence. Then fill in the missing stressed words.

Mari: I don't understand Americans.

Nancy: Huh?

Mari: Did you _____ what she said? "I'll call you, we'll go to a _____." But every time I try to pick a _____ day or time, she says she's _____, she has to check her _____. And then she _____ call.

Nancy: Mm hmm . . .

Mari: Why do Americans say things they don't _____? They _____ so nice, like they _____ say, "How are you," but then they keep on _____ and don't even wait for your _____. They're so . . . how do you say it . . . _____-faced?

Nancy: I know it _____ that way sometimes, Mari. But it's _____ _____. It's just that for Americans, friendliness and friendship _____ always the same thing.

Mari: What do you _____?

Nancy: Well, as you know, Americans can be very _____ and friendly. Like, they _____ you to sit down, they _____ you questions, they _____ you all about their families. So naturally you think they're trying to make _____ with you. But actually, friendship, _____ friendship, doesn't happen so _____.

Mari: So, when people say "How are you," they're just being _____? They don't really _____?

Nancy: Not exactly. The thing you have to _____ is that "How are you" isn't a _____ question. It's more like a _____, a way of saying hello.

Mari: Aha, I _____ it! And "Have a nice day" is just a _____ _____ way to say good-bye?

Nancy: Exactly. _____ you're catching on.

Mari: But I'm _____ in the dark about Yolanda. Does she _____ to be my friend or _____?

Nancy: It's _____ to say. Maybe she's just too _____ these days. I guess you'll just have to be _____.

Mari: Hmm. That's good _____, I guess. Thanks.

Check your answers using the listening script on page 286. Then read the conversation with a partner. Pronounce stressed words louder, higher, and more clearly than unstressed words.

Intonation

STATEMENTS WITH RISING INTONATION

You heard the following exchange in the conversation:

Mari: So when people say "How are you," they're just being polite? They don't really care?

Nancy: Not exactly.

Note that Mari's questions are actually statements—"They're just being polite?" "They don't really care?"—with rising intonation. This way of talking is often used in rapid, informal English, especially when the speaker is surprised or expects an affirmative answer.

5 Understanding Statements with Rising Intonation Listen to the following "statement questions" and rewrite them as "true" questions in the spaces.

Example

You hear: "You're going to work?"
You write: "Are you going to work?"

1. _____

2. _____

3. _____

4. _____

5. _____

After You Listen

6 Using Vocabulary Work in pairs to practice the new vocabulary. Student A should look at page 249. Student B should look at page 258.

Using Language Functions

CONTRADICTING POLITELY

To contradict means "to say the opposite of what someone has just said."
For example:

Mari: Why do Americans say things they don't mean? They're so . . . how do you say it . . . two-faced?

Nancy: I know it seems that way sometimes, Mari. But it's not true.

In her answer, Nancy contradicts Mari and corrects her wrong idea.

There are polite and impolite ways to contradict people. Here are some common expressions that are used for this purpose:

Polite Well, you might think . . . but actually . . .
Well, actually . . .
It's true that . . . but . . .
It seems . . . but . . .
That's not completely true.

Rude You're wrong.
What are you talking about?
That's ridiculous.

7 **Contradicting Stereotypes** Discuss stereotypes with your classmates and practice contradicting each other politely.

Language Tip

stereotype (noun) A too-general, overly simplified, and often negative idea about *all* members of a group or culture.
Example
"Americans are rich and care only about money." This description is a stereotype because it is too general and not true about all Americans.

1. Look at the picture. Describe this couple. Guess their nationality and explain your guess. Have you ever met people like this?

2. Complete the following sentence with adjectives or nouns. Share your sentences with your classmates and write your adjectives and nouns on the board.

   Americans are ——————————— , ——————————— ,
   ——————————— , and ——————————— .

3. With your class and teacher, discuss the following questions:

   a. Which of the words listed on the board are stereotypes? Which ones are facts? Remember, a stereotype is an idea that is too simple, too general, and cannot possibly be true for all members of a group or culture.

   b. How can you change your statements so that they are not stereotypes?

4. Work with a partner. Take turns stating stereotypes about these groups and then politely correcting those stereotypes. Use the expressions from the list on page 154.

   Americans are . . .
   Movie stars are . . .
   Athletes are . . .
   Women/Men are . . .

   People from ——————————— are . . .
             (your culture)

▲ Stereotypical tourists

Example

Student 1: Americans are only interested in money.

Student 2: I know it seems that way, especially if you don't know many American people personally. But actually, Americans can be very generous. They donate a lot of food and money to charities.

8 **What Is Friendship?** Look at the list of situations in the box. Then, in small groups discuss the questions that follow.

Situations

- take care of you when you are sick
- lend you money
- take you to or pick you up from the airport during school or work hours
- give you a gift on your birthday
- help you with your homework
- disagree with you
- tell you secrets
- help you move to a new house or apartment
- always tell you the truth
- take care of your pets or your children if you go away on vacation
- invite your relatives to his or her home
- other _____

Questions

1. Which of these things would you expect a friend to do for you? Which would you not expect? Why?

2. Which of these things would you do for a friend? Which wouldn't you do? Why?

▲ A group of friends on campus

Before You Listen

This lecture is about some differences between British and American English.

▲ "Do you have an elevator?"   ▲ "Have you got a lift?"

 1 **Prelistening Discussion** Discuss these questions in small groups.

1. Which English-speaking countries have you visited (if any)?

2. What special ways of speaking English did you notice there?

3. Which accent of English is easiest for you to understand: American, British, Australian, or something else? Why?

 2 **Previewing Vocabulary** Listen to these words from the lecture. Check (✓) the ones you think you know. Then work with a partner to define the ones you checked. Check the other words later as you learn them.

Nouns	Adjectives	Adverbs
❑ category	❑ identical	❑ while
❑ dialect	❑ noticeable	❑ whereas
❑ majority	❑ unique	
❑ sample		
❑ standard		

Strategy

Classifying and Taking Notes on Classification

Lectures are often organized by classification. That is, the lecture topic is classified, or divided, into several smaller topics. These smaller topics are called *subtopics*. A well-organized lecturer will announce these topics in the introduction. You should listen for this information because it helps you plan and organize your notes.

A graphic organizer like the one below can help you organize topics and details. Use this type of graphic organizer when you're taking notes on a lecture about several topics, or when you're organizing your own thoughts or research.

 3 **Classifying Lecture Organization** Listen to the introductions from three lectures. Write the subtopics in the spaces under each topic.

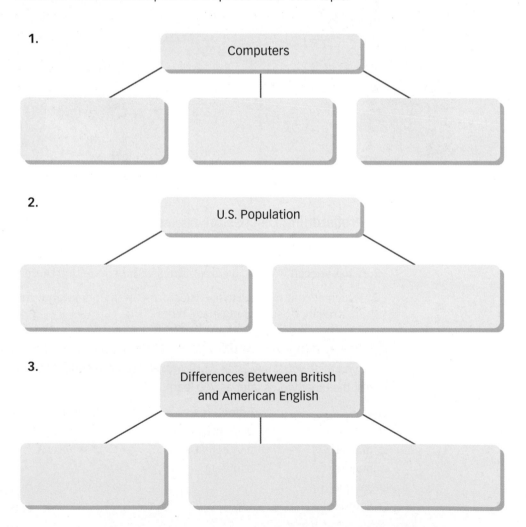

1.

Computers

2.

U.S. Population

3.

Differences Between British and American English

SOME VOCABULARY DIFFERENCES BETWEEN AMERICAN AND BRITISH ENGLISH

American English	British English
apartment	flat
bathroom	toilet
garbage can	dustbin
soccer	football
raincoat	mackintosh
quotation marks (punctuation)	inverted commas
lawyer	solicitor
pharmacist	chemist
truck	lorry
elevator	lift
cookie	biscuit
dessert	sweet

 4 **Taking Notes (Part I)** Listen to the first part of the lecture about British and American English. Take notes in the best way you can. Use your own paper.

 5 **Outlining the Lecture** Here is a sample outline of the first part of the lecture. Use your notes from Activity 4 to fill in the missing information. Remember to use abbreviations and symbols. Listen to the lecture again if necessary.

Differences Between American and British English

I. _____

_____

_____

Examples:

Sound	Am.E.	B.E.
1. "a"	/ae/	/a/
2. _____	_____	"New Yok"
3. _____	"liddle," "twenny-one"	_____

6 Taking Notes (Part II) Listen to the second part of the lecture. Continue taking notes on your own paper. After listening, use your notes to fill in the missing information below.

II. _____

_____

_____

   A. Eng. has over _____ words

   B. # of vocab diffs between Am.E. and B.E.:

     _____

     _____

   Examples:

<u>Am.E.</u>	<u>B.E.</u>
_____	_____
_____	_____
_____	_____
_____	_____

III. _____

_____

_____

   A. Am.E. almost = B.E.

   B. few diffs.:

<u>Grammar</u>	<u>Am.E.</u>	<u>B.E.</u>
1. Verbs	_____	_____
2. _____	_____	_____
3. _____	_____	_____

IV. _____

_____

7 **Discussing the Lecture** Discuss the following questions about the lecture and your own experience. Refer to your notes as necessary.

1. What is meant by standard English? How is the standard different in the United States or Canada and Great Britain?

2. Why are most speakers of American and British English able to understand one another with little difficulty?

3. In what category can you find the biggest difference between American and British English: pronunciation, vocabulary, or grammar? Where do you find the smallest variation? Give a few examples of differences between them. Use the words *while* and *whereas* to state the contrast.

Example

In standard American English, people use the verb *have,* whereas speakers of British English use *have got* to mean the same thing.

4. What language or languages are spoken by the majority of people in your community?

5. Do you speak a dialect of your first language? What are the unique characteristics of this dialect, and how is it different from the standard language? Use *while* or *whereas* to explain the differences.

6. If you ever have children, do you want them to be bilingual? Why is this important or useful?

8 **Reviewing Vocabulary** Work in small groups. Look back at the vocabulary list in Activity 2 on page 157. Quiz each other on the terms and their meanings.

9 **Comparing American and British English** Read the following sentences with a partner. Decide together if they are written in North American or British English. Check your answers by using an American-British–British-American dictionary on the Internet.

▲ The Statue of Liberty in New York

▲ The Queen's Guard in London

American	British	
_____	✓	**1.** A lorry hit my car on the motorway.
_____	_____	**2.** Can you help me lift this trash can?
_____	_____	**3.** Hundreds of people queued up at the cinema.
_____	_____	**4.** Please open the trunk so I can put in these suitcases.
_____	_____	**5.** Ask the chemist if this medicine is safe.
_____	_____	**6.** I need a new rucksack, but I'm not sure what color to get.
_____	_____	**7.** My family and I will be on holiday next week.
_____	_____	**8.** You can hang your raincoat in the closet.

Getting Meaning from Context

TOEFL® iBT

Focus on Testing

Using Context Clues Many tests such as the TOEFL® iBT measure your academic listening and speaking abilities. This activity, and others in the book, will develop your social and academic conversation skills, and provide a foundation for success on a variety of standardized tests. The following conversations are about language.

1. Listen to each conversation.

2. Listen to the question for each conversation. Stop the recording and choose the best answer to each question.

3. In the **Clues** column, write the words that helped you choose your answer.

Answers	Clues
Conversation 1	
1. (A) a city (B) a language (C) a country (D) a religion	
2. (A) from the television (B) from the radio (C) from a book (D) from a magazine article	
3. (A) It's easy to learn. (B) It has no native speakers. (C) The woman wants to learn it. (D) It sounds like Polish.	
Conversation 2	
4. (A) to buy more bees (B) to kill the bees (C) to repair the roof (D) to learn more about bees	
5. (A) direction (B) distance (C) quantity (D) taste	

Answers	Clues
6. (A) the study of language	
(B) the study of insects	
(C) the study of dancing	
(D) the study of communication	
Conversation 3	
7. (A) to improve her pronunciation	
(B) to save time	
(C) to practice typing	
(D) to finish her term paper	
8. (A) try Rita's software	
(B) finish his term papers	
(C) buy his own software	
(D) borrow the woman's computer	
9. (A) You have to type fast to use it.	
(B) It can save your life.	
(C) It's useful for students and writers.	
(D) It's expensive.	

Focused Listening

INTERJECTIONS

Interjections are sound combinations that have specific meanings in spoken English. They are not real words, so they are not usually written. Listen to these interjections.

Interjections	Meanings
Uh-huh.	Yes
Uh-uh.	No
Uh-oh.	I made a mistake.
	Something is wrong.
Huh?	What?
Oops.	I dropped something.
	I made a mistake.
Ouch!	That hurts!
Aha!	I finally understand.
Hmm.	I'm not sure; let me think.

1 **Understanding Interjections** Listen to the short conversations. Write the meaning of the *second* speaker's interjection in each blank.

Conversation 1: _____

Conversation 2: _____

Conversation 3: _____

Conversation 4: _____

Conversation 5: _____

Conversation 6: _____

2 **Using Interjections** Work in pairs to practice using interjections. Student A should look at page 250. Student B should look at page 258.

Using Language Functions

GUESSING

To show that you are unsure about something, use the following expressions:

I guess	I suppose	It might	It looks like
I think	I'd say	It could	

Example

A: What language is this? I don't recognize it.

B: Hmm. I suppose it's something Scandinavian. It looks like Swedish, but it might be Danish.

3 **Guessing Meanings of Slang Expressions** The chart on page 166 contains American slang expressions. Read the sentences with your classmates. Guess what the underlined slang words mean. Use expressions from the list above. Then turn to page 261 to check your answers.

Example

"That movie was a real <u>bomb</u>."

Student 1: I think it means the movie was terrible.

Student 2: Yeah, but it could also mean that the movie was great.

Student 3: I guess it means that the movie was long and boring.

Slang Expressions	Possible Meanings
1. Jenna <u>freaked out</u> when she saw her boyfriend on a date with another girl.	
2. On Saturday afternoon I like to go to the park and <u>shoot some hoops</u> with my brothers.	
3. The clothing in this store is really <u>cheesy</u>. I would never wear it.	
4. Teenage boys always act <u>goofy</u> when they're around girls.	
5. I really need a break. If I don't take a vacation soon, I'm going to <u>lose it</u>.	
6. To celebrate his birthday, we <u>pigged out</u> on pizza and ice cream.	
7. I told my dad about my bad grade, but he was totally <u>chill</u> about it.	
8. Kyle was <u>bummed out</u> when he got a D on his <u>chemistry</u> test.	
9. We were <u>wiped out</u> after playing two hours of <u>basketball</u>.	
10. I was going to ask my boss for a raise, but at the last minute I <u>chickened out</u>.	

Before You Listen

One common contest in American schools is called a spelling bee. In a spelling bee, competitors are given words to spell out loud. They remain in the game as long as they spell correctly, but if they make a mistake they must leave the game.

1 Prelistening Questions

1. Are you a good speller in your native language?

2. Do you spell well in English?

3. Give examples of words that are hard to spell in English.

4. How can a person become a better speller?

▲ A spelling bee

2 Identifying Spellings Listen to a spelling bee in a U.S. middle school class. The words are taken from a list of commonly misspelled words.* As you listen, choose the spelling you hear *even if it is wrong!* During the pause, check (✓) whether you think the spelling is right or wrong. Continue listening, and you will hear the correct spelling.

Spelling	Right	Wrong	Spelling	Right	Wrong
1. (A) tryes (B) tires (C) tries	✓		6. (A) ninty (B) ninety (C) ninnty		
2. (A) chose (B) choose (C) choise			7. (A) analyze (B) analize (C) analise		
3. (A) effect (B) affect (C) effete			8. (A) possibility (B) possibilety (C) possibilty		
4. (A) quizes (B) kwizzes (C) quizzes			9. (A) misterious (B) mysterious (C) mesterious		
5. (A) suceed (B) succede (C) succeed			10. (A) lightening (B) litening (C) lightning		

After You Listen

3 Class Spelling Bee Have a spelling bee in your English class. Use words that you have learned in Chapters 1 through 6 of this textbook.

---

* The list was published in the *Los Angeles Times*. The original list of the 25 most commonly misspelled words was taken from the *Student's Book of College English*.

Talk It Over

4 **Creating Dialogues** Look at the three photos on this page and page 170. Use your imagination to create a dialog for each photo. What are the people saying in each photo? Use as many of the expressions in the box as you can. Read or perform your dialog for the class.

Aha!	Huh?	Ouch!
catch on	I guess	That's not completely true.
chicken out	I suppose	two-faced
friendship	I think	Uh-oh
goofy	in the dark	Well, actually
Have a seat.	It's hard to say	wipe out
Hmmm.	make friends	

1.

▲ Alicia and Lee

_____

_____

_____

_____

_____

_____

2.

▲ Beth, Lee, and Alicia

_____

_____

_____

_____

_____

3.

▲ Ali and Lee

_____

_____

_____

_____

_____

Self-Assessment Log

Check the words you learned in this chapter.

Nouns
- ❑ category
- ❑ dialect
- ❑ friendliness
- ❑ friendship
- ❑ majority
- ❑ sample
- ❑ standard

Verbs
- ❑ catch on
- ❑ make friends

Adjectives
- ❑ identical
- ❑ in the dark
- ❑ noticeable
- ❑ two-faced
- ❑ unique

Adverbs
- ❑ whereas
- ❑ while

Expressions
- ❑ Have a seat.
- ❑ It's hard to say.

Check the things you did in this chapter. How well can you do each one?

	Very well	Fairly well	Not very well
I can use phrases for contradicting politely.	❑	❑	❑
I can talk about stereotypes.	❑	❑	❑
I can take notes on a lecture using an outline.	❑	❑	❑
I can classify information.	❑	❑	❑
I can talk about American and British English.	❑	❑	❑
I can guess meanings from context.	❑	❑	❑
I can participate in a spelling bee.	❑	❑	❑

Write about what you learned and what you liked in this chapter.

In this chapter,

I learned _____

_____

I liked _____

_____

Tastes and Preferences

❝ Markets change, tastes change, so the companies and the individuals who choose to compete in those markets must change. ❞

—Dr. An Wang
Chinese-American inventor,
co-founder of Wang Laboratories, (1920–1990)

Connecting to the Topic

1 What kind of music do you think the women are listening to?

2 What kind of music do you listen to? Where and when do you listen to music?

3 Tell your group about three things you've done that show your personal tastes and preferences.

Before You Listen

Jeff and his friend Dan play in a rock band. Last night Mari went to a club to hear them play. Today Dan has stopped by the house for a visit.

▲ Jeff, Mari, and Dan

 1 Prelistening Questions Discuss these questions with your classmates.

1. What do you think is happening in the photo?

2. Do you like to listen to music? What kind of music do you prefer? Do you like to go to clubs to listen to music?

3. In your opinion, is it important for two people to have the same tastes in order to be happy together?

4. What are some ways of asking about people's likes and dislikes in English?

2 Previewing Vocabulary Listen to the underlined words and phrases from the conversation. Then use the context to match them with their definitions.

Sentences

_____ **1. A:** Did you <u>have a good time</u> last night?
     B: Not really. The concert was boring.

_____ **2. A:** What do you think of this song?
     B: <u>I'm crazy about it!</u>
     A: I really like it, too.

_____ **3. A:** What is this delicious <u>dish</u>?
     B: It's vegetable lasagna. Carmen made it.

_____ **4. A:** I <u>can't stand</u> that old hat. When are
         you going to throw it out?
     B: Sorry, I like it.

_____ **5.** Harry and Renata don't <u>see eye to eye</u> on
     anything, but they are very happily married.

_____ **6.** Ahmed <u>doesn't care for</u> sports. He prefers
     to read and listen to music.

Definitions

a. to dislike a little

b. to dislike strongly; to hate

c. to enjoy oneself

d. to agree

e. "I love it!"

f. food cooked or prepared in a special way

Listen

3 Comprehension Questions Close your book as you listen to the conversation. Listen for the answers to these questions. After you listen, discuss your answers with a partner.

1. Do Mari and Dan like most of the same things?

2. At the end of the conversation, what do Dan and Mari agree to do together?

3. Fill in the chart with details about Dan's and Mari's tastes and preferences. If information is not given, fill in the box with an *X*.

	Dan Likes	Mari Likes
Music	rock	jazz
Food		
Art		
Sports		
Movies		

Stress

4 Listening for Stressed Words Now listen to part of the conversation again. Some of the stressed words are missing. During each pause, repeat the phrase or sentence. Then fill in the missing stressed words.

Dan: What did you think of our _____?

Mari: Well, your music is _____ for _____, but to tell you the truth, it was kind of _____. I guess I really prefer _____.

Dan: Do you go to _____ much?

Mari: No, not very often. I _____ _____ them. They're _____ expensive!

Dan: Yeah, I know what you _____. Well, what do you like to do for _____?

Mari: I _____ to _____! I love going to different _____ restaurants and trying new _____.

Dan: What's your _____ kind of food?

Mari: Well, _____, of course. What about you?

Dan: Well, I'm _____ _____ about sushi or sashimi. But I really like _____ food.

Mari: Ooh, I _____ _____ beans, and I don't like _____. Uh . . . What about _____ food?

Dan: I don't _____ for it. Too _____. Um . . . do you like _____ food? You know, hamburgers, hot dogs, French fries . . .

Mari: _____! All that fat and salt and sugar . . . We don't see eye to eye on _____, do we?

Dan: Well, let's see. What's your opinion of _____ art? There's a _____ show at the county _____ right now.

Mari: To be _____, I don't _____ the modern stuff. I prefer _____ century art, you know, Monet, van Gogh, Renoir.

Dan: Hmm. How do you feel about _____? Are you interested in _____?

Mari: _____ football? I _____ it!

Dan: Basketball?

Mari: It's OK.

Dan: How about tall musicians with _____ hair?

Mari: It _____.

Dan: OK, I got it. How about _____ musicians with

_____ hair who invite you to a _____?

Mari: Science fiction?

Dan: Sounds _____!

Mari: _____ we agree on _____!

Check your answers using the listening script on pages 290–291. Then read the conversation with a partner. Pronounce stressed words louder, higher, and more clearly than unstressed words.

Reductions

The following exchange is from the conversation:

Dan: Are you interested in football?

Mari: American football? I hate it!

Dan: Basketball?

Note the form of Dan's second question. The complete question should be "Do you like basketball?" However, Dan drops the subject and the verb because his meaning is clear to Mari from the context of the first question. This kind of reduction is common in rapid, informal speech.

5 **Listening for Reductions** Listen to the following short exchanges. Write the full questions instead of the reduced ones.

1. _____

2. _____

3. _____

4. _____

5. _____

After You Listen

6 **Reviewing Vocabulary** Work in pairs to practice the new vocabulary. Student A should look at page 250. Student B should look at page 259.

Using Language Functions

TALKING ABOUT LIKES AND DISLIKES

Like Very Much

It's fantastic/terrific/cool*/
super*/awesome.*

I love it.

I'm crazy about it.

Cool!*

Like a Little

It's nice/all right/
not bad.

I like it.

Neutral

It's OK.

It's so-so.

I can take it or leave it.

Dislike Very Much

It's terrible/horrible/awful/gross.*

It stinks.*

I can't stand it.

I hate it.

Yuck!*

Dislike a Little

I don't care for it.

I don't like it.

I'm not crazy about it.

_____

* These expressions are slang.

7 **Asking About Likes and Dislikes** Read the conversation on page 176.
Complete the questions that Dan asks to find out about Mari's likes and dislikes.

1. _____ *What did you think of* _____ our band?

2. _____ kind of food?

3. _____ American food?

4. _____ modern art?

5. _____ sports?

6. _____ football?

7. _____ tall musicians with curly hair?

Work with a partner. Use expressions from Using Language Functions at the top of the
page to answer the questions above.

8 Talking About Likes and Dislikes Here is a list of the topics and examples mentioned in the conversation. Work with a partner. First, add other examples of each topic. Then take turns asking and answering questions about each other's likes and dislikes. Use the language from Activity 7 and from the Using Language Functions box on page 178.

Examples   **Q:** How do you feel about heavy metal?
              A: I don't care for it much.

Topics	Examples
Music	*rock*
Food	*Italian*
Art	*modern*
Sports	*baseball*
Movies	*science fiction*

Talk It Over

9 Giving an Impromptu Speech

1. Write one specific question about people's tastes and preferences. Use language from Activity 8. You may choose a topic from the following list or pick your own, but be sure your question is specific.

   Too general: How do you feel about sports?
   Specific: Are you interested in golf?

Topics		
animals	foods	sports
cars	music	things to do on a Saturday night
cities	places to be alone	times of the day
colors	places to eat	TV shows
days of the week	places to take	writers, artists, actors, singers
flowers	a vacation	seasons

2. Your teacher will collect all the questions and put them in a box.

3. Students will take turns picking a question from the box and speaking about it for about one minute. In your speech, you can:
   - give your opinion about the topic, using expressions for talking about likes and dislikes
   - give reasons for your opinion
   - talk about your experience with the topic

Before You Listen

You are going to hear a radio interview with Dr. Stuart Harris, a professor of marketing, about a part of the U.S. population known as Generation Y.

Baby Boomers
born 1946–1964*
population: 72 million

Generation X
born 1964–1976
population: 40–45 million

Generation Y
born 1977–1993
population: 70+ million

1 **Prelistening Discussion** Discuss these questions in small groups.

1. What do you know about the three generations in the photos above?

2. Into which generation do you fit? What are some characteristics of your generation in your native country?

*Numbers and dates are approximate.

2 **Previewing Vocabulary** Listen to these words and phrases from the interview. Check (✓) the ones you think you know. Discuss their meanings with a partner. Check the other words and phrases later as you learn them.

Nouns
- ❑ brand
- ❑ conflict
- ❑ consumer
- ❑ developed country
- ❑ income
- ❑ phenomenon
- ❑ standard of living

Verb
- ❑ identify with

Adjectives
- ❑ Caucasian — *from Europe*
- ❑ confident
- ❑ diverse
- ❑ hip (informal) *cool, guapil*
- ❑ loyal
- ❑ optimistic
- ❑ significant
- ❑ tolerant

Listen

Strategy

Recognizing Paraphrases

To paraphrase means to say something again with different words. Speakers paraphrase often in order to make sure their listeners understand what they are saying or to emphasize something important.

When you are taking notes, you need to recognize paraphrases so that you don't write the same idea or information twice in your notes. The following phrases signal that a speaker is paraphrasing:

> In other words . . .
>
> That is . . . (abbreviated as *i.e.*)
>
> That is to say . . .
>
> I mean
>
> To put it another way . . .

Paraphrase signals can connect two complete sentences, a sentence and a phrase, or a phrase and another phrase. They can be at the beginning of a sentence or in the middle.

3 **Practicing Paraphrase Signals** Match each sentence on the left with a paraphrase on the right. Then add a paraphrase signal from the strategy box on page 181 and write or say complete sentences.

Example

Generation Y refers to people who were born between the late 1970s and the early 1990s, *in other words,* between 1977 or 1978 and 1993 or 1994.

_____ **1.** Generation Y refers to young Americans who were born between the late 1970s and the early 1990s.

_____ **2.** One-fourth of the people in this generation grew up in single-parent homes.

_____ **3.** One-third of Generation Y-ers are not Caucasian.

_____ **4.** These young people want to be modern.

_____ **5.** Three-fourths of the members of Generation Y have mothers who work.

a. seventy-five percent

b. between 1977–78 and 1993–94

c. one in four

d. This is the most diverse generation in U.S. history.

e. They're not interested in the traditional way of life.

4 **Predicting Note Organization** In this chapter you are going to hear an interview, not a lecture. An interview consists of questions and answers. With your teacher and classmates, discuss the form your notes might have.

 5 **Taking Notes (Part I)** Listen to the first part of the interview about the characteristics of Generation Y. Take notes in the best way you can. Use your own paper.

 6 **Rewriting Your Notes** Look at the sample notes on page 183. They are in the form of two columns. Use your notes from Activity 5 to fill in the missing information. Remember to use abbreviations and symbols. Listen to the interview again if necessary.

Generation Y	
Questions/Topics	Answers
A. Meaning of Gen Y?	1. Young Am. born late 1970s-early 1990s, i.e. 1977-1994
	2. Number = _____
	_____
B. Number–significant?	Yes. Reason: _____
	→ _____
	→ _____
	_____
C. _____ _____ _____ _____	1. _____ _____
	2. _____
	3. $\frac{1}{3}$ not Caucasian
D. Tolerant?	_____ _____
	Also _____
	_____
	_____
	_____
E. _____ _____ _____	Stats:
	1. Total income/yr: _____
	_____
	2. Spend: _____
	_____

7 **Taking Notes (Part II)** Listen to the second part of the lecture. Continue taking notes on your own paper. After listening, use your notes to fill in the missing information below.

F. _____ | Fashion, fast food, _____
_____ | _____
 | _____
G. Preferred brands? | _____
 | _____
H. _____ | 1. have grown up w/ media → smart shoppers
_____ | 2. Don't like trad. advert.
 | 3. _____
 | 4. _____
I. _____ | Not only U.S. Internat'l, but diff. in other countries, e.g.:
 | 1. _____
 | 2. _____

After You Listen

8 **Discussing the Lecture** Discuss the following questions about the interview and your own experiences. Refer to your notes as necessary.

1. Who are the members of Generation Y in the United States?

2. How old are they now?

3. What are some characteristics of this group?

4. What are some adjectives to describe Generation Y?

5. How much money do Generation Y-ers have?

6. What do they spend their money on?

7. How do Generation Y-ers feel about brand name items?

8. What are some characteristics of Generation Y in other countries?

9 **Reviewing Vocabulary** Work in small groups. Look back at the vocabulary list in Activity 2 on page 181. Quiz each other on the terms and their meanings.

10 Talking About Fads In the interview, Dr. Harris mentioned graphic T-shirts and flip-flops as examples of fads that are popular with Generation Y-ers in the first decade of this century. Look at the chart on page 186. Work in small groups. Answer the following questions.

1. For each category, give other examples of Generation Y fads that you know about.

2. Are these fads popular with young people in your country, community, or school?

3. Who follows them? Do you?

FYI

fad (noun) a temporary fashion, notion, manner of conduct, etc., especially one followed enthusiastically by a group

Language Tip

Expressions for Saying That Something Is Popular

popular

in style

fashionable

trendy

in

▲ What fads can you identify in this photo?

Current Fads	
Categories	**Examples**
Clothing	*Flip-flops, graphic tees, low-rise jeans*
Hair	
Body decoration and jewelry	
Food	
Electronics	
Musicians	
Cars	
Sports	
Entertainment	
Activities	
Books	

Focused Listening

YES/NO QUESTIONS WITH *DO, DOES,* OR *DID*

It can be difficult to understand present and past *yes/no* questions with pronoun subjects. Such questions are often reduced and linked, so it can be hard to hear the difference between *do/does* and *did*. For example:

Long	Short
Do I look tired?	du‿wi look tired?
Did he own a car?	did‿ee‿own‿a car?

It may be almost impossible to hear the difference between *Do we* and *Did we* or between *Do they* and *Did they*. In those cases, you may need to listen to the context to tell if the question is present or past.

1 *Yes/No* Questions with *Do, Does,* or *Did* Listen for the difference between unreduced and reduced pronunciation. Repeat both forms after the speaker.

Unreduced Pronunciation	Reduced Pronunciation
1. Do I look tired?	d'way look tired?
2. Did I look tired?	did-ay look tired?
3. Do you live with your parents?	d'yuh live with your parents?
4. Did you live with your parents?	didjuh live with your parents?
5. Does he own a car?	duzee own a car?
6. Did he own a car?	didee own a car?
7. Does she need any help?	dushee need any help?
8. Did she need any help?	ditshe need any help?
9. Do we have any homework?	duwee have any homework?
10. Did we have any homework?	diwee have any homework?
11. Do they live together?	d'they live together?
12. Did they live together?	di-they live together?

2 **Distinguishing Among *Do, Does,* and *Did*** You will hear one sentence from each pair that follows. Listen and choose the sentence you hear.

1. Ⓐ Do you have time to eat lunch?
   Ⓑ Did you have time to eat lunch?

2. Ⓐ Does he play the piano?
   Ⓑ Did he play the piano?

3. Ⓐ Do they need help?
   Ⓑ Did they need help?

4. Ⓐ Do I look like my sister?
   Ⓑ Did I look like my sister?

5. Ⓐ Does she understand the instructions?
   Ⓑ Did she understand the instructions?

6. Ⓐ Did we sound good?
   Ⓑ Do we sound good?

7. Ⓐ Do they own a house?
   Ⓑ Did they own a house?

8. Ⓐ Did we need to rewrite the composition?
   Ⓑ Do we need to rewrite the composition?

3 ***Do, Does,* and *Did* in Questions** Listen to the questions and write the missing words.

1. _____ _____ decide to take the job?

2. When _____ _____ eat?

3. _____ _____ have to rewrite this composition?

4. Where _____ _____ park the car?

5. _____ _____ know what to do?

6. _____ _____ miss the bus again?

7. _____ _____ usually walk to school?

8. _____ _____ remember to turn off the light?

Focus on Testing

Using Context Clues Many tests such as the TOEFL® iBT measure your academic and speaking abilities. This activity, and others in the book, will develop your social and academic communication skills, and provide a foundation for success on a variety of standardized tests. The following conversations are about people's tastes and preferences.

1. Listen to the beginning of each conversation.

2. Listen to the question for each conversation. Stop the recording and choose the best answer to each question.

3. In the **Clues** column, write the words that helped you choose your answer.

4. Listen to the last part of each conversation to hear the correct answer.

Answers	Clues
1. (A) a car (B) a painting (C) a television set (D) a movie	
2. (A) a T-shirt (B) a tie (C) a suit (D) a wallet	
3. (A) ice-skating (B) snow skiing (C) water-skiing (D) snowboarding	
4. (A) She likes it. (B) She does not like it. (C) She thinks it's funny. (D) She's angry.	
5. (A) She likes it. (B) She is not sure. (C) She thinks it's funny. (D) She's angry.	

Using Language Functions

EXPRESSING APPROVAL AND DISAPPROVAL

To approve means "to believe that someone or something is good or acceptable." *Disapprove* has the opposite meaning. As an example, many people approve of tattoos these days, but they probably disapprove of them for children.

The following expressions are used to express approval and disapproval.

Approval	Disapproval
I approve of + (noun/verb + ing)	I disapprove of + (noun/verb + ing)
I'm in favor of + (noun)	I'm against + (noun)
I'm for + (noun)	

4 **Practicing Expressions of Approval and Disapproval** Complete each statement with an expression of approval or disapproval. Then work with a partner and discuss your answers.

1. I _____ laws that forbid smoking in restaurants.

2. I _____ speed limits on highways.

3. I _____ uniforms for high school students.

4. I _____ unmarried couples living together.

5. I _____ women working as police officers and firefighters.

On the Spot!

5 **What Would You Do?** The chart on page 191 lists behaviors and fashions that are popular among many young people. In the "You" column, write a plus (+) sign if you approve of these things or a minus (−) sign if you disapprove. Do the same thing in the column marked "Your Parents."

▲ Body piercing

Activity/Product	You	Your Parents
pierced ears		
body piercing (nostril, lips, tongue, eyebrows)		
tattoos		
smoking		
rap music		
Internet dating		
living with roommates of the opposite sex		
dating a person from a different race or religion		
a couple living together before marriage		
downloading songs from the Internet (without paying)		
online chat rooms		

Discuss the following questions in small groups. Use expressions from Using Language Functions on page 190.

1. Why do you approve or disapprove of each item?

2. In which cases do you agree with your parents? Disagree?

3. Do your opinions about any particular activities depend on whether a male or female does it? Which activities?

▲ Do you approve of online chat rooms?

Part 4

Real-World Task:
Choosing Someone to Date

In this section you will hear about David, a 35-year-old professional man. For the past year he has been occasionally dating two women, Katherine and Jean. He likes both of them very much. David would like to get married and start a family soon, so he feels it's time to choose one woman and "get serious." Both women are interested in him, but David is having a hard time choosing between them.

Before You Listen

1 Describing Your Ideal Partner On a piece of paper, list at least five qualities you value in a romantic partner. Then share your list with one or more classmates.

Examples

(Unmarried people)
"My ideal wife would be intelligent."
"My ideal partner would have a good job."

(Married people)
"The qualities I admire most in my husband are his intelligence and sense of humor."

Listen

2 Comparing People's Qualities Listen as David describes Katherine and Jean. Take notes on their positive and negative qualities in the chart on the next page.

▲ David tries to choose between two women.

	Katherine	Jean
Positive Qualities		
Negative Qualities		

After You Listen

3 Discussion Compare your answers from Activity 2 with a partner. Then discuss the following questions:

1. Are Jean's and Katherine's positive qualities important to you too?

2. What other positive qualities do you want in a partner?

3. Would Jean's and Katherine's negative qualities bother you?

4. What other qualities would you want to avoid in a partner?

5. What do you think David should do? Why?

Talk It Over

4 Reading Personal Ads Read the ads. Then choose the ad that sounds most interesting to you. Tell the members of your group which ad you chose and why.

ance & more. Box 385.

share tennis,

FROM WOMEN:

Tall, attractive brunette, enjoys music, dancing, hiking, travel. Seeks good-looking, honest, secure man with sense of humor for friendship, possible relationship. Box 192.

Elegant, petite, grad student, marriage-minded, seeks professional man to share tennis, skiing, reading, sailing, opera. Box 120.

Artistic, bookish elementary school teacher, vegetarian. Seeks marriage with witty man who loves classical music, kids, pets. Box 239.

European grad student, 5'6", seeks fun-loving man to achieve perfect relationship. Box 923.

Brainy redhead, financially independent seeks ski companion with refined taste and great sense of humor. Box 329.

Fun-loving, 23, college

FROM MEN:

Easygoing guy, 33, college grad, good-looking, mature; seeks woman, slim, educated, for romance & more. Box 385.

Want to laugh? Talkative male, 24, seeks partner for dating fun. I'm smart, handsome, educated & hip. Into rock music, dancing & partying. Box 127.

Stockbroker 5'11", attractive, spontaneous, traveler; seeks attractive, fit, honest female. Box 383.

Firefighter, athletic, attractive, 28, seeks woman for companionship & adventure. Must enjoy life. Race/religion/age not important. Box 472.

Poetic, marriage minded professional pilot, 6'3", seeks non-smoking, energetic, adventurous woman for serious relationship. Box 489.

Professional, sports-minded, 26, seeks non-smoking female

5 **Writing Personal Ads** In this activity, you will write a personal ad. Read the information in the boxes and follow the directions.

How to Write an Interesting Personal Ad

1. Begin your ad by describing yourself. You may choose to include some of the following information:
   - your age
   - nationality
   - profession
   - religion
   - what you look like ("tall, nice-looking man")
   - what you enjoy doing ("loves intelligent conversation")
   - what kind of person you are ("honest, caring")
   - something unique about you ("bird lover")

2. In the second part of the ad, write about the person you would like to meet. List the characteristics that are important to you.

3. State what you want from a relationship: Marriage? A good time? A serious relationship? Friendship? Someone to share a hobby with? A tennis partner?

The Language of Personal Ads

1. Do not write complete sentences. Notice that the ads on page 193 begin with adjectives or descriptive phrases.

2. Use the word *seeks* (meaning "looking for") when you describe the person you would like to meet.

3. Use commas to separate a series of adjectives ("honest, attractive, funny guy")

4. Use adjective clauses ("seeks woman who loves golf") and prepositional phrases ("lawyer with a great sense of humor")

Write an ad about yourself. Follow the instructions in the boxes above. Don't write your name on your ad. Your teacher will collect all the ads and post them on the bulletin board.

Read all the ads and try to guess which classmate wrote each one. Finally, each person in the class should say which ad he or she wrote.

Self-Assessment Log

Check the words you learned in this chapter.

Nouns	**Verbs**	**Adjectives**	**Expression**
❏ brand	❏ identify with	❏ Caucasian	❏ can't stand
❏ conflict		❏ confident	❏ don't/doesn't care for
❏ consumer		❏ diverse	❏ have a good time
❏ developed country		❏ hip (informal)	❏ I'm crazy about it!
❏ dish		❏ loyal	❏ see eye to eye
❏ income		❏ optimistic	
❏ phenomenon		❏ significant	
❏ standard of living		❏ tolerant	

Check the things you did in this chapter. How well can you do each one?

	Very well	Fairly well	Not very well
I can hear and use stress and reductions.	❏	❏	❏
I can talk about my likes and dislikes.	❏	❏	❏
I can give a one-minute speech.	❏	❏	❏
I can recognize paraphrases.	❏	❏	❏
I can take notes on an interview using an outline.	❏	❏	❏
I can talk about fads.	❏	❏	❏
I can distinguish between *do, does,* and *did.*	❏	❏	❏
I can use phrases to express approval and disapproval.	❏	❏	❏
i can guess meanings from context.	❏	❏	❏
I can talk about my ideal partner.	❏	❏	❏

Write what you learned and what you liked in this chapter.

In this chapter,

I learned _____

_____

I liked _____

_____

New Frontiers

> **"** I never did anything worth doing by accident, nor did any of my inventions come by accident; they came by work. **"**
>
> —Thomas Alva Edison
> U.S. inventor (1847–1931)

Connecting to the Topic

1. Where is this person? What is this person doing?

2. What are some other jobs related to science?

3. What are some examples of science topics that have been in the news in the last few years?

Before You Listen

In the following conversation Andrew, Nancy, and Mari talk about medical research.

▲ Nancy, Andrew, and Mari

1 Prelistening Questions Discuss these questions with your classmates.

1. What interesting medical discoveries have you heard about lately?

2. What is cloning? What kinds of animals have scientists cloned?

2 Previewing Vocabulary Listen to the underlined words and phrases from the conversation. Then use the context to match them with their definitions.

Sentences

_____ **1.** We heard some <u>weird</u> noises last night. We didn't know what they were.

_____ **2.** Walking alone in a strange city at night <u>scares</u> me. I always try to walk with other people or take a taxi.

_____ **3.** Chimpanzees need our protection because they are an <u>endangered species</u>. There aren't many of them in the world anymore.

_____ **4.** If they're not protected, pandas could soon become <u>extinct</u> in the wild.

_____ **5.** After many years of <u>research</u>, scientists developed a way to repair a human heart.

_____ **6.** Some people think smoking should be illegal in all public places, but I'm <u>all for</u> letting people smoke where they want.

_____ **7.** The doctors were able to grow <u>stem cells</u> in the laboratory and to create healthy body parts from them.

Definitions

a. to make someone feel afraid

b. to support and agree with something very much

c. serious study of a subject to discover new ideas or information

d. animals that may not exist in the future

e. strange

f. not existing anymore

g. a type of cell in the body that can divide and develop into any other kind of cell in the body

Listen

3 Comprehension Questions Listen to the conversation. Listen for the answers to these questions. After you listen, compare answers with a partner.

1. What kind of animals have been cloned in the past?

2. What kind of cloning does Nancy disagree with?

3. What are some positive ways cloning might be used in the future?

4. The pet cloning service costs
- (A) $5,000.
- (B) $50,000.
- (C) $15,000.

5. Scientists in Korea have cloned a

    (A) sheep.

    (B) panda.

    (C) dog.

6. Andrew thinks cloning and stem cell research are

    (A) similar.

    (B) different.

    (C) scary.

Stress

4 **Listening for Stressed Words** Listen to the conversation again. Some of the stressed words are missing. During each pause, repeat the phrase or sentence. Then fill in the missing stressed words.

Mari: Your dog is so _____, Nancy. How old is he?

Nancy: Eleven.

Mari: Wow, that's pretty _____.

Nancy: Yeah. I just love him so much. I don't know what I'll do when he's

_____.

Mari: Well, you can _____ him, you know.

Nancy: Clone him? You're _____, right?

Mari: Yeah, of course. But actually, it _____ possible.

_____ in Korea have cloned a dog, you know; I saw

a _____ of it in *Time* magazine.

Nancy: Really? I've heard of cloned _____, and mice and

rabbits. But not _____ like dogs.

Andrew: Oh, yeah. _____ it or not, there is a company in

California that _____ a pet cloning service. For $15,000,

you can have an _____ copy of your pet.

Nancy: That's so _____. Actually, it kind of scares me. Pretty

soon, they'll start cloning _____, and then . . .

Andrew: Nah, I don't think that's going to _____. I think cloning

will be used in _____ ways.

Nancy: Like what?

Andrew: Like saving endangered species. For example, scientists could save the

giant _____ and other animals before they become

_____.

Mari: Oh, yeah, and _____ thing. I heard that scientists will

be able to clone _____ parts. You know, just grow a new

heart, or a new _____.

Andrew: Uh-huh. That's what stem cell research is all _____,

which is _____ to cloning. A lot of medical problems are

going to be _____ with that for sure.

Nancy: Well, I'm all _____ that. Especially if it can help us live

_____.

Mari: Or if they can help your _____ live longer, right?

Nancy: Right!

Check your answers using the listening script on page 294. Then read the conversation with a partner. Pronounce stressed words louder, higher, and more clearly than unstressed words.

After You Listen

5 Using Vocabulary Discuss the following questions with a partner. Use the underlined vocabulary in your answers.

1. If you could <u>clone</u> one animal or one person, what or who would it be?

2. What are some examples of <u>endangered species</u>?

3. Why do some animals become <u>extinct</u>?

4. Are you <u>for</u> spending government money on medical <u>research</u>? Or should private companies pay for it?

5. Does the idea of <u>cloning</u> humans <u>scare</u> you? Why or why not? Do you think it would be <u>weird</u> if a clone of you existed?

6. Does the government of your native country support <u>stem cell</u> research? Do you?

Pronunciation

PRONOUNCING *TH*

The English language has two sounds that are written with the letters *th*. The two sounds are almost the same, but one of them is voiced and the other is voiceless.

Example

Voiced: *there*   Voiceless: *think*

To pronounce both sounds, follow these steps:

1. Place the tip of your tongue between your teeth.

2. Keep your lips relaxed.

3. Exhale air from your lungs.

4. Be sure to do steps 1 to 3 *all at the same time.*

To produce the voiced /th/ sound, make your vocal cords vibrate as you exhale.

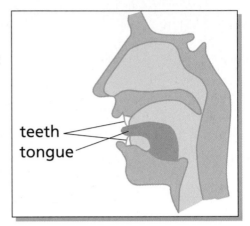

teeth
tongue

6 Pronouncing Voiced and Voiceless *th* Listen to two lists of words. Repeat the words after the speaker.

Voiceless *th*	Voiced *th*
think	this
thought	that
thumb	those
author	rather
nothing	other
mouth	father
both	breathe
throat	smooth

7 Distinguishing Between Voiced and Voiceless *th* Now listen to the following sentences. Repeat them after the speaker. Underline every voiceless *th* you hear. Circle every voiced *th*.

Examples   th̲ink   (th)ere

1. That's so weird.

2. There's no weather on the moon.

3. I don't think that's going to happen.

4. There's another thing to talk about.

5. They discovered something new.

6. Can they grow a new tooth in a laboratory?

7. What's the coldest place on Earth?

Using Language Functions

INTRODUCING SURPRISING INFORMATION

To introduce surprising or unexpected information, speakers often use special phrases such as:

It's weird/strange/funny, but . . .

Believe it or not,

Surprisingly,

You're not going to believe this, but . . .

Example

It's weird, but, there is a company in California that offers a pet cloning service.

▲ Tigers are an endangered species. Believe it or not, scientists think there are fewer than 2,500 tigers left in the world.

---

8 Fact or Fiction Game

1. Your teacher will hand out a card to each student in the class. The card will say "fact" or "fiction." Don't show your card to anyone.

2. Use one of the expressions from the list above to tell something surprising or unexpected about yourself. If your card says "fact," your story must be completely true. If it says "fiction," you must invent a story, but it should sound true.

3. Take turns telling your stories. After you are finished, the class should vote on whether you told the truth or not. Your purpose, of course, is to fool your classmates.

Before You Listen

1 **Prelistening Discussion** Discuss these questions in small groups.

▲ An illustration of the Mars Rover

1. Based on the picture, what does Mars look like? Describe it.

2. What do you think is the function of the rover in the picture?

3. What facts do you know about Mars (for example: distance from Earth, size, atmosphere, climate, etc.)?

4. What scientific news have you heard recently about Mars?

2 Previewing Vocabulary Listen to the following words from the lecture. Check (✓) the words you think you know. Discuss their meanings with a partner. Check the other words later as you learn them.

Nouns
- ❑ disaster
- ❑ evidence
- ❑ planet
- ❑ resources
- ❑ solar system
- ❑ telescope

Verbs
- ❑ analyze
- ❑ explore
- ❑ fascinate

Adjectives
- ❑ critical
- ❑ fascinating

Listen

Strategy

Recognizing Facts and Theories

When listening to lectures, especially about science, you need to recognize the difference between *facts* and *theories*.

Fact: proven, true information
Theory: unproven idea, may or may not be true

To hear the difference, listen for signal words and phrases like these:

FACT	THEORY
It's a well-known fact that . . .	(It) may/might /could + verb
(It) has been proven	(It's) possible that . . .
(Scientists) know . . .	(There's) a chance . . .
(There's) strong evidence . . .	possibly/probably

3 Listening for Fact and Theory in the Lecture Pay attention to signal words and phrases. Check (✓) Fact or Theory.

        Fact   Theory

1. _____   _____

2. _____   _____

3. _____   _____

4. _____   _____

5. _____   _____

6. _____   _____

4 Taking Notes and Outlining (Part I) Listen to the first part of the lecture and take notes in the best way you can. Use your own paper. After listening, use your notes to fill in the missing information on the lines that follow. Remember to use abbreviations and symbols.

Part 1
  I. Intro
    A. Mars—popular topic
    B. NASA & ESA: _____

       _____

    C. Lecture topic: _____

       _____

  II. Reasons
    A. _____

       _____

       _____

    B. Similar to Earth (_____

       _____)

       _____

  III. Life on Mars?
    A. Most scientists think _____

       _____

    B. It's possible that _____

       _____

       1. in 2003: _____

       _____

       2. If water → _____

5 Taking Notes and Outlining (Part II) Listen to the second part of the lecture. Continue taking notes on your own paper. After listening, use your notes to fill in the missing information below.

Part 2

IV. _____

    A. Exploring Mars → _____

    B. People need to live on M. if

        1. _____

        2. _____

        3. _____

After You Listen

 6 Discussing the Lecture Discuss the following questions about the lecture. Refer to your notes as necessary.

    1. Why are scientists interested in exploring Mars?

    2. What do we know about life on Mars?

    3. What critical evidence was discovered in 2003?

    4. How could we benefit from Mars exploration?

    5. Do you agree with the speaker that it's important to continue exploring Mars? Explain.

▲ A view of Mars from Earth

7 Reviewing Vocabulary Work in small groups. Look back at the vocabulary list in Activity 2 on page 205. Quiz each other on the terms and their meanings.

Talk It Over

8 **Solving a Science Problem** Imagine you are a member of a space crew. Your spaceship has crash-landed on the lighted side of the moon. Another spaceship will pick you up about two hundred miles away. Because you will have to walk there, you can take only a limited number of items with you.

1. Following is a list of 13 items your crew will have to choose from. Read the items and use your dictionary if necessary to understand their meanings.

2. Decide which items are the most important and which are the least important. Place the number 1 by the most important item, the number 2 by the second most important, and so on.

3. When you have finished, compare your rankings with those of your classmates. Explain the choices you made. Then turn to page 261 to check your answers.

_____ box of matches

_____ dried food

_____ 50 feet of nylon rope

_____ parachute silk

_____ portable heating unit

_____ three gallons of milk

_____ two 100-pound tanks of oxygen

_____ map of the moon's surface and rock formations

_____ life raft

_____ magnetic compass

_____ five gallons of water

_____ first aid kit containing injection needles

_____ solar-powered FM receiver-transmitter

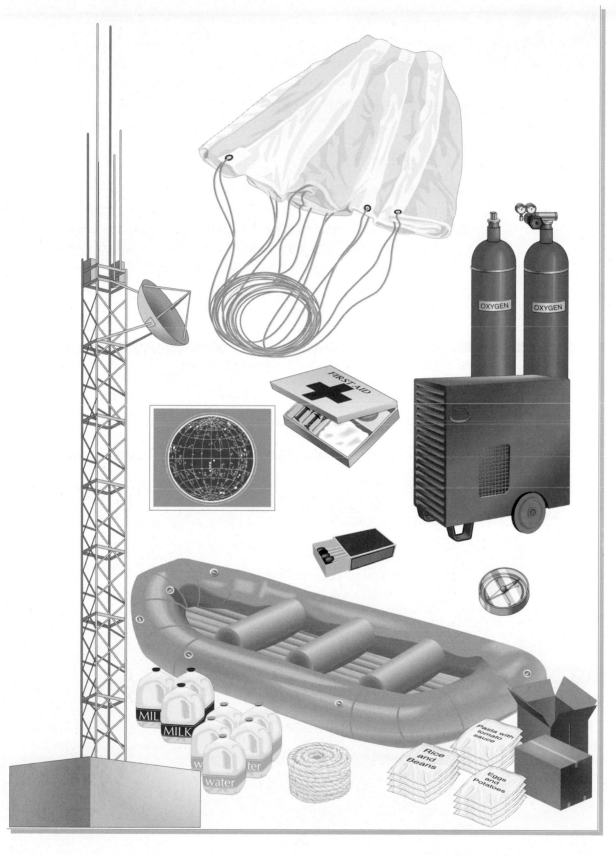

Getting Meaning from Context

Focus on Testing

Signal Words for Guessing the Correct Answer

Many tests such as the TOEFL® iBT measure your academic listening and speaking abilities. This activity, and others in the book, will develop your social and academic conversation skills, and provide a foundation for success on a variety of standardized tests. The following vocabulary is often used in such questions:

infer	What can you infer from the story?
imply	What does the speaker imply?
conclude	What can you conclude from this information?

Using Context Clues You are going to hear five short talks about discoveries.

1. Listen to each passage.

2. Listen to the question for each passage. Stop the recording and choose the best answer to each question.

3. In the **Clues** column, write the words that helped you choose your answer.

Answers	Clues
1. Ⓐ Discoveries and inventions usually happen at the same time. Ⓑ An invention helped Columbus make an important discovery. Ⓒ All discoveries depend on inventions. Ⓓ Columbus invented ships because he hoped to discover a new land.	
2. Ⓐ It requires expensive technology. Ⓑ It is a very old practice. Ⓒ It will decrease in the future. Ⓓ It began in ancient Rome.	
3. Ⓐ It was invented in the 12th century. Ⓑ It makes adding and subtracting easier. Ⓒ It is used in outlines. Ⓓ It was a European invention.	

FYI

Roman Numerals:
I, II, III, IV, V, VI, VII, VIII, IX, X, and so on

Arabic Numbers:
0, 1, 2, 3, 4, 5, 6, 7, 8, 9, 10, and so on

4.
(A) It was the greatest accomplishment of the ancient Chinese.
(B) It led to improvements in people's health.
(C) It was accidental.
(D) It was a big mistake.

5.
(A) Columbus used rubber to build his boats.
(B) Rubber comes from a tree.
(C) *Rubber* was originally a French word.
(D) Rubber was discovered in Europe.

1 **Talking About Inventions and Discoveries** The following discoveries and inventions were discussed above. What role, if any, do they play in your life?

1. solar energy

2. tea

3. the number zero

4. rubber

5. America

▲ What role, if any, does tea play in your life?

Focused Listening

PRONUNCIATION OF -ED ENDINGS

The -ed ending is found on regular past tense verbs and their past participles. For example:

- We finish**ed** the work at 8 P.M. (Past tense verb)
- We're very excit**ed** about your visit. (Past participle used as adjective)
- The papers were correct**ed** by the TA. (Past participle used in passive voice)

The -ed ending has three different pronunciations in English.

1. In words ending with /t/ or /d/, it is pronounced as a separate syllable, /id/.

   Examples

   wait; waited   decide; decided

2. In words that end with a voiceless consonant, it is pronounced as /t/.

   Examples

   step; stepped   wish; wished

   talk; talked   watch; watched

3. In words that end with a voiced consonant or a vowel, it is pronounced as /d/.

   Examples

   live; lived   die; died

   turn; turned   use; used

   enjoy; enjoyed   call; called

2 **Practicing -ed Endings** Listen and repeat the following words after the speaker.

/t/	/d/	/id/
passed	discovered	directed
developed	solved	existed
reached	used	started
looked	closed	invented
asked	cloned	fascinated

3 **Distinguishing Among -ed Endings** Listen to the past tense verbs and check the pronunciation that you hear. You will hear each word twice.

	/t/	/d/	/id/
1.	laughed		
2.		deescribed	
3.			Painted
4.	stoped		
5.		Changed	
6.			Ended
7.	helped		
8.		studied	
9.		invented	
10.	danced		
11.			realized
12.		Crowded	
13.	worked	Lis	
14.		Listened	
15.		Answered	

4 **Pronouncing -ed Endings** With a partner, decide on the -ed pronunciation of these words. In the blanks write /t/, /d/, or /id/. Then say the words.

1. _____ pointed

2. _____ dreamed

3. _____ traveled

4. _____ kissed

5. _____ thanked

6. _____ waited

7. _____ explored

8. _____ interested

9. _____ judged

10. _____ moved

Using Language Functions

EXPRESSING INTEREST OR SURPRISE

In Chapter 1, page 9, you learned several ways of showing that you are interested in what someone is saying. Here are some additional expressions you can use:

> That's (really) interesting.
>
> That's an interesting/great/nice story.

If you are surprised by something you hear, you can say:

> (That's) incredible!
>
> (That's) unbelievable!
>
> (That's) amazing!
>
> I can't believe it.
>
> I'm shocked.

5 **Talking About Discoveries** We discover things that are already there, just waiting for us to find them. Most discoveries are actually ordinary. For example, think of a baby discovering his or her toes.

Work in small groups and tell your classmates about discoveries that you have made in your life. If you are surprised by your classmates' comments, use the expressions above. See the chart below for examples of discoveries.

Personal Discoveries	
Categories	**Examples**
▪ A skill you found you have	the ability to sing, to make bread perfectly
▪ A place	a new restaurant, a vacation spot
▪ A new form of entertainment	jazz, bungee jumping
▪ Something you never noticed before about something familiar	Your dog has different-colored eyes. Your left thumb is longer than your right one.
▪ Something unusual about another country or its people	In Italian, the word for "hello" and "goodbye" is the same.

In this section you are going to listen to a game show called "Explorations, Inventions, and Discoveries." You will play along with the contestants.

Before You Listen

1 Prelistening Questions Discuss the following questions with your classmates.

1. What are the people in the photos doing?

2. Are game shows popular in your community? Do you enjoy watching them?

3. Do you enjoy watching English-language game shows? Which one(s)?

4. Would you like to be a contestant on a game show? What kind?

2 Listening to a Game Show Listen to a game show with questions about explorations, inventions, and discoveries. As you hear each question, choose *your* answer in the column titled "Your Answer." Then listen and choose the answer given by the contestant, Roger. Finally, the host will provide the correct answer. You can find the correct answers on page 261.

Question	Your Answer	Roger's Answer
1	(A) Apple (B) Microsoft (C) Intel	(A) Apple (B) Microsoft (C) Intel
2	(A) Mt. Everest in Nepal (B) Mt. Fuji in Japan (C) Mt. Whitney in the United States	(A) Mt. Everest in Nepal (B) Mt. Fuji in Japan (C) Mt. Whitney in the United States
3	(A) Spain (B) Portugal (C) Italy	(A) Spain (B) Portugal (C) Italy
4	(A) Italy (B) Egypt (C) China	(A) Italy (B) Egypt (C) China
5	(A) penicillin (B) aspirin (C) ginseng	(A) penicillin (B) aspirin (C) ginseng
6	(A) the motion picture (B) the telephone (C) the lightbulb	(A) the motion picture (B) the telephone (C) the lightbulb
7	(A) Isaac Newton (B) Galileo Galilei (C) Nicolaus Copernicus	(A) Isaac Newton (B) Galileo Galilei (C) Nicolaus Copernicus

After You Listen

3 **Reviewing the Listening** Answer the questions with your class.

1. How many questions did you answer correctly? Who got the most correct answers in your class?

2. Using the answers as cues, try to reconstruct the questions.

Talk It Over

4 **Ordering Events in a Story** Read the paragraph below.

The Travels of Marco Polo

Marco Polo was born in Venice in the year 1254. With his father and uncle, he traveled to Asia and eventually reached China, where he met the famous emperor Kublai Khan. Late in his life Marco Polo spent some time in prison. There he wrote a book about his travels in Asia, which became a valued source of information about the lands of the East. Marco Polo died in 1324.

The lettered sentences on page 218 give information about Marco Polo's travels. This information is not in the correct order. Your task will be to put the events in the correct sequence.

1. Divide into groups of seven students each, if possible.

2. Each person in the group should choose one lettered set of sentences. (If your group has only six people, one person should select two sets.)

3. Read your sentences. If necessary, use a dictionary to understand the important information. On the map, mark the part of Marco Polo's voyage that is described in your sentences.

4. When everyone has finished preparing,

   a. Without looking at your sentences, tell your part of the story to your group. Use the map on page 218 for illustration as you speak. As your group members tell their parts of the story, ask for repetition or clarification if you don't understand.

   b. As a group, decide what the correct order of the story is.

   c. Complete the route of Marco Polo's voyage on your map.

5. Check the correct order on page 261.

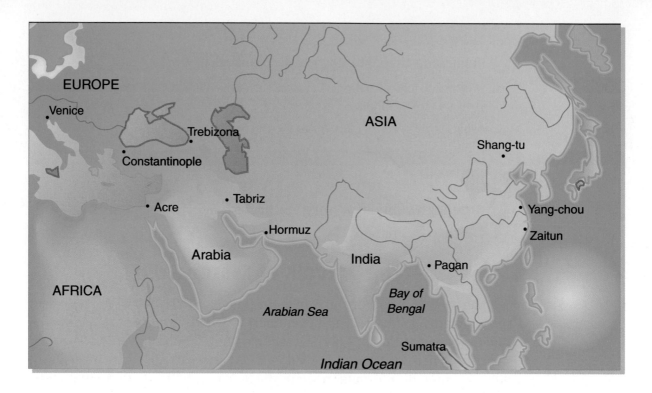

Story

A. The Polos finally left China in 1292. They sailed south from Yang-chou, through the Straits of Sumatra, and around the tip of India.

B. More than three years after leaving Venice, they finally arrived at the palace of the emperor Kublai Khan in Shang-tu, China.

C. Marco Polo, his father, and his uncle sailed on their famous voyage to the Orient in 1271. First they traveled to the port city of Acre in Palestine. From there they traveled by camel to the Persian port of Hormuz.

D. They then sailed up the western coast of India and across the Arabian Sea, returning to the port of Hormuz. After that they traveled by land to Tabriz, Trebizona, and Constantinople.

E. They arrived back in Venice in the year 1295 after traveling more than 15,000 miles.

F. The Polos stayed in China for 17 years. During that time, Marco traveled to Southeast Asia and India and back. After that, he became a government official in the Chinese city of Yang-chou.

G. They wanted to sail from Hormuz to China, but they could not find a ship. Therefore, they continued traveling by camel across the deserts and mountains of Asia.

Self-Assessment Log

Check the words you learned in this chapter.

Nouns
- ❏ clone
- ❏ disaster
- ❏ endangered species
- ❏ evidence
- ❏ planet
- ❏ research
- ❏ resources
- ❏ solar system
- ❏ stem cell
- ❏ telescope

Verbs
- ❏ analyze
- ❏ explore
- ❏ fascinate
- ❏ scare

Adjectives
- ❏ critical
- ❏ extinct
- ❏ fascinating
- ❏ weird

Expressions
- ❏ (all) for

Check the things you did in this chapter. How well can you do each one?

	Very well	Fairly well	Not very well
I can hear and use stress and pronunciation.	❏	❏	❏
I can use phrases to introduce surprising information.	❏	❏	❏
I can talk about scientific discoveries.	❏	❏	❏
I can distinguish between facts and theories.	❏	❏	❏
I can take notes on a lecture using an outline.	❏	❏	❏
I can solve a science problem.	❏	❏	❏
I can distinguish between -ed endings.	❏	❏	❏
I can use phrases to express interest and surprise.	❏	❏	❏
I can guess meanings from context.	❏	❏	❏
I can talk about personal discoveries.	❏	❏	❏
I can participate in a game show.	❏	❏	❏
I can order events in a story.	❏	❏	❏

Write what you learned and what you liked in this chapter.

In this chapter,

I learned _____

_____

I liked _____

_____

Ceremonies

In This Chapter

Conversation: A Baby Shower

Lecture: Water in Traditional Ceremonies

Using the Context: Conversations About Ceremonies

Real-World Task: Making Wedding Plans

❝ There is nothing like a ritual for making its participants think beyond their own appetites, and for making them feel that they belong to something greater, older and more important than themselves. ❞

—Tom Utley, British journalist (1921–1988)

Connecting to the Topic

1. Who are these people? Where are they from?

2. What are some reasons people have ceremonies?

3. Describe a ceremony that you know about.

Before You Listen

In the following conversation, Mari, Jeff, and Sharon talk about an invitation to a baby shower.

▲ A baby shower

1 Prelistening Questions Discuss these questions with your classmates.

1. What are the women in the picture doing? What kind of celebration is this?

2. How do people in your culture celebrate the birth of a baby?

2 **Previewing Vocabulary** Listen to the underlined words and expressions from the conversation. Then use the context to match them with their definitions.

Sentences

_____ **1.** The Olympic Games were <u>hosted</u> by Greece in 2004.

_____ **2.** My family members <u>shower</u> each other <u>with</u> dozens of gifts every Christmas.

_____ **3.** In some cultures, couples are not <u>allowed</u> to see each other before the wedding ceremony.

_____ **4.** My sister's new baby is <u>due</u> next week, so we are all very excited.

_____ **5.** When Jane was <u>pregnant</u> with her first baby, she gained 15 kilos in nine months.

_____ **6.** Everyone laughed at the <u>silly</u> costumes worn by the guests at the Halloween party.

_____ **7.** That store sells everything a <u>mother-to-be</u> could possibly need.

_____ **8.** When the bride came in wearing her long white dress, everyone <u>went ooh and aah</u>.

_____ **9.** You will need to <u>register</u> at the store's website before you can buy gifts online.

Definitions

a. to give someone a lot of things

b. not serious, childish

c. expecting to have a baby

d. to offer a place and arrange everything necessary for a special event such as a party

e. to sign up for an online service, organization, mailing list, etc.

f. permitted

g. expected to happen or arrive at a specific time

h. a woman who is going to have a baby

i. to express surprise and joy (informal)

Listen

3 **Comprehension Questions** Listen to the conversation. Listen for the answers to these questions. After you listen, compare answers with a partner.

1. What kind of invitation did Mari receive?

2. Who are the hosts?

3. Is Jeff invited too? Why or why not?

4. When is Nancy and Andrew's baby due?

5. What are three things people do at baby showers?

6. How is gift-giving different in Japan and in the United States?

7. Where is Mari probably going to buy a gift for the baby?

Stress

 4 Listening for Stressed Words Now listen to part of the conversation again. Some of the stressed words are missing. During each pause, repeat the phrase or sentence. Then fill in the missing stressed words.

Mari: Hmm. But isn't Nancy and Andrew's baby due at the end of

_____? And this invitation says April

_____.

Sharon: Well, yes. The custom is to have a shower _____ the baby is born, when the woman is seven or eight months

_____.

Mari: Very interesting. And everybody brings a _____?

Sharon: Right. Something for the baby: You know, _____ or

clothes or something for the baby's _____.

Mari: OK. The _____ says it's for lunch, so . . .

Sharon: Yeah, we'll have lunch, and _____ we'll play

_____.

Mari: Games? What _____ of games?

Jeff: _____ games.

Sharon: _____ games like bingo, or guessing games, or baby

trivia games. And the _____ get small prizes.

Mari: It _____ like fun.

Sharon: It is. And then, at the _____ of the party there's

usually a cake with _____ decorations, and then the

mother-to-be opens her _____.

Mari: While the _____ are still there?

Sharon: Sure. That's my _____ part! Everybody gets to see

the gifts.

Jeff: And go "oooh, aaah . . ."

Sharon: And see how _____ the woman is.

Mari: Wow. That's so _____ from our custom. In Japan

we usually _____ _____ a gift in

front of guests.

Sharon: Really? That _____ different.

Mari: Well what kind of gift do you think I should _____

for her?

Sharon: She's registered _____, so you can see what she's

already _____ and what she still needs. Would you

like me to write down the _____ address for you?

Mari: Sure, _____ would be great.

Check your answers using the listening script on page 298. Then read the conversation with a partner. Pronounce stressed words louder, higher, and more clearly than unstressed words.

After You Listen

5 Using Vocabulary Discuss the following questions with a partner. Use the underlined vocabulary in your answers.

1. Discuss a recent event that you were invited to. Who <u>hosted it</u>? What did the hosts do to make the event successful?

2. When was the last time your family <u>showered</u> you <u>with</u> advice? Example: after graduation, before getting married, before traveling abroad, and so on.

3. What are some real activities in your life that you have to complete before a specific date? For example, when are the following <u>due</u>?
   - a rented DVD
   - a borrowed library book
   - a telephone bill
   - the rent
   - homework

4. What kinds of things were you not <u>allowed</u> to do when you were a child?

5. In your culture, is it a custom to give a <u>pregnant</u> woman and her husband gifts before the baby is born?

6. What advice do people in your culture traditionally give to a <u>mother-to-be</u>?

7. In what situation do you feel comfortable acting <u>silly</u>?

8. Would you <u>go "ooh and aah"</u> if you met your favorite movie star? Why or why not?

9. What do you think of the modern custom of couples <u>registering</u> online for wedding or baby shower gifts they want?

Pronunciation

STRESS IN COMPOUND PHRASES

Compound phrases combine two nouns or an adjective and a noun.

- **Stress in Noun + Noun Combinations**

  The first word of the phrase is normally stressed.* For example:

  baby + shower = baby shower

- **Stress in Adjective + Noun Combinations**

  In most cases both words are stressed equally. For example:

  silly + games = silly games

---

*This is true whether the compound is spelled as one word (e.g. *bridesmaid*) or two words (e.g. *baby shower*).

---

6 Pronouncing Noun + Noun Combinations Listen to the following noun + noun combinations. Notice where the stress is placed and repeat each phrase after the speaker.

baby decorations	dinner party	graduation gift
welcoming ceremony	wedding invitation	flower arrangement

7 Pronouncing Adjective + Noun Combinations Listen to the following adjective + noun combinations and repeat them after the speaker. Remember to stress both words equally.

female relative	favorite part	instant message
traditional ceremony	white dress	funny hat

8 Predicting Stress Read the examples of compound nouns and adjective + noun combinations. Based on the rules above, mark the stressed word(s) in each item. Then listen to check your answers.

1. young mother	stepmother
2. coffeepot	large pot
3. nice place	fireplace
4. flashlight	green light
5. wedding cake	delicious cake
6. hair dryer	dry hair
7. busboy	tall boy
8. fast reader	mind reader

Using Language Functions

OFFERING TO DO SOMETHING

At the end of the conversation, notice the expressions Mari and Sharon use to offer each other help:

Sharon: Would you like me to write down the Internet address for you?
Mari: Sure. That would be great.

Mari: Is there anything I can do to help with the party?
Sharon: Thanks, but it's not necessary.

Study these expressions commonly used in English to offer, accept, or decline help:

OFFER

Would you like me to . . .?

Is there anything I can do to . . .?

May I . . .?

Could I . . .?

What can I do to . . .?

ACCEPT	**DECLINE**
Sure.	No, that's OK, thanks.
Yes.	No, but thanks anyway.
I'd appreciate it.	Thanks, but it's not necessary.
If you wouldn't mind.	No, but thanks a lot for asking.

▲ Could I help you with those strawberries?

9 **Role-Play** Work with a partner. Create a conversation about each photo. Use some of the expressions from the list on page 227 to offer, accept, or decline help.

Before You Listen

You are going to hear a talk about the uses of water in ceremonies and celebrations around the world.

▲ Young people celebrating the New Year in Thailand.

▲ A baptism

▲ Washing with water before prayer

1 **Prelistening Discussion** Discuss this question in small groups.

1. What are some symbolic meanings that water has? Check the ones you know about:
   - ❑ purity
   - ❑ danger
   - ❑ fertility
   - ❑ death
   - ❑ change
   - ❑ wealth
   - ❑ good luck
   - ❑ other _____

2 **Previewing Vocabulary** Listen to these words and phrases from the lecture. Check (✓) the ones you think you know. Discuss their meanings with a partner. Check the other words and phrases later as you learn them.

Nouns	**Verbs**	**Adjectives**
❑ prayer	❑ cleanse	❑ fascinating
❑ priest	❑ focus on	❑ pure
❑ ritual	❑ involve	
❑ sin	❑ narrow (something) down	
❑ symbol	❑ play a part in	
❑ symbolism	❑ pour	
	❑ pray	
	❑ purify	
	❑ sprinkle	
	❑ symbolize	

Listen

Strategy

Digressing from (Going off) and Returning to the Topic
Lecturers often include personal stories, jokes, or other information not directly related to the main topic. When speakers "go off the subject" (digress) like this, do not take notes. Start taking notes when the speaker signals a return to the main subject.

Study the expressions below:

Going off the Topic	**Returning to the Topic**
By the way	As I was saying
That reminds me	Anyway
Before I forget	Back to our topic
	Where was I?

3 **Recognizing Digressions** Listen to part of the lecture. Listen carefully for the place where the speaker goes off and then returns to the topic. After you listen, look at the following notes and cross out any unnecessary information.

A. Thailand

Speaker's experience

- April: hottest time of year
- Thail. doesn't have four seasons.
- dry season: Nov.-Feb.
- hot season: March-June
- rainy season: July-Oct.
- spkr was walking down street & teens threw water on him
- reason: April 13th = Songkran

Songkran = water festival

- people throw water on each other
- wash hands of elders w/scented water
- belief = water will wash away bad luck

 4 **Taking Notes** Listen to the whole lecture. Take notes in the best way you can. Use your own paper.

 5 **Outlining the Lecture** Use your notes from Activity 4 to fill in the missing information in the outline on page 232. Remember to use abbreviations and symbols. Listen to the lecture again if necessary.

 Culture Note

The Peace Corps
The Peace Corps is a U.S. government organization that tries to help developing countries by sending volunteers (people who work without payment), especially young people, to teach skills in education, health, farming, and so on.

I. Intro

Speaker: _____

General Topic: _____

II. Specific Topic: _____

A. _____

_____

_____

_____

_____

_____

_____

B. _____

_____

_____

_____

_____

C. Christian ceremony: baptism

_____

_____

_____

_____

_____

III. Conclusion _____

After You Listen

6 **Discussing the Lecture** Discuss the following questions about the lecture. Refer to your notes as necessary.

1. What is the speaker's background?

2. What similarity did he find among different cultural celebrations?

3. What role does water play in each of the ceremonies that the speaker described?

4. Does water play a role in any of the major celebrations or festival in your culture?

 7 **Reviewing Vocabulary** Work in small groups. Look back at the vocabulary list in Activity 2 on page 230. Quiz each other on the terms and their meanings.

Talk It Over

Strategy

Graphic Organizer: Multi-Column Chart
A multi-column chart can help you organize different characteristics of one or more items, events, people, and so on. You can use a multi-column chart to organize facts or your thoughts about a topic.

 8 **Interview** Choose a ceremony or celebration that is found in most cultures, for example, New Year's Eve, a birthday, a wedding, and so on. Interview a classmate or a friend from a different culture, community, or religion and ask about his or her way of celebrating these events. Take notes in the chart below. Note any similarities between their customs and yours in the last column.

Celebration	Country	What People Do	Reason for Celebration	Other Notes
Baby shower— 1 or 2 mos. before baby's birth	United States	Women give party and bring gifts for mother-to-be	Welcome new baby, shower baby and mother with gifts and good wishes	

Choose the most interesting or unusual ceremony from your chart and share the information with your class in a short presentation.

Getting Meaning from Context

Focus on Testing

Using Context Clues Many tests such as the TOEFL® iBT measure your academic listening and speaking abilities. This activity, and others in the book, will develop your social and academic conversation skills, and provide a foundation for success on a variety of standardized tests. You are going to hear five short conversations about ceremonies.

1. Read the list of ceremonies below. Define the unfamiliar items with the help of your teacher.

2. Listen to the conversations.

3. Stop the recording after each conversation. In each blank, write the letter of the ceremony that the conversation is about.

_____ **1.** Conversation 1	a. anniversary	e. promotion
_____ **2.** Conversation 2	b. baptism	f. retirement
_____ **3.** Conversation 3	c. funeral	g. wedding
_____ **4.** Conversation 4	d. graduation	
_____ **5.** Conversation 5		

1 **Talking About Ceremonies** Which of the ceremonies in the activity above have you attended in the last year? Work in groups. Describe your experiences.

Focused Listening

AFFIRMATIVE TAG QUESTIONS
In affirmative tag questions, the main verb is negative, and the tag is affirmative.

Example
George <u>isn't</u> married, <u>is</u> he?

This question can have different meanings, depending on the intonation.

Falling Intonation

Purpose: to start a conversation, to make an observation. The speaker already knows the answer.

Example

George isn't married, is he?

Rising Intonation

Purpose: to get information. The speaker doesn't know the answer.

Example

George isn't married, is he?

Speakers also use affirmative tag questions with rising intonation to express a hope. For example, in Focus on Testing: Using Context Clues, Conversation 5, you heard:

Mother: You and Robert aren't going to shove cake in each other's faces, are you?

Daughter: No, Mom, don't worry.

The mother hopes that the bride and groom will not shove cake in each other's faces. We can infer that she disapproves of this custom.

---

2 **Recognizing the Meaning of Affirmative Tag Questions** Listen to tag questions and decide the speaker's meaning.

Question	The Speaker . . .
1.	(A) is sure Alia bought flowers.
	(B) isn't sure if Alia bought flowers.
2.	(A) thinks the ceremony wasn't long.
	(B) isn't sure the ceremony was long.
3.	(A) is sure he needs to bring a present.
	(B) isn't sure if he needs to bring a present.
4.	(A) hopes the listener is not going to wear that shirt to the party.
	(B) knows the listener is not going to wear that shirt to the party.
5.	(A) is asking a question.
	(B) is making an observation.
6.	(A) is certain the listener is not bringing a dog.
	(B) hopes the listener is not bringing a dog.
7.	(A) is not sure if the wedding has started.
	(B) knows the wedding has started.
8.	(A) is asking a question.
	(B) is sure the listener didn't like the party.

ANSWERING AFFIRMATIVE TAG QUESTIONS

Many English learners get confused about the correct way to answer affirmative tag questions. Look at these examples:

Question	Answer	Meaning of Answer
1. It's not your birthday today, is it?	No, it's not.	The speaker was correct. It's not the listener's birthday.
2. It's not your birthday today, is it?	Yes, it is.	It is the listener's birthday. The speaker was wrong.

3 **Asking and Answering Affirmative Tag Questions** Work in pairs to ask and answer affirmative tag questions. Student A should look at page 251. Student B should look at page 259.

Using Language Functions

OFFERING CONGRATULATIONS AND SYMPATHY

It is polite to offer congratulations on happy occasions such as anniversaries, graduations, promotions, and birthdays. In contrast, we offer sympathy in cases of death, injury, illness, accident, unemployment, or bad luck.

	Congratulations	**Sympathy**
Offering	Congratulations! Congratulations on . . . I'm very happy for you. It's great that . . .	Please accept my sympathy. (formal) I was so sorry to hear (that/about) . . . I'm (so) sorry. It's (really) (awful, terrible) that . . .
Accepting	Thank you (very much). Thanks (a lot).	Thank you for your concern. (formal) You're very kind. (formal) I appreciate it. Thank you.

4 **Role-Play** Prepare conversations with a partner for the following situations. Add details to each situation. Take turns offering and expressing congratulations and sympathy. Then role-play one of the situations for the class.

1. One of your classmates had a serious car accident and spent two weeks in the hospital. He or she is now at home recovering. Call your classmate, express sympathy, and offer to help.

2. You have just been accepted to a university. You call your friend to tell him or her about it. Your friend congratulates you.

3. You run into an acquaintance you haven't seen in a while. She tells you that she quit smoking and hasn't had a cigarette in six months. Offer your congratulations.

4. Your good friend tells you he or she was promoted and is moving to a new city for work. He or she is excited about the new job but sorry about moving. Express both congratulations and sympathy to your friend.

5. Your teacher announces that he will be absent from the next class because he has to go to his aunt's funeral. Offer your sympathies.

▲ A sympathy card

Katsu and Sandra are engaged to be married. He is a first-generation Japanese-American. She is a fourth-generation American. They met at college. Although Katsu and Sandra were both raised in the United States, their backgrounds are very different. For that reason they have decided to hire a professional wedding consultant to help them plan their wedding. In this section you will hear each of them talking to the consultant.

Katsuhiro Mata
Age 25
San Francisco, CA

Sandra Bennett
Age 26
Dallas, TX

Culture Note

Participants in Traditional North American Weddings

- Justice of the peace: A nonreligious official who performs a wedding ceremony.
- Bridesmaid: A female friend or relative who helps the bride and stands by her during the wedding ceremony.
- Groomsman: A male friend or relative who helps the groom get ready for the wedding, usher wedding guests to their seats, and escort bridesmaids during the wedding ceremony.
- Flower girl: A young girl who walks before the bride and groom carrying flowers or scattering flower petals.

1 **Comparing Wedding Preferences** Imagine that you are planning your wedding ceremony. Read the questionnaire. Take notes on your preferences. Then sit in groups and compare your preferences.

My Wedding Preferences	
Location	
Date/time of year	
Type of service/ceremony (e.g., religious, traditional, modern)	
Number of guests (approx.)	
Number and types of attendants (bridesmaids, groomsmen, etc.)	
Role of parents/grandparents	
Clothing	
Music	
Colors	
Other	

2 **Taking Notes on Wedding Preferences** Listen as Katsu and Sandra talk separately to the wedding consultant. Divide into two groups. Each group will listen to one of the conversations and take notes. If a detail is not mentioned, leave it blank.

	Sandra	Katsu
Location		
Date/time of year		
Type of service/ceremony (e.g., religious, traditional, modern)		
Number of guests (approx.)		
Attendants (bridesmaids, groomsmen, etc.)		
Role of parents/grandparents		
Clothing		
Music		
Colors		
Other details		

3 **Discussion** Work with a student who listened to the other conversation. Tell each other about the conversation you heard and fill in the chart with the information your partner gives you. Pay attention to the similarities and differences between Katsu and Sandra.

▲ A garden wedding

4 Role-Play

1. Work in groups. Imagine that you are wedding planners. Look at your chart of Katsu and Sandra's preferences and make recommendations regarding each of the details below. Give reasons for your decisions in cases where Sandra and Katsu disagree.

   Example "I recommend that Katsu and Sandra's parents walk down the aisle with them. That way Sandra gets her wish to walk with her father, and Katsu gets his wish to walk with his parents. And Sandra's mother will also feel included."

   - Location
   - Date/time of year
   - Type of service/ceremony
   - Number of guests
   - Number and types of attendants
   - Role of parents/grandparents
   - Clothing
   - Music
   - Colors
   - Other details

2. Role-play a conversation among Katsu, Sandra, and the wedding planner. Discuss two or three details that Sandra and Katsu don't agree on. The wedding planner should:
   - congratulate Katsu and Sandra on their engagement
   - offer his or her recommendations

   Sandra and Katsu should respond by asking questions, discussing, and finally making decisions about the details of their ceremony.

Self-Assessment Log

Check the words you learned in this chapter.

Nouns
- ❏ mother-to-be
- ❏ prayer
- ❏ priest
- ❏ ritual
- ❏ sin
- ❏ symbol
- ❏ symbolism

Verbs
- ❏ cleanse
- ❏ focus on
- ❏ host
- ❏ involve
- ❏ narrow (something) down
- ❏ play a part in
- ❏ pour
- ❏ pray
- ❏ purify
- ❏ register
- ❏ shower
- ❏ sprinkle
- ❏ symbolize

Adjectives
- ❏ allowed
- ❏ due
- ❏ fascinating
- ❏ pregnant
- ❏ pure
- ❏ silly

Expressions
- ❏ go "ooh and ah"

Check the things you did in this chapter. How well can you do each one?

	Very well	Fairly well	Not very well
I can hear and use stress and pronunciation.	❏	❏	❏
I can use expressions to make and respond to offers.	❏	❏	❏
I can recognize digressions.	❏	❏	❏
I can take notes on a lecture using an outline.	❏	❏	❏
I can talk about celebrations and ceremonies.	❏	❏	❏
I can use and answer tag questions.	❏	❏	❏
I can use expressions to offer congratulations and sympathy.	❏	❏	❏
I can guess meanings from context.	❏	❏	❏
I can compare preferences.	❏	❏	❏

Write what you learned and what you liked in this chapter.

In this chapter,

I learned _____

_____

I liked _____

_____

Appendix 1: Pairwork Activities for Student A

5 Describing Map Locations page 24   Ask your partner for the locations of the places listed under your map. Ask "Where is _____?" Your partner will use expressions of location. Then ask your partner to repeat the description. Write the name of the place on the map. When you are finished, your two maps should be the same.

Example

Student A: Where is the Undergraduate Library?

Student B: It's on Campus Road, up the street from the Administration Building.

Student A: Is it north or south of College Boulevard?

Student B: North.

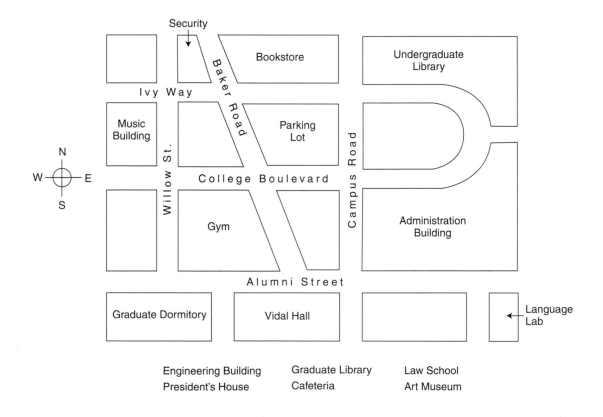

Engineering Building   Graduate Library   Law School

President's House   Cafeteria   Art Museum

Chapter 2 Part 1

8 Role-Play page 35   Role-play these phone conversations. Take turns playing Student A and Student B. Read the information for your role and be sure to use the expressions for opening and closing a phone conversation.

Student A

Situation 1   You are a student. Your friend told you about a very nice room for rent with an American family. Call the family to get information about the room. Then make an appointment to go see it.

You can ask about the following things (choose three or four):

- ❑ who lives in the house
- ❑ rent and utilities
- ❑ furniture, telephone
- ❑ any restrictions (smoking, visitors, pets, etc.)

Situation 2   You are the manager of an apartment building. You have a vacant apartment. It has two bedrooms, one bathroom, air conditioning, and parking for two cars. It is fully furnished in a security building. The rent is $800 a month. It is 30 minutes away from the local college. You will only rent to someone serious and mature. A smoker is OK, but pets are not. A student calls and asks about the apartment.

Chapter 2 Part 3

1 Listening for Clues to Relationships Between People page 45

Pair A

1. You will read the following short conversation with your partner.

Conversation

A: Can I get you anything to drink?

B: Just water, thanks.

Add titles or pet names to show the following relationships between A and B, and practice the conversation three times.

a. two male friends

b. secretary and boss

c. child and mother

2. With the other pair of students in your group, take turns role playing your three conversations. Listen for titles and pet names. Use them to guess the relationships. The other pair will say if you guessed correctly.

2   Role-Play   page 46   Role-play situations in an apartment building.

Student A

Situation 1   You are a tenant in a large apartment building. Your refrigerator has broken for the third time in less than six months. Call the manager to express your frustration and to tell him or her you also want the refrigerator replaced.

Situation 2   You are a music major in college. You love to play your CDs while you do your homework at night. The problem is that your downstairs neighbor goes to bed early and does not like your music. This neighbor complained once, and since then you have tried to be quieter at night. However, you refuse to stop listening to music. Now it is 12:30 A.M., and someone is knocking on your door.

Chapter 2   Part 4

3   Requesting and Giving Directions   page 48   Look at the map. Ask your partner for directions to the places listed at the bottom of your map. When you find the place, write its name on your map. Then give your partner directions to the places that he or she asks about, from where it says, "Start here each time." At the end of this activity, your two maps should look the same.

Example

Student A: How do I get to the print shop?

Student B: That's easy. Go two blocks north on Pine Street. Turn left and go one block west on 3rd Avenue. The print shop will be on your left, in the middle of the block, next to the hardware store.

Student A: Thanks!

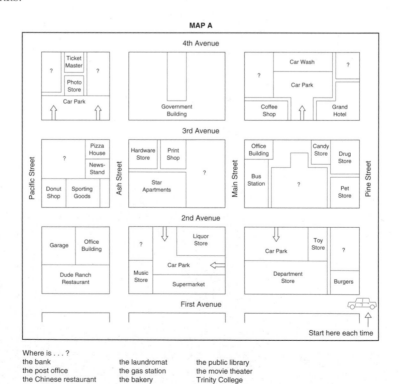

Where is . . . ?

the bank	the laundromat	the public library
the post office	the gas station	the movie theater
the Chinese restaurant	the bakery	Trinity College

7 Using Vocabulary page 57   The following box contains statements using the idioms from this section. Read an item from your box. Student B will select the appropriate response from his or her box.

Student A

1. You look worried. What's wrong?

2. I can't make ends meet on $600 a month. I need more money!

3. My father won't give me any more money this month.

4. What's the secret to living on a budget?

5. Why didn't you go to the concert?

Chapter 3 Part 3

4 Pair Practice with Teens and Tens page 67

Student A

1. Your partner will read some sentences with numbers to you. Circle the numbers you hear.

   1. 13   30
   2. 115   150
   3. $14.05 $40.05
   4. $16.60 $60.60
   5. 1919   1990
   6. 7040   7014
   7. 1.14   1.40

2. Now read the following sentences to your partner.

   1. I pay $70 a month for parking.
   2. She is 160 centimeters tall.
   3. The president's house has 19 rooms.
   4. She paid $50.50 for a haircut.
   5. Her family has lived here since 1830.
   6. Please deliver the package to 1670 Loyola Street.
   7. That cookie contains only 114 calories.

Chapter 4 Part 1

7 Reviewing Vocabulary page 80   The following box contains statements using the new vocabulary from this section. Read an item from your box. Student B will select the appropriate response from his or her box.

Student A

1. How was your trip to New York last December?

2. Did you do anything about the broken elevator in your building?

3. Do you want to go to the beach this afternoon?

4. I heard your mother got a full-time job.

5. What's your brother doing these days?

Chapter 4 Part 3

4 Asking and Answering Negative Tag Questions page 93   Use the statements in the box to make negative tag questions. Decide if the intonation should rise or fall. Then ask your partner the questions.

Student A

1. You're from _____ (name of country, city, or area), aren't you?

2. Last night's homework was _____ (hard, easy, boring, confusing, etc.) . . .

3. This _____ (book, pen, etc.) is yours . . .

4. It's _____ (cold, hot, pleasant) today . . .

5. Our next test is _____ (day or date) . . .

6. This classroom is _____ (comfortable, too small, etc.) . . .

Chapter 5 Part 1

7 Using Vocabulary page 106   The following box contains statements using the new vocabulary from this section. Read an item from your box. Student B will select the appropriate response from his or her box.

Student A

1. It's 3 o'clock in the morning! Why aren't you sleeping?

2. Are you leaving?

3. Wake up, Sally. It's 7 A.M.

4. Hello? Is anybody home?

5. Who takes care of your kids while you're working?

6. What's wrong with this light? It's not working properly.

7. How's the baby doing?

8. Why did George quit his job?

Chapter 5 Part 1

8 Asking for a Favor page 107 Read the situations in the following box and ask your partner for help or for a favor. Your partner must give an appropriate response.

Example It's Thursday. Your library books are due tomorrow. Ask your partner to return the books to the library for you.

A: My library books are due tomorrow. Could you please return them to the library for me?

B: I'm sorry, but I'm not going there today.

Student A

1. Your arms are full of books. Ask your partner to open the door for you.

2. It's raining and you don't have a car. Ask your partner to drive you home after class.

3. You're trying to concentrate. Ask your partner to speak on the phone more quietly.

Chapter 7 Part 1

6 Using Vocabulary page 154 The following box contains statements using the new vocabulary from this section. Read an item from your box. Student B will select the appropriate response from his or her box.

Student A

1. Do you understand tonight's homework assignment? I don't.

2. When do you think you'll be able to speak English fluently?

3. I'm here to see Dr. Brown at 3 P.M.

4. Jerry is a two-faced liar. He told my girlfriend I was seeing another woman!

5. Claudette's friendliness is the reason everyone likes her.

6. I've known my best friend since we were three years old.

7. I've told John six times that I don't want to go out with him, but he keeps asking me.

8. Why is it so hard to make friends with Americans?

Chapter 7 Part 3

2 Using Interjections page 165 Work in pairs to practice using interjections.

Student A

1. Say the following sentences to your partner and wait for a response.

    1. Did you understand last night's homework?

    2. Oops! I forgot my listening book at home.

    3. Ouch! My leg!

    4. The teacher looks really annoyed.

2. Now listen to your partner and choose the proper response from the following list.

    a. Huh? Could you repeat that?

    b. Uh-huh. Let's go home before it starts.

    c. Let's go see if it's still there.

    d. I'll pick it up.

Chapter 8

6 Reviewing Vocabulary page 177

Student A

1. What is this delicious dish?

2. Sally has a new boyfriend. To be honest, I'm not crazy about him.

3. What do you think of action movies?

4. Did you have a good time in San Diego last weekend?

5. Why did you break up with your girlfriend?

6. I don't care for this new chair you bought. It's not very comfortable.

3 **Asking and Answering Affirmative Tag Questions** page 236 Use the statements in the box to make affirmative tag questions with rising intonation (asking for information). Your partner should answer truthfully.

Example

You read: You're not from France.

You ask: You're not from France, are you?

Your partner answers Yes, I am (if he or she is from France).

No, I'm not (if he or she is not from France).

Student A

1. You don't smoke . . .

2. There's no homework tonight . . .

3. It isn't raining . . .

4. You don't have children (grandchildren, sisters, brothers) . . .

Chapter 1 Part 4

5 Describing Map Locations page 24   Ask your partner for the locations of the places listed under your map. Ask "Where is _____?" Your partner will use expressions of location. Then ask your partner to repeat the description. Write the name of the place on the map. When you are finished, your two maps should be the same.

Example

Student B: Where is the Undergraduate Library?

Student A: It's on Campus Road, up the street from the Administration Building.

Student B: Is it north or south of College Boulevard?

Student A: North.

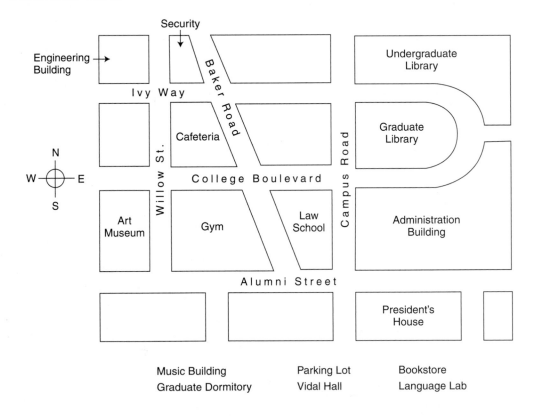

Music Building   Parking Lot   Bookstore
Graduate Dormitory   Vidal Hall   Language Lab

8 Role-Play page 35   Role-play these phone conversations. Take turns playing Student A and Student B. Read the information for your role and be sure to use the expressions for opening and closing a phone conversation.

Student B

Situation 1 You live in a large house with your husband or wife and two children. You have an extra bedroom that you want to rent to a student. The room is furnished. It has a private phone and bath. The rent is only $300, but the student must agree to do ten hours a week of babysitting. Also, you have two large dogs, so the student cannot have any pets. You definitely do not want a smoker. A student calls and asks about the room.

Situation 2 You are a university student looking for a place to live. You saw the following ad in the campus housing office. You can afford to spend $900 a month on rent, and you don't have a car. Therefore, it's important for you to rent an apartment close to the college. Call the owner and get more information about the apartment. Decide if you want to see the place or not. If so, make an appointment with the manager.

Chapter 2 Part 3

1 Listening for Clues to Relationships Between People page 45

Pair B

1. You will read the following short conversation with your partner.

Conversation

A: Can I get you anything to drink?

B: Just water, thanks.

Add titles or pet names to show the following relationships between A and B, and practice the conversation three times.

a. grandson and grandfather

b. boyfriend and girlfriend

c. waiter and customer

2. With the other pair of students in your group, take turns role playing your three conversations. Listen for titles and pet names. Use them to guess the relationships. The other pair will say if you guessed correctly.

2 Role-Play page 46   Role-play situations in an apartment building.

Student B

Situation 1 You are the manager of a large apartment building. You have one tenant who frequently complains about problems in his or her apartment. This takes up a lot of your time. Now the tenant calls you with a new complaint. You feel that this tenant should pay for the repairs because you think the tenant doesn't take good care of the apartment.

Situation 2 The neighbor above you plays loud music late at night. You wrote this neighbor a polite note about it, but the problem has not stopped. Now it is 12:30 A.M. and you cannot sleep because of the music. You are very frustrated. You go upstairs, knock on the neighbor's door, and tell the neighbor you want the problem to stop.

Chapter 2 Part 4

3 Requesting and Giving Directions page 48   Look at the map. Ask your partner for directions to the places listed at the bottom of your map. When you find the place, write its name on your map. Then give your partner directions to the places that he or she asks about, from where it says, "Start here each time." At the end of this activity, your two maps should look the same.

Example

Student A: How do I get to the print shop?

Student B: That's easy. Go two blocks north on Pine Street. Turn left and go one block west on 3rd Avenue. The print shop will be on your left, in the middle of the block, next to the hardware store.

Student A: Thanks!

MAP B

Where is . . . ?

the coffee shop	the pet store	the donut shop
the pizza house	the garage	the toy store
the government building	the supermarket	the candy store

7 **Using Vocabulary** page 57   The following box contains statements using the idioms from this section. Student A will read an item from his or her box. Select the appropriate response from your box.

Student B

   a. Don't spend more than you earn.

   b. Because the tickets cost an arm and a leg.

   c. I'm broke again. I can't pay my rent.

   d. Maybe you should get a part-time job.

   e. My dad is a tightwad too.

Chapter 3 Part 3

4 **Pair Practice with Teens and Tens** page 67

Student B

   1. Read the following sentences to your partner.

      1. I have only 30 cents in my wallet.

      2. She weighs 115 pounds.

      3. The sweater cost $40.05.

      4. Your change is $60.60.

      5. She was born in 1919.

      6. Our business office is at 7040 Adams Street.

      7. Today one U.S. dollar traded for 1.14 Euros.

   2. Now listen as your partner reads sentences with numbers to you. Circle the numbers you hear.

      1. $17 $70

      2. 160   116

      3. 90   19

      4. $15.50 $50.50

      5. 1813   1830

      6. 1617   1670

      7. 140   114

7 Reviewing Vocabulary page 80   The following box contains statements using the new vocabulary from this section. Student A will read an item from his or her box. Select the appropriate response from your box.

Student B

   a. Yeah. I complained about it to my apartment manager.

   b. Yeah. She's supporting me while I finish my B.A.

   c. It was the worst. It snowed for five days straight.

   d. He spends all his time studying. I almost never see him.

   e. No thanks. I'm not in the mood.

Chapter 4 Part 3

4 Asking and Answering Negative Tag Questions page 93   Use the statements in the box to make negative tag questions. Decide if the intonation should rise or fall. Then ask your partner the questions.

Student B

   1. You speak _____ (language) . . . , don't you?

   2. _____ (an actor or actress) is from England . . .

   3. The verb tenses in English are difficult to understand . . .

   4. The textbook for this class is (expensive, useful, etc.) . . .

   5. The capital of Canada is Toronto* . . .

   6. The _____ (type of food) at _____
      (name of restaurant) is _____ (delicious, terrible, etc.) . . .

---

* The capital of Canada is not Toronto; it's Ottawa.

7 **Using Vocabulary** page 106   The following box contains statements using the new vocabulary from this section. Student A will read an item from his or her box. Select the appropriate response from your box.

Student B

4 **a.** Yeah, come on in.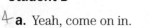

1 **b.** I have to finish this paper by 10 A.M. Time is running out.

7 **c.** I just checked up on her. She's sleeping.

3 **d.** I'm tired! I don't want to go to school today!

8 **e.** He decided to stay home for a couple of years and bring up his kids.

5 **f.** My mother.

2 **g.** Yes, it's getting dark. I'd better take off.

6 **h.** I know. I told the manager, and he's going to look into it.

Chapter 5 Part 1

8 **Asking for a Favor** page 107   Read the situations in the following box and ask your partner for help or for a favor. Your partner must give an appropriate response.

Example It's Thursday. Your library books are due tomorrow. Ask your partner to return the books to the library for you.

B: My library books are due tomorrow. Could you please return them to the library for me?

A: I'm sorry, but I'm not going there today.

Student B

1. Your partner speaks English very well. Ask your partner to read your composition and check the grammar.

2. Ask your partner to help you paint your bathroom on Saturday.

3. You need to move a heavy table. Ask your partner to help you.

6 Using Vocabulary page 154   The following box contains statements using the new vocabulary from this section. Student A will read an item from his or her box. Select the appropriate response from your box.

Student B

  a. I guess he's a little slow to catch on.

  b. Please have a seat. The doctor is with another patient right now.

  c. Really? You're lucky to have such a close friendship.

  d. No, I'm in the dark too.

  e. That's hard to say. In just a few years, I hope.

  f. You have to be patient. Friendships don't happen so quickly.

  g. He did? I thought he was your best friend!

  h. I agree. She always smiles when I see her.

Chapter 7 Part 3

2 Using Interjections page 165   Work in pairs to practice using interjections.

Student B

  1. Listen to your partner and choose the proper response from the following list.

    a. Uh-oh, I wonder what's wrong.

    b. What happened? Are you hurt?

    c. Uh-uh. The directions were too confusing.

    d. You can share mine.

  2. Now say the following sentences to your partner and wait for a response.

    1. Do you think it's going to rain tonight?

    2. You need the past participle here, not the present.

    3. Uh-oh, I left my wallet in the restroom!

    4. Here's your dictionary . . . oops!

6 **Reviewing Vocabulary** page 177   The following box contains statements using the new vocabulary from this section. Student A will read an item from his or her box. Select the appropriate response from your box.

Student B

  a. I can't stand them. I prefer comedies.

  b. It's humus. It's from the Middle East. I love it too.

  c. No. It rained all day Saturday and Sunday, so we came home early.

  d. Really? What's his name?

  e. OK, I'll take it back to the store.

  f. Because we didn't see eye to eye on anything.

Chapter 10 Part 3

3 **Asking and Answering Affirmative Tag Questions** page 236   Use the statements in the box to make affirmative tag questions with rising intonation (asking for information). Your partner should answer truthfully.

Example

You read: You're not from France.

You ask: You're not from France, are you?

Your partner answers: Yes, I am (if he or she is from France).

No, I'm not (if he or she is not from France).

Student B

  1. You don't eat meat . . .

  2. There's no test tomorrow . . .

  3. You don't have a computer (cell phone) . . .

  4. Milk isn't good for adults . . .

Appendix 3: Activity Information

11 What Would You Do? page 89

Read about your background and qualifications before the interview.

A. Applicants for Manager

1A.
Education: High school graduate
Experience: Two years as the night manager at another supermarket
Skills: Well-organized; good communication skills with the workers

2A.
Education: B.A. in management
Experience: Managed a fast-food restaurant in London for five years; good recommendations
Skills: None specifically related to managing a supermarket, but highly motivated and eager to learn

3A.
Education: B.A. in chemistry
Experience: Four years managing another supermarket; had some trouble communicating with the workers there
Skills: Have also worked as a checker, stock clerk, butcher, and truck driver

B. Applicants for Butcher

1B.
Education: High school graduate and completed trade school for butchers
Experience: None
Skills: Know how to cut and prepare every kind of meat

2B.
Education: High school graduate
Experience: Worked in parents' butcher shop during the summers since age 12
Skills: Know how to cut and prepare most kinds of meat

3B.
Education: Master's degree in sociology
Experience: Worked as a butcher's helper at another supermarket for four years

Skills: Know how to cut and prepare most kinds of meat; speak three languages

C. Applicants for Stock Clerk

1C.
Education: High school graduate
Experience: None
Skills: Honest and willing to work hard; need this first job in order to get experience

2C.
Education: Tenth grade
Experience: Worked as a stock clerk in another supermarket; work was good but sometimes was late
Skills: Nothing special

3C.
Education: High school graduate
Experience: Worked in an office for six months; excellent references
Skills: Can read and follow directions very well

D. Applicants for Butcher

1D.
Education: Eighth grade
Experience: Worked as a checker at another market for 15 years
Skills: Know how to operate cash register; polite and helpful

2D.
Education: High school graduate
Experience: None in a supermarket
Skills: Learned how to operate cash register while working in a department store; received Employee of the Month award for outstanding customer service

3D.
Education: B.A. in English
Experience: Worked at another market as a stock clerk and bagger* for four years
Skills: Don't know how to use a cash register yet, but learn quickly

---

* This is the person who puts groceries in bags after the checker has entered the price in the cash register.

Appendix 4: Answers

Chapter 5 Part 2

9 What Would You Do? page 112

"The Tokyo District Court . . . rejected the husband's demand for damages but did ask the woman to return her wedding rings and a cash gift of $8,000."

Chapter 7 Part 3

3 Guessing Meanings of Slang Expressions page 165

1. freaked out—to become extremely upset
2. to shoot some hoops—play basketball
3. cheesy—tacky
4. goofy—silly
5. lose it—to lose control, or lose one's temper
6. pigged out—to overeat
7. chill—relaxed
8. bummed out—discouraged, depressed
9. wiped out—exhausted
10. chickened out—to back out of something because of fear

Chapter 9 Part 2

8 Solving a Science Problem page 208

1. two 100-pound tanks of oxygen—no air on the moon
2. five gallons of water—you can't live long without water
3. map of moon's surface and rock formations—needed for navigation
4. dried food—you can live for some time without food

5. solar-powered FM receiver-transmitter—communication
6. 50 feet of nylon rope—for travel over rough terrain
7. first aid kit containing injection needles—kit is useful, but needles are useless
8. parachute silk—carrying
9. life raft—some value for shelter or carrying
10. three gallons of milk—could be useful as food
11. portable heating unit—useless, the lighted side of the moon is hot
12. magnetic compass—useless, moon's magnetic field is different
13. box of matches—useless, no oxygen

2 Listening to a Game Show page 216

1. a. Apple
2. a. Mt. Everest in Nepal
3. c. Italy
4. c. China
5. a. penicillin
6. b. the telephone
7. c. Nicolaus Copernicus

4 Ordering Events in a Story page 217

Correct order: C, G, B, F, A, D, E

Appendix 5: Note-taking Abbreviations

Sample Abbreviations and Symbols to Use in Taking Notes

Mathematical symbols to use in expressing relationships among ideas:

=	is like, equals, means (in defining a term)
≠	is unlike, not the same as
#	number
<	is smaller than
>	is larger than
+	plus, in addition, and

Other useful symbols:

&	and
%	percent
$	dollars
@	at
?	question, something unclear
~	approximately
↑	increase, go up
↓	decrease, go down
→	causes (as in A → B)
♂	male
♀	female
"	same as above (repeated or used again)
∴	therefore, as a result

Some common abbreviations:

A.M.	morning	w/o	without
P.M.	afternoon or evening	yr.	year
e.g.	for example	mo.	month
i.e.	that is, in other words	wk.	week
re:	concerning or regarding	no.	number
etc.	and so on	pd.	paid
vs.	versus	ft.	foot
ch.	chapter	lb.	pound
p., pp.	page, pages	cm	centimeter
w/	with	km	kilometer

Audioscript

Chapter 1 Education and Student Life

Part 1 Conversation: On a College Campus

3 Comprehension Questions page 5

4 Listening for Stressed Words page 6

Mari: Excuse me. Could you tell me where Kimbell Hall is?

Nancy: Oh, you mean Campbell Hall?

Mari: Oh yeah, right.

Nancy: Do you see that brown building over there?

Mari: Uh, behind the fountain?

Nancy: Yeah, that's it. Come on, I'm going there too. Are you here for the English placement test?

Mari: Yes, I am. How about you?

Nancy: Actually, I'm one of the English teachers here.

Mari: Oh really? Maybe I'll be in your class!

Nancy: It's possible. What's your name?

Mari: Mariko Honda, but most people call me Mari. And you?

Nancy: I'm Nancy Anderson. So, where are you from?

Mari: Japan.

Nancy: Aha. And, uh, how long have you been here?

Mari: Just three weeks.

Nancy: Really? But your English sounds great!

Mari: Thanks. That's because my family used to come here every summer to visit my grandmother when I was little. I can speak pretty well.

Nancy: Mmm—hmmm.

Mari: But now I want to go to college here, so I need to improve my skills, especially writing. Yeah, so, uh, that's why I signed up for this English program.

Nancy: I see. Uh, what do you want to major in?

Mari: International business. My father has an import-export company, and he does a lot of business here in the States.

Nancy: Oh, I see.

Mari: And I also want to take art classes, because I'm really into art.

Nancy: Art and business. Wow. That's an interesting combination. But, can't you study those things in Japan?

Mari: Well, sure, but you have to speak good English these days to get ahead in business. It's better for my career if I go to college here.

Nancy: Well, here's Campbell Hall. Good luck on the placement exam. It was nice meeting you, Mari.

Mari: Thanks. You too.

Nancy: See you later.

Mari: Bye-bye.

6 Listening for Reductions page 8

A: Could you help me, please? I used to be a student at this school.

B: Oh yeah, I remember you. How are you?

A: Fine, thanks.

B: Can I help you with something?

A: Yes, I want to get an application for the TOEFL® test.

B: You mean the International TOEFL® iBT? Let's see. They used to be here on this shelf. It looks like they're all gone. I'm sorry, you'll have to wait until they come in next week.

A: How about sending me one when they come in?

B: No problem. What's your name and address?

Part 2   Lecture: Undergraduate Courses in North America

Good morning, everyone. My name is Richard Baldwin, and I am the academic advisor here at the English Language Center. If you have any questions about applying to a university, or if you need help with your application, you can come see me in my office.

So . . . uh, this . . . this morning I want to give you a general introduction to the university system in the United States and Canada. First, I'm going to tell you about three types of university courses. And then my second main topic is course requirements . . . uh, course requirements, which means what you have to *do* in order to pass the course. OK? So I'll talk about those two topics, and then you'll have time to ask questions before we take a break. OK?

Good morning, everyone. My name is Richard Baldwin, and I am the academic advisor here at the English Language Center. If you have any questions about applying to a university, or if you need help with your application, you can come see me in my office.

So . . . uh, this . . . this morning I want to give you a general introduction to the university system in the United States and Canada. First, I'm going to tell you about three types of university courses. And then my second main topic is course requirements . . . uh, course requirements, which means what you have to *do* in order to pass the course. OK? So I'll talk about those two topics, and then you'll have time to ask questions before we take a break. OK?

All right, now as I said, first I want to tell you about three types of university courses. And I should explain that I'm talking about undergraduate courses now, because the system

is different at the graduate level. All right. The most common type of undergraduate course is called a lecture course. Got that? A lecture course. Now basically, in a lecture course, the professor talks and the students sit and take notes. This is very important—taking notes, I mean . . . because most of the time the information in a lecture is not the same as the information in your books, and you can expect to have questions on your exams that are based on the lectures. So you see, it isn't enough to just read your textbooks, like it is in some countries; in the U.S. and Canada the system is that you have to attend lectures. And during the lecture you can't just sit there and listen, you have to take notes. Then later you use the notes to study for your exams. I hope that's clear.

Now, as an undergraduate in almost any major, you'll probably spend four to six hours a week attending lectures. But that's four to six hours for each lecture course. Do you understand? And students normally take three or four lecture courses per semester, so figure it out . . . you're going to spend a lot of hours each week listening to lectures. And the last thing about lecture courses is that they're often held in very large rooms because undergraduate courses like Introduction to Psychology can have two or three hundred students in them, especially at large universities.

And so . . . Well, what if you have a question or need help? There's no w—there's no way that one professor can meet with 300 students, right? That's why, each week, all the students in a lecture course are divided into groups for a special kind of class called a discussion section, which meets for two or three hours a week, and it's smaller, maybe 20 or 30 students. Your discussion section is the place where you can ask questions about the lectures and the readings and go over homework. But this class isn't taught by your professors. At large universities it's taught by graduate students called teaching assistants, or TAs.

Let's see. So far I've told you about lecture courses and discussion sections. The third kind of class I want to mention is especially important for science majors, and that's the lab class. Lab is short for "laboratory." If your major is chemistry or physics or any other kind of science, you'll have to spend several hours a week in the lab. This is where you do your experiments.

Let's move on now to the second major topic I mentioned, which is course requirements. As I told you, "course requirements" means the things you have to do in order to pass a course. First of all, nearly every class you take will have one or more tests, or exams. Most university courses have at least two big exams: one in the middle of the course, called a midterm, and another big one at the end, called the final exam. You might also have smaller tests from time to time. A small test is called a quiz.

Also, in many courses you might also have to do something called a term paper or research paper, so let me tell you a little about that. A term paper is a large written report that has several steps. First, you choose a topic related to the course. Then you do research on this topic, either in a library or on the Internet. "Do research" means that you read and take notes on the topic. And finally, you use your notes to write a paper in your own words. A research paper can be anywhere from 5 pages to 25 pages long.

Now, this is a good place for me to introduce you to something called plagiarism. That's spelled P-L-A-G-I-A-R-I-S-M. Plagiarism is a kind of cheating, and it's a serious problem at American universities. Do you remember I just said that when you write a term paper, it has to be in your own words? That means you can't copy your paper or even small parts of your paper from another student or a book or the Internet. If you do, I mean if you copy, that's plagiarism. If you plagiarize and you get caught, the punishment can be very serious. You can fail the course or even get kicked out of the university. So as I said, this is a very serious thing, and you need to be very careful about it.

OK; does anyone have questions at this point about types of university courses, about course requirements, or about plagiarism? No? Then let's stop here and take a break.

Part 3   Strategies for Better Listening and Speaking

Using Context Clues   page 17

Conversation 1

A: What's wrong?

B: Well, I've got a term paper due in a week, and all the books I need are checked out!

A: I know what you mean. There are a million books in this place, and I can never find what I need.

Question 1: Where are the speakers?

B: Maybe I'll try the other library.

Conversation 2

A: Can I come see you tomorrow?

B: Sure, what's the problem?

A: I am totally confused about this week's chemistry experiment.

B: Didn't you come to the lab yesterday?

A: Yeah, but I had to leave early and I missed part of your demonstration.

Question 2: Who is the student probably talking to?

B: OK, can you come to the TA's office tomorrow at noon?

Conversation 3

A: What are the requirements for the course?

B: There'll be a grammar quiz every Monday and a final exam. Also, you're required to go to the language lab two hours every week. And, of course, your attendance and class participation are very important.

Question 3: What class is this?

B: And one more thing. Each student is required to give a short speech in German.

Conversation 4

A: You asked to see me, Professor Jansen?

B: Yes, Sheila. Would you like to explain what happened on this research paper?

A: What do you mean, sir?

B: It is almost exactly the same as a paper I received from another student two years ago.

Question 4: The student probably . . .

B: I'm going to let you rewrite your paper this time. But if you ever plagiarize again, you will fail the course. Is that clear?

1 **Listening for Intonation Clues** page 18

Conversation 1A

Kathy: Hello?

Ron: Kathy? Uh, this is Ron, you know, from your history class?

Kathy: Oh, hi!

Ron: Listen, I was wondering . . . um, were you planning to go to Ali's party Saturday?

Kathy: Hmm. I haven't really thought about it yet.

Ron: Well, would you like to go?

Kathy: You mean, with you?

Ron: Yeah.

Question 1: How does the woman feel about the invitation?

Kathy: Well sure, Ron, I'd love to go.

Conversation 1B

Kathy: Hello?

Ron: Kathy? Uh, this is Ron, you know, from your history class?

Kathy: Oh, hi.

Ron: Listen, I was wondering . . . um, were you planning to go to Ali's party Saturday?

Kathy: Hmm. I haven't really thought about it yet.

Ron: Well, would you like to go?

Kathy: You mean, with you?

Ron: Yeah.

Question 2: How does the woman feel about the invitation?

Kathy: Well thanks, Ron, but I just remembered that I'm busy that night.

Conversation 2A

A: Did you hear the news? Professor Bradley had to go out of town suddenly. All his classes are cancelled this week.

B: Cancelled?

Question 3: How do the students feel about the situation?

A: I'm really worried about my score on the last test. Now I'll have to wait until next week to find out.

Conversation 2B

A: Did you hear the news? Professor Bradley had to go out of town suddenly. All his classes are cancelled this week!

B: Cancelled? Oh, wow!

Question 4: How do the students feel about the situation?

A: I'm so happy! Now I'll have an extra week to work on my term paper.

Part 4 Real-World Task: Reading a Map

3 **Expressions of Location in Context**
page 23

1. The Math Building is down the street from Memorial Cafeteria.

2. The Computer Science building is across the street from the theater.

3. The Business Hall is at the intersection of Campus Road and Jones Street.

4. Memorial Cafeteria is in the middle of the block on Bridge Road.

5. There is a park beside the Math Building.

6. The boathouse is between Lakeshore Drive and College Lake.

7. There are buildings on both sides of Bradford Avenue.

8. Smith Library is opposite the Science Hall.

Chapter 2 City Life

Part 1   Conversation: Finding a Place to Live

3 **Comprehension Questions** page 29

4 **Listening for Stressed Words** page 30

Nancy: Hello?

Mari: May I speak to Nancy, please?

Nancy: Speaking.

Mari: Uh hi, uh, my name is Mari, and I'm calling about the room for rent. I saw your ad at the campus housing office.

Nancy: Oh, right. OK, uh, are you a student?

Mari: Well, right now I'm just studying English, but I'm planning to start college full-time in March.

Nancy: I see. Where are you living now?

Mari: I've been living in a house with some other students, but I don't like it there.

Nancy: Why? What's the problem?

Mari: Well, first of all, it's really noisy, and it's not very clean. The other people in the house are real slobs. I mean they never lift a finger to clean up after themselves. It really bugs me! I need a place that's cleaner and more private.

Nancy: Well, it's really quiet here. We're not home very much.

Mari: What do you do?

Nancy: I teach English at the college.

Mari: Wait a minute! Didn't we meet yesterday at the placement exam?

Nancy: Oh . . . you're the girl from Japan! What was your name again?

Mari: Mari.

Nancy: Right. What a small world!

Mari: It really is. By the way, who else lives in the house? The ad said there are three people.

Nancy: Well besides me there's my husband, Andrew, and my cousin, Jeff. He's a musician and a part-time student. Uh, are you OK with having male roommates?

Mari: Sure, as long as they're clean and not too noisy.

Nancy: Don't worry. They're both easy to live with.

Mari: OK. Um, is the neighborhood safe?

Nancy: Oh sure. We haven't had any problems, and you can walk to school from here.

Mari: Well, it sounds really nice. When can I come by and see it?

Nancy: Can you make it this evening around five? Then you can meet the guys too.

Mari: Yeah, five o'clock is good. What's the address?

Nancy: It's 3475 Hayworth Avenue. Do you know where that is?

Mari: No, I don't.

Nancy: OK. From University Village you go seven blocks east on Olympic Avenue. At the intersection of Olympic and Alfred, there's a stoplight. Turn left and go up one and a half blocks. Our house is in the middle of the block on the left.

Mari: That sounds easy.

Nancy: Yeah, you can't miss it. Listen, I've got to go. Someone's at the door. See you this evening.

Mari: OK, see you later. Bye.

Nancy: Bye-bye.

6 **Listening for Reductions** page 33

Conversation 1

Mari: Hey Jeff, where are you going?

Jeff: I want to get a present for Nancy. It's her birthday, you know.

Mari: Yeah, I know. What do you think I should get her?

Jeff: Well, she likes music. How about a CD?

Conversation 2

Nancy: How do you like my new haircut, Mari?

Mari: It's great! Who's your hairstylist?

Nancy: His name's José.

Mari: Can you give me his phone number?

Nancy: Sure, but he's always very busy. You can try calling him, but he might not be able to see you until next month.

Conversation 3

Andrew: What do you want to do tonight, Nancy?

Nancy: Nothing special. I've got to stay home and correct my students' compositions.

Part 2 Lecture: Neighborhood Watch Meeting

4 **Taking Notes on Statistics** page 38

1. A year ago there were 48 burglaries in your area; this year it's gone up to 60 so far.

2. The number of car thefts has almost doubled.

3. Did you know that in half of all burglaries, 50 percent, the burglars enter through unlocked doors or windows?

5 **Listening for Transitions** page 39

6 **Taking Notes** page 40

Part 1

Police Officer: Good evening. My name is Officer Jenkins. Thanks for inviting me tonight. OK, so, as you know, there have been a number of break-ins recently in your neighborhood, and even though it's true that there's been very little *violent* crime, um, especially compared to other parts of the city, burglary and car theft are both up in this area. Let me give you some statistics. OK, a year ago there were . . . 48 burglaries in your area; this year it's gone up to 60 so far, and the number of car thefts has almost doubled, too. Now, I'm not here to try to scare you. What I want to do tonight is to give you some simple suggestions that will make your homes and automobiles safer. OK?

So first of all, let's talk about lights outside the house. If you live in a house, you need to have lights both in the front of your house and in the back, and be sure to turn on those lights at night. In my opinion this is the most important thing you can do to prevent burglaries.

Next, let's talk about lights inside the house. It's . . .

Woman in Audience: Excuse me, what about apartments? I mean, I live in an apartment building . . .

Police Officer: Yeah, good question. If you live in an apartment building, you want to have good, bright lighting in the garage, the hallways, and by the door to your apartment. If a light is broken, don't ignore it. Report it to your manager immediately. And whether you live in a house or an apartment, it's a good idea to put automatic timers on your lights. You know what a timer is, right? It's like a clock that turns on your lights automatically, so it looks like someone is home even if you're out. Are you with me on that?

All right, then . . . the next topic I want to discuss is locks. First of all, forget cheap locks 'cause they're not safe. Every door in your place should have a deadbolt . . . um, a deadbolt at least one inch thick. Also, there are special locks you can buy for your windows. By the way, did you know that in half of all burglaries, 50 percent, the burglars enter through unlocked doors or windows? I'm telling you, even in a peaceful neighborhood like this, where you know all your neighbors, you have to get into the habit of keeping your windows and doors locked.

Part 2

Police Officer: OK, now let's move on and talk about how you can prevent car theft. First, if you have a garage, use it for your car, not for your ping-pong table! But seriously, the most important thing is—and I hope this is obvious—if you've got valuables in the car, hide them in the trunk. Don't leave them out on the seat, not even for five minutes! Last week we got a report from a guy who left his laptop on the car seat while he ran in to buy a cup of coffee. When he came back it was gone. The thief just broke the car window and reached in and took it. And also . . .

Man in Audience: What about a car alarm?

Police Officer: Well, most research shows that noisy alarms don't do anything to prevent car theft. It's better to have the kind of device thieves can see, like a lock on your steering wheel. But the best thing of all is just to lock your car and keep valuables out of sight.

All right. Now my last point is what you, as neighbors, can do to help each other. The main thing is that when you go on vacation, ask someone to watch your house for you, to collect your mail, take in your newspaper, stuff like that. Also, if you see something unusual, like a strange van or truck in your neighbor's driveway, or people carrying furniture out, *don't* go out there and try to stop it. Just call the police! And one more thing. Each of you should put this Neighborhood Watch decal—

this picture right here of the man in a coat looking over his shoulder—in your front window. This tells criminals that this area has a Neighborhood Watch and that someone might be watching them. OK, are there any questions?

Man in Audience: Yeah, there's something I want to know . . . Do you think it's a good idea to keep a gun in the house?

Police Officer: Well now, that is a very complicated question. I think that it's a bad idea to have a gun in your house, especially if you have kids. Thousands of people die in gun accidents each year in this country. So, in my opinion, it's just not safe to have a gun in your house. But of course it *is* legal to have a gun, if that's what you want. Just make sure you get the proper license and that you take a course in gun safety, OK? All right. Anything else?

Part 3 Strategies for Better Listening and Speaking

Using Context Clues page 44

Conversation 1

Manager: Yes? Who is it?

Tenant: It's Donna from 206. I've got a check for you.

Manager: Oh, it's you. Do you know it's the fifth of the month?

Tenant: Yes, Mr. Bradley. I'm sorry. I know it was due on the first, but my grandma got sick, and I had to go out of town suddenly.

Question 1: Who is the man?

Manager: Look, my job as manager here is to collect the rent on the first. If you're late again next month you'll have to look for another place to live.

Conversation 2

Tenant: OK, Mr. Bradley. But look, while I'm here, I need to talk to you about a couple of things.

Manager: Yeah?

Tenant: First, about the cockroaches. They're all over the kitchen again. I'm sick of them!

Manager: Have you used the spray I gave you?

Tenant: It's no good. I need something stronger to kill those horrible bugs once and for all.

Question 2: Who will the manager probably need to call?

Manager: OK, I'll call the exterminator next week.

Conversation 3

Tenant: Next week?! Last week you said you'd fix the hole in the ceiling, and you still haven't done that! I'm fed up with waiting for you to fix things around here!

Question 3: What can you guess about Donna's apartment?

Tenant: Why should I pay so much rent for a place in such bad condition?

Manager: Well, you're not the only tenant in this building. If you don't like it, why don't you move out?

Conversation 4

John: Hi, Donna. What do you need this time?

Donna: Hello, John. A couple of eggs. Do you mind?

John: No, come on in.

Question 4: How does John feel about Donna's request?

Donna: Thanks so much, John!

John: You're welcome!

Conversation 5

John: Hi, Donna. What do you need this time?

Donna: Hello, John. A couple of eggs. Do you mind?

John: No, come on in.

Question 5: How does John feel about Donna's request?

Donna: Thanks, John.

John: OK, but next time go ask somebody else, all right?

Part 4 Real-World Task: Following Directions

2 Following Directions page 48

1. You are at the X. Go two blocks west on 2nd Avenue. Turn left and go down one block. What's on your left?

2. You are at the intersection of Main Street and 3rd Avenue. Go one block south on Main. Turn left. Go straight for half a block. What's on your left?

3. You have just eaten dinner at the French restaurant on the corner of 4th and Pine. Go south on Pine Street to 2nd Avenue. Turn right. Go one block west on 2nd. Turn left. Go down Main Street for half a block. What's on your right?

4. You work in the office building at the intersection of 3rd and Main. After work you decide to go shopping. Go one block east on 3rd. Turn left and go one block up Pine Street. Turn right. Go one block east until you reach Oak Street. What's on your right?

Chapter 3 Business and Money

Part 1 Conversation: Borrowing Money

3 Comprehension Questions page 53

4 Listening for Stressed Words page 54

Dad: Hello?

Jeff: Hi, Dad.

Dad: Jeff! How are you?

Jeff: I'm fine Dad. How's Mom? Did she get over her cold?

Dad: Yes, she's fine now. She went back to work yesterday.

Jeff: That's good. Um, Dad, I need to ask you something.

Dad: Sure, son, what is it?

Jeff: Well, uh, the truth is, I'm broke again. Could you lend me $200 just till the end of the month?

Dad: Broke again? Jeff, when you moved in with Nancy and Andrew, you said you could make ends meet. But this is the third time you've asked me for help!

Jeff: I know, I know, I'm sorry. But, see, my old guitar broke, and I had to buy a new one. I can't play on a broken guitar, right?

Dad: Look Jeff, if you want to play in a band, that's OK with me. But you can't keep asking me to pay for it!

Jeff: OK, OK, you're right. But what do you think I ought to do? Everything costs an arm and a leg around here.

Dad: Well, first of all, I think you'd better go on a budget. Make a list of all your income and all your expenses. And then it's simple. Don't spend more than you earn.

Jeff: But that's exactly the problem! My expenses are always larger than my income. That's why I need to borrow money from you.

Dad: Then maybe you should work more hours at the computer store.

Jeff: Dad! I already work 15 hours a week! How can I study and work and find time to play with my band?

Dad: Come on, Jeff, when I was your age . . .

Jeff: I know, I know. When you were my age you were already married and working and going to school.

Dad: That's right. And if I could do it, why can't you?

Jeff: Because I'm not you, Dad, that's why!

Dad: All right, Jeff, calm down. I don't expect you to be like me. But I can't lend you any more money. Your mother and I are on a budget too, you know.

Jeff: Maybe I should just drop out of school, work full-time, and play in the band in the evenings. I can go back to school later.

Dad: I wouldn't do that if I were you.

Jeff: Yeah, but you're not me, remember? It's my life!

Dad: All right, Jeff. Let's not argue. Why don't

you think about this very carefully and call me back in a few days. And in the meantime, you'd better find a way to pay for that new guitar.

Jeff: Yes, Dad.

Dad: All right. Good-bye, son.

Jeff: Bye.

6 Listening for Reductions page 56

Customer: Hi, my name is Chang Lee.

Teller: How can I help you?

Customer: I want to check my balance.

Teller: OK. Can I have your account number, please?

Customer: 381335.

Teller: Your balance is $201.

Customer: OK. And I asked my father to wire me some money. I'd like to know if it's arrived.

Teller: I'm sorry, your account doesn't show any deposits.

Customer: Oh, no. I need to pay my rent tomorrow. What do you think I ought to do?

Teller: Well, we're having some computer problems today. So, why don't you call us later to check again? Or you can come back. We're open till 5:00.

Customer: OK, thanks.

Teller: You're welcome.

9 Distinguishing Between *Can* and *Can't* page 58

1. Sue can pay her bills by herself.

2. Jeff can't work and study at the same time.

3. I can't find my wallet.

4. You can pay with a credit card here.

5. You can't open an account without identification.

6. Anna can't work in the United States.

7. I can lend you five dollars.

8. We can't make ends meet.

9. You can apply for a loan at the bank across the street.

10. Jeff can play the guitar very well.

Part 2 Lecture: Entrepreneurs

3 Taking Notes page 61

4 Outlining the Lecture page 63

How many of you know the name Jeff Bezos? OK, how about Amazon.com? Have you heard of that? Well, Amazon is the world's first and largest Internet bookstore. And Jeff Bezos is the man who started Amazon back in 1995. Five years later, Amazon was serving millions of customers in 120 different countries. Amazing, right? And this is the reason why, in 1999, Jeff Bezos was selected as *Time* Magazine's Person of the Year, a very great honor.

Now, Jeff Bezos is actually not the topic of my lecture today, but he is a perfect example of my topic, which is entrepreneurs. That's *entrepreneurs*, spelled E-N-T-R-E-P-R-E-N-E-U-R-S. *Entrepreneur* is a French word meaning a person who starts a completely new business or industry; um, someone who does something no one else has done before; or who does it in a completely new way, like Jeff Bezos. Entrepreneurs like Jeff Bezos are very highly respected in American society and, I think, in many other countries too. So, in today's lecture I want to talk about three things. First, the characteristics of entrepreneurs—I mean, what kind of people they are. Second, the kind of background they come from. And third, the entrepreneurial process, that is, the steps entrepreneurs follow when they create a new business.

OK, let's begin by looking at the characteristics or, um, the qualities, of entrepreneurs. There are two qualities that I think all entrepreneurs have in common. First, entrepreneurs have vision. I mean that they have the ability to see opportunities that other people simply do not see. Let's look again at the example of Jeff Bezos. One day in 1994, he was surfing the Internet when suddenly he had a brilliant idea: why not use the Internet to sell products? Remember, at that time, no one was using the Internet in that way. After doing some research, Bezos decided that the product he wanted to sell was books. That's how Amazon got its start.

The other quality that I think all entrepreneurs have is that they're not afraid to take risks. I mean they're not afraid to fail. As an example, let me tell you about Frederick Smith. He founded FedEx, the company that delivers packages overnight. Smith first suggested the idea for his company in a college term paper. Do you know what grade he got on it? A C! Clearly, his professor didn't like the idea, but this didn't stop him. Today FedEx is worth more than 20 billion dollars and employs more than 130,000 people.

OK, we've just seen that all entrepreneurs have at least two important qualities in common. But now let's take a look at some differences. We'll see that their backgrounds can be very different. First of all, some entrepreneurs are well educated, like Jeff Bezos, who graduated from Princeton University. But others, like Bill Gates, the founder of Microsoft, never even finished college. Next, some entrepreneurs come from rich families, like Frederick Smith, the founder of FedEx. In contrast, other entrepreneurs come from poor families, and many are immigrants or the children of immigrants. A great example is Jerry Yang, one of the men who started Yahoo.com. He was born in Taiwan and came to America as a young boy in the 1970s.

OK, another difference is that although many entrepreneurs start their businesses at a young age, lots of others don't start until age 40 or later. And finally, I think it's important to remind you that entrepreneurs are not always men. A famous woman entrepreneur, for example, is Anita Roddick. She founded The Body Shop. You can find her natural cosmetics shops all over the world. So, to conclude this section, you can see that entrepreneurs come from many different backgrounds.

5 **Taking Notes on a Process** page 64

I want to move on now and take a look at the entrepreneurial process. There are six basic steps that most entrepreneurs follow when they start their businesses. In the first step, they identify a problem; in other words, they see a need or a problem that no one else sees. Then, in the second step, they think of a solution, what needs to be done to solve the problem or meet the need. I think we've already seen several examples today of people who saw a need or an opportunity and then came up with a creative solution.

Step three is to prepare a business plan. This means looking at things like equipment, location, financing, marketing, and so on. There are thousands of details to think about when you start a new business; as a result, this stage can take months or even years.

The next step, the fourth step, is putting together a team—in other words, hiring the right people to work with the entrepreneur in the new business. After that, the fifth step is something called test marketing. That's test marketing. This involves making and selling a small amount of the product or service just to try it out and see if customers like it. And if they do, then, finally, entrepreneurs go to the sixth step, which is raising capital. Capital is another word for money. The entrepreneur has to raise a lot of money, you know, from the bank, or friends, or family, in order to produce and sell the product or service in large quantities.

I want to say, in conclusion, that entrepreneurs like Jeff Bezos are among the most respected people in the United States. They are cultural heroes, like movie stars or sports heroes. Why? Because, starting with a dream and working very hard, these people created companies that solved serious, important problems. They provided jobs for millions of people, and in general their companies made life easier and more pleasant for all of us. If you ever order a book from Amazon, or use natural make-up from the Body Shop, say thanks to the remarkable people who created these companies.

Part 3 Strategies for Better Listening and Speaking

Using Context Clues page 66

Advertisement 1

Every person has valuable possessions that are difficult or impossible to replace, for example, family photographs, jewelry, a passport, old coins, or insurance policies. You should protect these priceless valuables by putting them in a safe place. Lock up your treasures in International Bank, and you'll never have to worry about losing your valuables again.

Question 1: The speaker is talking about . . .

The International Bank Safe-Deposit Box—safety and protection the easy way!

Advertisement 2

Right now International Bank can lend you money for dozens of projects. For instance, remodeling a kitchen or a bathroom can change an old house into an exciting new one. Thinking about solar heating? Need a new roof? International Bank can help you finance them.

Question 2: The speaker is talking about . . .

For any home improvement loan, talk to International Bank first.

Advertisement 3

With an Insta-Teller Card from International Bank, you're close to your money night or day. The Insta-Tellers operate 24 hours a day, seven days a week, 365 days a year. It's an easy way to get cash, pay your bills, make a deposit, or check your balance even when your bank is closed.

Question 3: The speaker is talking about . . .

Insta-Teller automated teller machines—any transaction, any time.

Advertisement 4

How would you like to earn 4.5 percent interest and still be able to take out money any time you need it? You can do both! Just deposit $5,000 and keep a minimum average balance of $500. Come in and ask about our investor's plan.

Question 4: The speaker is talking about . . .

International Bank Investor's Plan-a savings account and more!

3 Distinguishing Between Teens and Tens page 67

1. He paid $40.10 for the bottle of wine.

2. **Woman:** How much does this dictionary cost?
   Man: $16.99.

3. Most credit card companies charge 18 percent interest per month on your outstanding balance.

4. We drove at a speed of 90 miles per hour.

5. I bought my coat in Paris for 230 Euros.

6. The plane from Buenos Aires carried 260 passengers.

7. My dog weighs 14 and a half kilos.

8. The rent on this apartment is $2,215 a month.

9. My aunt lives at 1764 Wilson Avenue.

10. International Bank is located at 1890 West Second Street.

Part 4 Real-World Task: Balancing a Checkbook

3 Balancing a Checkbook page 70

George: Let's see here. Check number 200. October 25th. Did you write this check?

Martha: Hmm. $30.21. Oh, yes. That was last Thursday. ABC Market.

George: OK, so that leaves a balance of $490.31. Next: number 201. Electric bill. $57.82. So now we have $432.49. Next: October 27th. *Time* magazine. I forgot to enter the amount.

Martha: I remember that. It was $35.00.

George: OK. So that leaves $397.49. Now what's this $70?

Martha: That was for your sister's birthday present.

George: Oh, yes. OK . . . And here's check 205. When did we pay the dentist?

Martha: The same day I deposited my paycheck. November first.

George: Fine. So after the deposit, the balance was $1,397.18. And then I made the house payment, check number 206. That's $412, and the credit card payment—that's $155, so now our balance is $830.18.

Martha: You know, George, we should really pay off our credit card balance. The interest is 18 percent a year.

George: You're right. But we can't afford it right now. Look at this car insurance bill! $305 to Auto Insurance of America. And that's just for four months. And what's this . . . another traffic ticket?

Martha: Last month it was you, this month it was me.

George: Oh, man . . . How much was it this time?

Martha: $68. OK, so what's the balance now?

George: $457.18. I guess we're OK for the rest of the month as long as we don't get any more traffic tickets.

Part 1 Conversation: Finding a Job

Mari: Hey, Jeff, what's going on?

Jeff: Oh, I'm looking at the classified ads. It looks like I have to get a job.

Mari: I thought you had a job, at a computer store or something.

Jeff: Yeah, but that's part-time. I need something full-time.

Mari: Really? But what about school? What about your band? How can you work full-time?

Jeff: Well, to tell you the truth, I'm probably going to drop out of school for a while. I'm just not in the mood for studying these days. I'd rather spend my time playing with my band. But my father won't support me if I'm not in school.

Mari: I see . . . Well, what kind of job do you want to get?

Jeff: Well ideally, something involving music, like in a record store. But if that's not possible . . . I don't know, but whatever I do, it'll be better than my first job.

Mari: Oh yeah? What was that?

Jeff: Believe it or not, the summer after I finished high school I worked at Burger Ranch.

Mari: You? In a fast-food place? What did you do there?

Jeff: I was a burger flipper. You know, I made hamburgers all day long.

Mari: That sounds like a pretty boring job!

Jeff: It was the worst. And I haven't gone inside a Burger Ranch since I quit that job.

Nancy: Hi, what's so funny?

Jeff: Do you remember my job at the Burger Ranch?

Nancy: Oh yeah. That was pretty awful. But actually, it doesn't sound so bad to me right now.

Mari: Why, Nancy? What's wrong?

Nancy: Oh, I'm just really, really tired. I'm teaching four different classes this term, and two of them are really large. Sometimes I think I've been teaching too long.

Mari: How long have you been teaching?

Nancy: Twelve years. Maybe it's time to try something else.

Mari: Like what?

Nancy: Well, I've always wanted to be a writer. I could work at home . . .

Jeff: Oh, don't listen to her, Mari. She always talks this way when she's had a bad day at school. At least you have a good job, Nancy. Look at me: I'm broke, and Dad won't lend me any more money . . .

Nancy: Oh, stop complaining. If you're so poor, why don't you go back to the Burger Ranch?

Mari: Listen you two, stop arguing. Look at me! I can't work at all because I'm an international student.

Jeff: OK, OK. I'm sorry, Nancy. Tell you what. Let's go out to dinner. I'll pay.

Nancy: But you're broke!

Jeff: All right, *you* pay!

6 Listening for Reductions page 80

Manager: I'm going to ask you some questions, OK? What kind of jobs have you had?

Applicant: Mostly factory jobs. The last five years I worked in a plastics factory.

Manager: What did you do there?

Applicant: I used to cut sheets of plastic.

Manager: What do you want to do here?

Applicant: I don't know. I'll do anything. I'm good with my hands and I'm a hard worker.

Manager: Why don't you fill out an application in the office. It looks like we're going to have an opening next week. I'll call you.

Applicant: Thanks.

Part 2 Lecture: Changes in the U.S. Job Market

5 Listening and Taking Notes on Causes and Effects page 85

1. Because of technology, we're able to manufacture goods by using machines instead of human workers.

2. As a result, thousands of manufacturing jobs don't exist anymore.

3. We're going to need more medical services because people are living longer and longer.

4. Also, because of developments in medical technology, people with serious illnesses are able to live much longer than they could in the past.

5. The main reason for the huge growth in this category is that most married women now work outside the home.

6 Taking Notes on Statistics page 85

1. According to the United States government, approximately 2.5 million manufacturing jobs have disappeared just since the year 2001.

2. At the same time that the number of manufacturing jobs is decreasing, the number of service jobs is probably going to grow by more than 20 million just in the next ten years!

3. Almost half of the jobs on the list are in the field of health care.

4. According to the United States Department of Labor, the number of health care jobs will increase by almost 3 million in the next ten years.

5. The number of jobs in the computer industry is expected to grow by almost 30 percent in the next ten years.

7 Taking Notes page 86

8 Outlining the Lecture page 86

Part 1

Lecturer: If you'll be graduating from high school or college in the next year or two, then I'm sure you're very concerned about finding a job. There are two questions that young people like you always ask me. First, what are the best jobs going to be? And second, how can I prepare myself to get one of those good jobs? Well in the next few minutes, I want to try to answer these questions for you, and I hope this information will help you make the right choices about your future career.

Let's start with a little history. In the last 100 years, there's been a big change in the U.S. job market, from a manufacturing economy to a service economy. What does that mean? Well, in a manufacturing economy people make things, like cars or furniture or clothes. In a service economy, people do things. Uh, they cut your hair, they fix your shoes, they sell you a computer. Uh, airline pilots, doctors, restaurant workers—all of these are examples of service workers. OK? So again, my point is that the number of manufacturing jobs has been going down for quite a long time. Now why do you think that is? What's the cause?

Student 1: I think automation, you know, robots, computers . . .

Lecturer: That's one reason, yes. Because of technology, we're able to manufacture goods by using machines instead of human workers. As a result, thousands of manufacturing jobs don't exist anymore. OK, can you think of another reason?

Student 2: Foreign competition. I mean . . . most manufacturing is done outside of the U.S. now, in countries where the labor costs are cheaper.

Lecturer: Yes, that's right. According to the U.S. government, approximately 2.5 million manufacturing jobs have disappeared just since 2001. And that trend is definitely going to continue as we move further into the 21st century.

But now let's talk about service jobs. Here the trend is exactly the opposite. At the same time that the number of manufacturing jobs is decreasing, the number of service jobs is probably going to grow by more than 20 million just in the next ten years! Now, would everybody please look at the handout I gave you, which shows a list of the occupations that will grow the fastest between the years 2002 and 2012. If you study the list carefully, you'll see that most of the jobs on the list are in three categories: health care, computers, and personal care and services. Let me say a few words about each of these categories.

Part 2

First, health care. Almost half of the jobs on the list are in the field of health care. Uh, medical assistants, physician assistants, physical therapy aides, dental hygienists—these are just a few examples. According to the U.S. Department of Labor, the number of health care jobs will increase by almost 3 million in the next ten years. And why is that? Simple. We're going to need more medical services because people are living longer and longer. Also, because of developments in medical technology, people with serious illnesses are able to live much longer than they could in the past. And many of them need a lot of special care and medical help.

All right, now, getting back to the list, you can see that there will be many new jobs related to computers. We're going to need people who can design and build computers, like engineers, but in addition, there will be lots of jobs for people who manage and operate computers, like database administrators. As you know, computers are used in everything these days from rockets to coffee machines, so it's no surprise that the number of jobs in the computer industry is expected to grow by almost 30 percent in the next ten years.

Now let me explain the third category, personal care services. Some examples of jobs in this group are caterers, home health workers, and day care providers. One reason for the huge growth in this category is that most women now work outside the home. So a lot of the work that women used to do in the home, like cooking and taking care of small children, is now done by service workers.

OK, now, while we're looking at the list, there's one more thing I'd like you to notice. Look at all the jobs that have a salary rank of 1. OK? And what do you notice about the educational requirements for those jobs? That's right. They all require at least a Bachelor of Arts degree.

So in conclusion, let me go back to the two questions I mentioned at the beginning of this talk. First, where will the good jobs be? We've seen today that the areas of greatest growth will be in the fields of computers, healthcare, and personal services. If you still haven't decided which career you want to follow, you should think about getting a job in one of these fields. However, it's important to remember that many service jobs don't pay very well. The best jobs all require a college education. So the answer to the second question—how you can prepare yourself to get a good job—the answer is simple. Go to college and get a degree. That's the bottom line.

Part 3   Strategies for Better Listening and Speaking

Using Context Clues page 91

Conversation 1

Woman: May I see your driver's license, please?

Man: What did I do?

Woman: You ran a red light.

Man: But I'm sure it was yellow.

Question 1: What's the woman's job?

Woman: Are you trying to argue with a police officer?

Conversation 2

Woman: Is this your first visit?

Man: No, I come in every six months for a check-up.

Woman: Oh, I see. Did you bring your insurance form with you?

Man: Here it is.

Woman: OK. Take a seat, and the dentist will be with you shortly.

Question 2: What is the woman's job?

Man: You're new here, aren't you? What happened to the other receptionist?

Conversation 3

Man: Do you have a reservation?

Woman: Yes, Jackson, party of four.

Man: Inside or out on the patio?

Woman: Outside. And could you bring us some coffee?

Question 3: What's the man's job?

Man: I'm the host. I'll ask the waiter to bring you some coffee right away.

Conversation 4

A: Hi Jim. It's Carl. It looks like I'm going to need your professional services this year.

B: I thought you always did your taxes by yourself.

A: Yeah, but this year things are too complicated. I lost money in the stock market, and then I inherited my uncle's house, remember?

B: Hmm. You need professional help, for sure.

Question 4: What is Jim's job?

B: But you know, it's not a good idea to use your best friend as your accountant. I think you should find someone else.

Conversation 5

Man: May I help you?

Woman: The sleeves on this jacket are too short. How much will it cost for you to make them longer?

Man: Let me look at it . . . I can do it for $30.

Woman: That much?

Question 5: What's the man's job?

Man: Well, that's what any tailor would charge.

3 Recognizing the Intonation of Tag Questions page 92

1. We're having a staff meeting tomorrow, aren't we?

2. You're the programmer from Turkey, aren't you?

3. This exercise is easy, isn't it?

4. The supervisor is married, isn't she?

5. Smoking is forbidden here, isn't it?

6. That test was really hard, wasn't it?

7. The secretary speaks Arabic, doesn't he?

8. That training video was really boring, wasn't it?

9. The marketing director speaks beautiful Japanese, doesn't she?

10. We need to sign our names on these reports, don't we?

Part 4 Real-World Task: A Homemaker's Typical Day

4 Sequencing Events page 95

Do you want to know what I do on a typical day? Well, I'll tell you what I did yesterday as an example. I woke up before my wife and son, and the first thing I did was to come into the kitchen and make the coffee. Then I made my son's lunch, you know, to take to school, and after that I started cooking breakfast. I made eggs, oatmeal, and toast because I always want my family to start the day with a full stomach. Then my wife and son came into the kitchen and sat down to eat. While they were eating, I threw a basket of laundry into the washing machine and then I also sat down to eat.

After breakfast I walked my son to the bus stop, and I waited with him until the bus came. I kissed him good-bye and walked home. As soon as I entered the house, the phone rang. It was my mother-in-law. She wanted to know if my wife was still there, but I told her she had just left. So I talked with her for a few more minutes, about the weather and her garden, and then I got off the phone. After that, uh, let's see, I spent three hours cleaning the house, and after lunch I went shopping for groceries. By then it was three o'clock, and it was already time to pick up my son at the bus stop. I helped him with his homework, and then my wife came home. Normally she gets home at about 6 P.M., but yesterday she was a few minutes early. I was so busy all day that I hadn't had time to water the garden, so I did it while my wife made dinner. Finally, after dinner I washed the dishes while my wife put our son to bed. And then both of us just collapsed in front of the TV.

And that was my day. Nothing glamorous—just really busy!

Chapter 5 Lifestyles Around the World

Part 1 Conversation: A Single Mother

3 Comprehension Questions page 103

4 Listening for Stressed Words (Part I) page 104

Jeff: Who's there?

Sharon: It's Sharon and Joey!

Jeff: Hi! Come on in. What's happening?

Sharon: Jeff, can you do me a big favor? I just got a call from the office. They want me to look into a computer problem right away. Would you mind watching Joey until I get back?

Jeff: Sure, no problem. Is he asleep?

Sharon: Yeah, he just fell asleep ten minutes ago. He usually sleeps for a couple of hours at this time of day. But if he wakes up, just give him a bottle.

Mari: Ooh, what a cute baby! He's so little!

Jeff: Mari, this is our neighbor, Sharon, and her son, Joey. Sharon, this is our new roommate, Mari.

Mari: Nice to meet you.

Sharon: You too. Listen, I've got to take off. Thanks so much, Jeff, for helping me out.

Jeff/Mari: Bye!

Mari: Hey, Jeff, I didn't know you liked babies.

Jeff: Well, Joey is special. I take care of him from time to time when Sharon's busy. And then she does favors for me in return. Like last week she lent me her car.

Mari: And her husband? Is he . . .

Jeff: She's not married. I don't think she ever was, actually.

Mari: Never?

Jeff: Nope, never. I think she's happy being a single mother.

Mari: Oh. Is that pretty common in America?

Jeff: Well, it's certainly becoming more and more common. Even Nancy used to talk about it. You know, before she got married.

Nancy: Hi, guys.

Mari/Jeff: Hi.

Nancy: Uh, what were you saying about me?

Jeff: That you used to talk about having a baby by yourself before you met Andrew.

Nancy: Oh yeah, I worried that time was running out. You know, like, what if I never got married . . .

Mari: Maybe I'm old-fashioned, but I could never bring up a baby by myself. I think it would be so difficult . . .

Nancy: Yeah, raising a child is tough. I'm really lucky I met Andrew.

Mari: And, if you have a baby, you'll have Jeff here to help you with babysitting.

Jeff: We'll see. Speaking of babysitting, I'd better check up on Joey.

5 Listening for Stressed Words (Part II)
page 104

1. Come on in.

2. They want me to look into a computer problem right away.

3. If he wakes up, just give him a bottle.

4. Listen, I've got to take off.

5. Thanks so much, Jeff, for helping me out.

6. I take care of him from time to time when Sharon's busy.

7. I worried that time was running out.

8. I could never bring up a baby by myself.

9. I'd better check up on Joey.

Part 2 Lecture: Changes in the American Family

3 Taking Notes on Examples page 109

1. Women today are working in professions that were not as open to them 30 or 40 years ago. To give just one example, today more than half the students in American medical schools are women.

2. Most American homes don't have a full-time homemaker anymore. And that creates new problems for families; problems like who takes care of babies and old people; who shops, cooks, and cleans; who volunteers at the children's school; and so on.

3. In some countries, companies are required by law to give new parents a paid vacation when they have a new baby. Canada, for instance, has a law like that, but the United States does not.

4 Taking Notes (Part I) page 110

5 Outlining the Lecture page 110

Have you ever seen the old television show *Father Knows Best?* You probably haven't because it was a popular comedy show in the 1950s—way before you were born. It was about a family: a father, who went to work every day; a mother, who stayed home and took care of the house; and the children—two or three, I can't remember. Anyway, in those days that was considered to be a typical American family.

But today, the American family is very different. First, families are smaller today than before. I mean, people are having fewer children. Second, more and more children are growing up in single-parent families—families with only a mother or only a father. I'm not going to go into the reasons for that here because I want to focus on the third and biggest change in the American family: the role of married mothers and the effects of this new role. Consider these statistics: In the 1950s, only 11 percent of married mothers worked outside the home. In 2002, about 70 percent of mothers were employed.

Why is that? Well, there are two important reasons. The first one, very simply, is that they need the money. These days the cost of living is so high that most families need two salaries in order to make ends meet.

The other reason why married mothers are working in larger and larger numbers is that they have more opportunities than they did 30 or 40 years ago. There are laws in the United States that give women the same opportunity as men to go to college and get jobs. As a result, women today are working in professions that were not as open to them 30 or 40 years ago. To give just one example, today more than half of the students in American medical schools are women.

So, to summarize so far, we've seen that the American family has changed dramatically since the days of those old television shows. In the typical two-parent family today, both the father and the mother have jobs. This means that most American homes don't have a full-time homemaker anymore. And that creates new problems for families: problems like who takes care of babies and grandparents; who shops, cooks, and cleans; who volunteers at the children's school; and so on.

6 Taking Notes (Part II) page 111

To help families with working parents deal with these new problems, some American businesses have introduced new programs and policies to make it easier to work and raise children at the same time. Let me give you five examples of these policies and programs.

The first policy is paid maternity leave. What we're talking about is a woman taking time off from work when she has a baby. American law requires companies to give a woman up to 12 weeks of leave when she has a baby. But the problem is that the companies aren't required to pay for those 12 weeks. As a result, many women are forced to go back to work much sooner than they want to. Recently some companies, at least the big ones, have started to offer paid maternity leave. But it's still kind of rare. By the way, a small percentage of companies now also offer *paternity* leave—that means that fathers can take time off for a new baby. I would like to see a

law that requires all companies to give paid leave to both mothers and fathers for a new baby. Canada, for instance, already has a law like that.

OK, moving along, here's another example of a policy that helps working families. As you know, big companies like IBM or General Motors often transfer their employees to other cities, right? Well, if a company transfers the husband, for instance, this might create a problem for the wife because now she has to find a new job too. So now there are companies that will help the husband or wife of the transferred worker find a new job.

A third policy that many companies now offer is called "flextime." Here's what that means. In the United States, a normal workday is from 9 A.M. until 5 P.M.—eight hours. With flextime, workers can choose the hour that they start work in the morning and can go home after eight hours. So, for instance, a worker who comes in at 7 can leave at 3. Or a worker can come in at 10 and leave at 6. You can imagine how useful this flexibility is for people who have children.

The fourth change I want to describe is telecommuting. Or sometimes we say "teleworking." With telecommuting, people work at home and use the computer or phone to communicate with their workplace. It's estimated that about 15 percent of the U.S. workforce telecommutes now. But the percentage is growing all the time because it saves people time and money. And if parents are allowed to work at home, their children might not have to spend as much time in child care.

And speaking of child care, the fifth program offered by many of the best companies is day care; that is, some companies have day care centers at the office where trained people take care of the employees' children. This means workers come to work with their young children, leave them at the center, and can visit them during lunch or whatever. Then the parents and kids drive home together at the end of the day. With day care at work, parents don't need to worry about their kids because they're right there.

OK, let me review what I've been talking about. I've given you five examples of company policies and programs that make life a little easier for working mothers and fathers. But it's important for me to tell you that only some large companies can afford these kinds of programs.

For most people, trying to work and take care of a family at the same time is still very, very difficult. In my opinion, our government and our society need to do a lot more to help working parents and their children.

Part 3 Strategies for Better Listening and Speaking

Using Context Clues page 115

Conversation 1

Senior Citizen Man: Well, I tell you, things get pretty tough by the end of the month. I don't have any pension—just Social Security—and that's only $800 a month. Sometimes the check is late, and the rent is due on the first of the month. Do you think the landlord cares?

Question 1: The speaker is . . .

Senior Citizen Man: Sometimes I think no one cares about retired people in this country.

Conversation 2

17-Year-Old Girl: Sometimes I feel like I'm in a prison. "Come home by ten." "Don't go there." "Don't do that." "Turn down the music." They treat me like a baby. They have no respect for my privacy.

Question 2: The speaker is talking about . . .

Girl: My parents forget that I'm 17 years old. I'm not a child anymore.

Conversation 3

Man: My ex-wife and I agreed that the kids would live with me. At first it was hard with all the work and no help. But it's exciting to watch my kids grow up.

Question 3: This man . . .

Man: And fortunately, there are organizations to help divorced fathers like me.

Conversation 4

Young Man: I lived with my parents until I was 18, then I left home to go to college and lived with roommates in an apartment near the campus. When I graduated, I got a job with an engineering firm and got my own place. But last year I lost my job and ran out of money. So what could I do? I came back home.

Question 4: This person probably lives . . .

Young Man: Boy, it's not easy living with your parents again after all these years.

Conversation 5

Senior Citizen Woman: After I broke my hip, it was too hard to go on living by myself. So I tried living with my son and his family for a while, but their house is small and noisy, and I want my privacy, too. So I came here. And it really isn't bad. I have my own doctor, good food, and plenty of friends my own age.

Question 5: This woman is living in . . .

Senior Citizen Woman: This retirement home is really the best place for me.

Part 4 Real-World Task: Using Numbers, Percentages, Graphs

2 Completing Line Graphs page 118

Graph number 1

Graph 1 gives statistics on American women in the U.S. labor force. In 1960, 37.8 percent of American women had jobs. By 1980, it had jumped to 51.1 percent. In 1990, it was 57.5 percent. And in 2003, 61 percent of American women were working.

Graph number 2

Graph 2 shows the divorce rate in the United States. In 1960, the divorce rate was just 2.2 per 1,000 people. In 1970, it rose to 3.5, and in 1980 it jumped to 5.2. However, it declined in 1990 to 4.7, and in 2003 declined even more, to 3.8 per 1,000 people.

Graph number 3

Graph 3 presents information on people over age 65 who lived alone from 1970 to 2000. You need to make two sets of points here. Use an O for men and an X for women.

In 1970, 35.9 percent of elderly women lived alone, compared to 10.8 percent of elderly men.

In 1980, the percentage was 31.9 for women and 8.1 for men. In 1990, 51.8 percent of women lived alone, compared to 21.5 percent for men. And finally, in 2000, 40 percent of women and 17 percent of men were living by themselves.

Chapter 6 Global Connections

Part 1 Conversation: Using Technology to Stay in Touch

3 Comprehension Questions page 128

4 Listening for Stressed Words page 128

Jeff: Come in!

Mari: Am I interrupting?

Jeff: It's OK, I was just catching up on my blog.

Mari: Oh yeah? What's it about?

Jeff: Mostly it's about hip-hop. Like, here's a comment from a guy named Hasan talking about, let's see . . . hip-hop in Istanbul.

Mari: In Turkey? Turkish hip-hop?

Jeff: Sure. And here's one from my friend Hiroshi, the drummer in Tokyo.

Mari: Hmm. Maybe I should start a blog about learning English.

Jeff: Well, it's a great way to meet new people, that's for sure. And all you need is an Internet connection.

Mari: Well, speaking of the Internet, I wanted to ask your advice about something.

Jeff: OK. What's up?

Mari: Well, I just got my cell phone bill for last month, and it was $160!

Jeff: Ouch.

Mari: Yeah, I can't believe it. Cell phone calls are so expensive here.

Jeff: Are they cheaper in Japan?

Mari: Much cheaper. And we use our cell phones for email, too. A lot of people don't even own a computer.

Jeff: It's amazing what you can do with cell phones these days. Talk, take pictures, send email . . .

Mari: Yeah. But anyway Jeff, I need to find a cheaper way to stay in touch with my parents and my friends in Japan. And I heard there's a way you can call overseas for free using your computer. Do you know anything about that?

Jeff: Of course, it's a technology called Voice over Internet. I use it all the time.

Mari: How does it work?

Jeff: Well, you need a computer with a sound card, if you've got that.

Mari: Yeah, I do . . .

Jeff: And you also need a microphone and a headset.

Mari: Hmm. I don't have those.

Jeff: No sweat, you can buy them at any electronics store.

Mari: OK. What else?

Jeff: Well, then you'll need to download the software, which is free, and then if the person you're calling installs the same software, there's no cost for calling.

Mari: But what if they don't? Can I call from my computer to someone's phone?

Jeff: Yes. There's a charge for that, but it's a lot cheaper than using your cell phone, believe me.

Mari: Could you show me how it works on your computer?

Jeff: Right now?

Mari: No, it's nighttime in Japan now. Can we do it in about three hours?

Jeff: No problem. I'll be here.

Mari: Great. See you later.

6 Identifying Intonation Patterns page 130

1. Are you working on the computer right now?
2. Can you help me?
3. Where do you want me to put this paper?
4. Could you please repeat that?
5. What kind of computer do you have?
6. Did you check your email today?

Part 2 Lecture: Customs Around the World

3 Taking Notes on Similarities and Differences page 135

1. Maybe you've noticed that many Americans use people's first names very freely, even if they've just met someone. Some people even call their bosses by their first names. In contrast, people in most other cultures are more formal . . .

2. In Egypt you should leave some food on your plate at the end of a meal. However, Bolivians expect visitors to eat everything on their plates.

3. Bolivians expect visitors to eat everything on their plates, and Americans also think that a clean plate means you were satisfied with the food.

4. Many Japanese people bow when they greet each other, while people from Thailand prefer to hold their hands in a prayer position.

5. In the United States, greetings often involve some sort of touching, such as a handshake, a hug, or a kiss if the people know each other very well. And most Western countries are similar to the United States in this way.

4 Taking Notes (Part I) page 135

5 Outlining the Lecture page 136

Lecturer: Good afternoon, class. I want to start today by telling you a little story. Once there was a young woman from Mexico named Consuela who came to New York to work. And she got a job at a factory owned by a man from Taiwan. One day, when Consuela came to work, her Taiwanese boss handed her a red envelope. She looked inside and saw $50. And what do you think she did? She became very upset and threw the envelope back at him! Of course her boss was totally shocked. Can you guess why? Well, he had given her the red envelope and the money because it was the Chinese New Year. And on the Chinese New Year it's traditional to give money to young, single people for good

luck. But Consuela didn't know about this Chinese custom. She thought her boss was asking her for sex. Naturally she was very insulted and refused to take the money.

Now, what does this story show us? What's the point? Yes?

Student: It shows that an action can have totally opposite meanings in different cultures. Like in this case, the boss thought he was being generous, but Consuela was insulted.

Lecturer: Exactly. Every culture has its own rules for appropriate and inappropriate behavior. And serious misunderstandings, like the one with Consuela and her boss, can occur if we don't know other people's cultural "rules." Um, to illustrate this point, I'd like to offer some examples from four areas. First, the way people greet each other in different cultures. OK . . . Second, the way they use names and titles. Third, the way people eat. And finally, the way they exchange gifts. All right?

So let's start with greeting customs—I mean, how people behave when they say hello. First of all, I'm sure you know that in the United States, greetings often involve some sort of touching, such as a handshake, a hug, or a kiss if the people know each other very well. And most Western countries are similar to the United States in this way. Also, did you know that people from France kiss almost everyone on the cheek, even strangers? On the other hand, people from most Asian countries don't usually feel as comfortable touching in public. I mean, it's normal for businessmen to shake hands; that's true. But many traditional Japanese prefer a bow, while people from Thailand, for example, normally hold their hands together in a kind of prayer position, like this, you see. So imagine what would happen if an American was invited to someone's home in Japan or Thailand and he or she tried to hug the host! It would be very embarrassing, right? And yet that behavior would be perfectly acceptable in the United States or Latin America.

OK, now, another behavior that differs from culture to culture is the use of names. Maybe you've noticed that many Americans use people's first names very freely, even if they've just met someone. Some people even call their bosses by their first names.

In contrast, people in most other cultures

are more formal and prefer to use family names to address people, like "Mr. Martinez" or "Ms. Schultz." In some countries, like Korea for example, it's polite to use a person's title or position with their family name. So you'd say, for example, Teacher Park or Manager Kim.

6 Taking Notes (Part II) page 137

Now moving on, the third area I want to look at is eating customs. I don't mean the foods that people like to eat in different countries but rather some of the behaviors that are connected with eating. Um, one of these is the use of utensils. You probably know that people in many Asian cultures use chopsticks while in the West they usually use forks, knives, and spoons. Or for example, in parts of India, and in traditional Arab families, too, it's customary to eat with your fingers or to use a piece of bread to scoop up food. Another example is that in some cultures eating everything on your plate is impolite. In Egypt, for example, you should leave some food in your dish at the end of the meal in order to show that your hosts were generous and gave you more than enough to eat. However, people from Bolivia, in South America, expect visitors to eat everything on their plates, and Americans also think a clean plate means you were satisfied with the food.

Finally, the last area of behavior that I want to mention today is gift giving. The rules of gift giving can be very complicated, and it can be embarrassing if you don't know them. For example, in the United States, if you're invited to someone's home for dinner, you can bring wine or flowers or a small gift from your country, but Americans generally don't give gifts in business situations. On the other hand, the Japanese, like many other people in Asia, give gifts often, especially if they want to thank someone like a teacher or a doctor for their kindness. In Japan, the tradition of gift giving is very ancient, and there are detailed rules for everything from the color of the wrapping paper to the time of the gift presentation. Another interesting fact about gift giving is that many cultures have strict rules about gifts you should not give. For example, never give yellow flowers to people from Iran, or they'll think you hate them!

So to conclude, I hope all these examples will help you to understand my main point today, which is that each culture has its own unique rules for social behavior. We should never assume that our way of doing things is the only way or the best way. Learning about other people's customs is part of being good international citizens.

Part 3 Strategies for Better Listening and Speaking

Using Context Clues page 141

Conversation 1

Harold O'Connor, a professor of English at an American university, invites his students to his home at the end of the semester. He asks them to come at 4 P.M. for coffee and cake. At 3:45 the doorbell rings. He opens the door and is surprised to see several of his Korean students standing there. He feels embarrassed.

Question 1: Why did the students arrive at 3:45?

Conversation 2

The feet are the lowest part of the body. For that reason, many people from the Middle East believe it is rude to point your feet at someone or to show them the bottoms of your shoes. Some people also think it is impolite to step over someone, for example, at a theater or sports event.

Question 2: Which of the following is probably a good idea if you are a visitor in a Middle Eastern home?

Conversation 3

Americans smile mainly to show friendliness or happiness. In Japan, people smile when they are sad, happy, apologetic, angry, or confused. In traditional Korean culture, smiling meant that a person was foolish or thoughtless. On the island of Puerto Rico, a smile can have many positive meanings, including "please," "thank-you," and "you're welcome."

Question 3: What can we conclude from these examples?

Conversation 4

In the United States, you can sometimes see old shoes attached to a newly married couple's car. What's the origin of this custom? Some people believe that old shoes can help a couple to have many children. Some people even put old shoes in trees that don't give enough fruit!

Question 4: What is this passage mainly about?

Conversation 5

A bribe is an amount of money that someone offers a public official, such as a police officer, to get some kind of special favor or treatment. In some countries, bribes are a normal part of doing business. However, in the United States, bribery is illegal.

Question 5: What could happen if you try to bribe a police officer in the United States?

Part 4 Real-World Task: A Trivia Quiz

2 Taking a Trivia Quiz page 145

Kevin: Hey, Joyce, what are you doing?

Joyce: I was just reading the paper. Oh, here's another one of those trivia quizzes that you love to take, Kevin.

Kevin: What's it about?

Joyce: The title is "Global Connections." It's about transportation and communication around the world. Want to try it?

Kevin: Sure, why don't you read it to me while I make a salad for dinner?

Joyce: OK, first question. Which country has the largest number of time zones: The United States, Canada, Russia, or China?

Kevin: That's easy. Russia.

Joyce: Right. OK, second question: which country is the most popular tourist destination in the world? Is it France, the United States, Italy, or China?

Kevin: France.

Joyce: Right again. Go Kevin! OK, next. Oh, the third one's hard: This region has 12.5 percent of the world's population and 29 percent of the world's Internet users. Is it North America, Europe, Latin America, or the Middle East?

Kevin: Hmm. Let me think. OK, I guess the Middle East.

Joyce: Wrong. It's Europe.

Kevin: OK, keep going.

Joyce: All right, number 4. Looks like another computer question. Which of the following countries has the largest actual number of Internet users? And the choices are China, the U.S., Russia, or Canada.

Kevin: Well, not Canada. Canada has a small population, compared to its size. I'll say . . . the United States.

Joyce: Right. Good job.

Kevin: Thanks. I hope the next question is easier.

Joyce: Let's see. Number 5. How many hours does it take to fly from New York to Cairo: 5 hours, 8 hours, 11 hours, or 15 hours?

Kevin: Wow. I have no idea. I think it's about six hours to London, so it's more than that. How about . . . 8 hours?

Joyce: No. Eleven.

Kevin: OK, what's next?

Joyce: Which of the following countries has the largest number of daily newspapers: Mexico, Russia, England, or Greece?

Kevin: I'm sure it's England.

Joyce: Wrong! It's Mexico!

Kevin: No kidding! I wonder why . . . OK, next.

Joyce: Number 7 . . . The most frequently used language on the Internet is English. Which language is second: German, Spanish, Japanese, or Chinese?

Kevin: Wow. That's a tricky question. I am going to say . . . Chinese.

Joyce: Yeah.

Kevin: Actually I wasn't sure if it was Chinese or Japanese.

Joyce: Well, you got it right. Do you want to keep going?

Kevin: Yeah, one more. Then we can eat.

Joyce: OK, question 8. Which city has the longest subway system? Moscow, New York, Tokyo, or London?

Kevin: London. For sure.

Joyce: You're right.

Kevin: Yeah, I studied in London last summer and I took the underground everywhere. So what's my score?

Joyce: Five right and three wrong. Not too bad.

Kevin: Yeah, but not great, either! All right. Let's eat. I'm starving!

Chapter 7 Language and Communication

Part 1 Conversation: What Do People Really Mean?

3 **Comprehension Questions** page 152

4 **Listening for Stressed Words** page 152

Mari: Yolanda! Hi!

Yolanda: Hi, Mari, how are you?

Mari: Fine, thanks. Um, is anyone sitting here?

Yolanda: No, have a seat.

Mari: Thanks. So how have you been?

Yolanda: Oh, you know, busy. I've got school, and work, and I'm getting ready for my brother's wedding next month.

Mari: Oh, yeah.

Yolanda: Anyway, it's going to be a huge wedding and . . .

Mari: Oh, excuse me, uh . . . Nancy! Over here!

Nancy: Hi!

Mari: Nancy, this is Yolanda. She works in the library. Yolanda, this is my housemate, Nancy. She teaches English here.

Nancy: Nice to meet you, Yolanda.

Yolanda: You too. Well, listen, actually, I've got to go. I have to be at work in ten minutes. I'll see you soon, Mari. We'll go to a movie or something.

Mari: Sure. How about Thursday night?

Yolanda: Uh, I have to check my calendar. I'll call you, OK?

Mari: OK, see you.

Mari: I don't understand Americans.

Nancy: Huh?

Mari: Did you hear what she said? "I'll call you, we'll go to a movie." But every time I try to pick a specific day or time, she says she's busy, she has to check her calendar. And then she doesn't call.

Nancy: Mm hmm . . .

Mari: Why do Americans say things they don't mean? They act so nice, like they always say, "How are you," but then they keep on walking and don't even wait for your answer. They're so . . . how do you say it . . . two-faced?

Nancy: I know it seems that way sometimes, Mari. But it's not true. It's just that for Americans, friendliness and friendship aren't always the same thing.

Mari: What do you mean?

Nancy: Well, as you know, Americans can be very open and friendly. Like, they invite you to sit down, they ask you questions, they tell you all about their families. So naturally you think they're trying to make friends with you. But actually, friendship, real friendship, doesn't happen so quickly.

Mari: So, when people say "How are you," they're just being polite? They don't really care?

Nancy: Not exactly. The thing you have to understand is that "How are you" isn't a real question. It's more like a greeting, a way of saying hello.

Mari: Aha, I get it! And "Have a nice day" is just a friendly way to say good-bye?

Nancy: Exactly. Now you're catching on.

Mari: But I'm still in the dark about Yolanda. Does she want to be my friend or not?

Nancy: It's hard to say. Maybe she's just too busy these days. I guess you'll just have to be patient.

Mari: Hmm. That's good advice, I guess. Thanks.

5 Understanding Statements with Rising Intonation page 154

1. You're going?

2. You remember my friend Yolanda?

3. He hasn't done his homework yet?

4. It's at the intersection of First and Main?

5. Jack is Rose's brother?

Part 2 Lecture: Differences Between British and American English

3 Classifying Lecture Organization
page 158

Lecture 1

Personal computers have revolutionized the way people work and communicate. I could talk for hours about the wide use of personal computers, but today we only have time to introduce three major uses of computers: at home, in business, and in education.

Lecture 2

In today's lecture I will provide the most recent information concerning the growth and characteristics of the U.S. population.

Lecture 3

You may have guessed by now that my topic for today's lecture is differences between American and British English. In particular I want to examine three categories of difference. First, and most obvious, is pronunciation; second, vocabulary; and third, grammar.

4 Taking Notes (Part I) page 159

5 Outlining the Lecture page 159

Lecturer: Good afternoon. To introduce my topic today, I'd like you to listen to two speech samples and tell me where the speakers are from. Ready? OK, here's the first one.

Speaker 1: "Today's weather forecast calls for partly cloudy skies in the morning, clearing by mid afternoon with winds up to 15 miles an hour out of the west. The high temperature will be 80 degrees Fahrenheit, and the low will be 64."

Lecturer: OK. Now, where do you think that speaker was from?

Audience: America . . . the United States . . . Canada.

Lecturer: Yes, most of you got it. That was what we call a *standard* American accent. Which means the accent that is spoken by the majority of people who live in the United States and Canada.

Now, listen to a different speaker reading the same text.

Speaker 2: "Today's weather forecast calls for partly cloudy skies in the morning, clearing by mid afternoon with winds up to 15 miles an hour out of the west. The high temperature will be 80 degrees Fahrenheit, and the low will be 64."

Lecturer: And where is that speaker from?

Audience: England . . . the United Kingdom . . . Great Britain.

Lecturer: Yes, of course. That was British English. So you may have guessed by now that my topic for today's lecture is differences between standard American and British English. In particular I want to examine three categories of difference. First, and most obvious, is pronunciation; second, vocabulary; and third, grammar.

So to begin, let's go back to the subject of accent, or pronunciation. You had no trouble identifying the North American and British accents because each of them has a unique sound. What is it? Well, one obvious difference is in the pronunciation of the letter a. For example, most Americans say /kænt/, but the British say /kant/. Or Americans say /bæth/ and the British say /bath/. The /æ/ sound is very common in American English, but not very common in British English.

Another noticeable difference between American and British pronunciation is the /r/ sound. In British English, the /r/ sound is very often dropped; it disappears. To give some examples, Americans say /kar/ but the British say /ka/. Americans say /fɤrst/ but British say /fʌst/. A big American city is "New /yɔrk/ " for Americans, but "New /yok/" to the British. In the two speech samples you heard at the beginning of this lecture, the American speaker said /forekæst/, but the British said /fohcast/. In that single word you can hear the difference both in the a vowel and in the pronunciation of /r/. Listen again: /forkæst/, /fohkast/.

A third difference is the pronunciation of the /t/ sound in the middle of words. In British English it is normally pronounced, but in American English it changes to a /d/ or disappears. For example: a British person will say "little," but an American says "liddle." You can hear this difference particularly with numbers: Brits say "twenty one, twenty two," and so on, but Americans drop the /t/ and say "twenny one, twenny two," and so on.

So there you have just three of the differences that give American and British pronunciation their unique sounds. There are many more. But now let's go on to talk about vocabulary.

6 Taking Notes (Part II) page 160

Some people believe that American English vocabulary and British English vocabulary are very different, but actually they are not. The English language has more than one million words. Yet there are only a few hundred words and expressions that are different in American and British English. You can see a few of them in the chart right here. So for instance, Americans say "truck," but the Brits say "lorry." Another well-known example is "elevator," which is used in the United States and "lift," which is the British term. Now, although the number of vocabulary differences is small, funny misunderstandings can sometimes occur. For instance, if an American says, "I'm going to wash up," he would go into the bathroom and wash his hands and face. But a British person may be quite surprised to see him go to the bathroom because in England, to "wash up" means to wash the dishes.

Vocabulary differences can also create some confusing situations in restaurants. If an Englishman traveling in the United States enters a restaurant and orders "bangers and mash," the American waiter would be totally confused. He wouldn't know that the man wanted sausage and mashed potatoes.

Finally, let's talk a bit about grammar. I've left this category for last because in the area of grammar, standard American and British English are nearly identical. One common difference, however, involves the past participle of the verb *get*. For example, An American might ask, "Have you gotten your grade yet?" whereas a Brit would ask, "Have you got your grade yet?" Another difference is in the use of the verb *have*, especially in questions. Americans say, "Do you have any ideas?" but the British say, "Have you any ideas?" There are also differences in prepositions. So for instance in the United States, it's correct to say that John is different *from* Mary, but the British will say that John is different *than* Mary. But these differences are very small and few in number.

And this brings me to my conclusion, which is this: Standard British and standard American English are so similar that most speakers of these two types will have no trouble understanding one another. American and British English are not two different languages. Rather, they are two dialects, two varieties, of the same language, English.

Part 3 Strategies for Better Listening and Speaking

Using Context Clues page 163

Conversation 1

A: Have you ever heard of Esperanto?

B: Huh?

A: Esperanto. It's a language.

B: Really? I've never heard of it. Where is it spoken?

A: Lots of places. According to this article, it's actually an artificial language; it was invented in 1887 by a man from Poland.

B: That's interesting. So who speaks this language now?

A: Well, it says here that there may be as many as 15 million people who speak Esperanto as a second language.

B: What does *Esperanto* mean, anyway? It doesn't sound like Polish.

A: It's not. The vocabulary of Esperanto comes from lots of different languages. Esperanto means "hope" in Latin.

B: Well, I hope I never have to learn it. It's hard enough trying to learn English.

Question 1: What is Esperanto?

Question 2: Where did the woman get her information about Esperanto?

Question 3: Which of the following is probably true about Esperanto?

Conversation 2

A: Look, there's a beehive under the roof.

B: I guess we'd better call an exterminator.

A: Yeah, you're right . . . But I really don't want to kill them. Did you know bees can communicate with one another?

B: Really? How?

A: They use body language to show where food is, how far away it is, and how much food is available.

B: No kidding . . .

A: Yeah, see that one there? See how she's going around and around in circles, like she's dancing? That means food is nearby. If the food is farther away, the bee points to it with her body. And the faster she dances, the more food is available.

B: How do you know so much about bees?

A: I took an entomology class in college. I was a biology major, and I thought it would be interesting to learn something about bugs.

Question 4: Why does the man want to call an exterminator?

Question 5: Which information about food is *not* conveyed by the bee's body language?

Question 6: What is entomology?

Conversation 3

Man: Why are you talking to your computer?

Woman: I'm not talking to it. I'm giving a dictation.

Man: What do you mean?

Woman: It's this great software program. It understands what I'm saying and writes down the words.

Man: Wow. So you don't have to type at all?

Woman: No, that's the point. I'm a slow typist, so this program is a lifesaver.

Man: Can I try it?

Woman: Well, first you have to train the computer to recognize your voice.

Man: Oh. Why?

Woman: Because everybody's pronunciation is different. If it doesn't know your voice, it makes mistakes.

Man: I see. I should get one of these for my computer. I have three term papers due this month.

Question 7: Why does the woman use this software program?

Question 8: What will the man probably do next?

Question 9: What is probably true about this computer program?

1 Understanding Interjections page 165

Conversation 1

Student: Can we use a dictionary on the test?

Teacher: Uh-huh.

Conversation 2

Mother: Here, let me brush your hair.

Child: Ouch! Not so hard!

Conversation 3

Father: Could you please carry this bag of groceries into the house? Be careful; it's heavy.

Son: Sure . . . oops! Sorry.

Conversation 4

A: The computer is down because of a virus that crashed the hard drive.

B: Huh?

Conversation 5

A: I'm expecting an important letter. Has the mail arrived yet?

B: Uh-uh.

Conversation 6

A: Did you remember to buy stamps when you went to the post office?

B: Uh-oh.

Part 4 Real-World Task: Spelling Bee

2 Identifying Spellings page 168

Teacher: Our contestants in today's spelling bee are Jack, Marisa, Yolanda, Evan, and Tony. As you know, I will say the word and then say it in a sentence. Are you ready to begin?

All: Ready. Yes.

Teacher: All right. The first word is for Tony. The word is *tries*. "He always tries to do a good job."

Tony: Tries. OK, T-R-I-E-S.

Teacher: Correct. All right. The next word is for Jack. Your word is *choose*. "Which flavor ice cream will you choose?"

Jack: Choose. C-H-O-S-E.

Teacher: I'm sorry, but that is wrong. The correct spelling of *choose* is C-H-O-O-S-E. Good try, Jack. OK, the next word goes to Marisa. Your word is *effect*. "Jogging has a good effect on our health."

Marisa: Effect. E-F-F-E-C-T.

Teacher: Right! Marisa, you stay in the game. The next word is for Evan. Your word is *quizzes*. "We had two grammar quizzes last week."

Evan: OK, quizzes. Uh, Q-U-I-Z-Z-E-S.

Teacher: Yes, that's right. Now, for Yolanda, your word is *succeed*. "You must study hard if you want to succeed."

Yolanda: Hmm. Succeed. S-U-C-C-E-D-E.

Teacher: I'm sorry, Yolanda, that's wrong. It's S-U-C-C-E-E-D. Good try. OK, let's see who's still in the game: Marisa, Evan, and Tony. Are you ready for the second round?

All: Yes, yeah, let's go.

Teacher: OK, Tony. Your word is *ninety*. "The shoes cost ninety dollars."

Tony: N-I-N-E-T-Y. Ninety.

Teacher: You're right! Well done. The next word is for Marisa. *Analyze*. "After a test, you should analyze your mistakes."

Marisa: Wow, that's hard. OK: A-N-A-L-I-Z-E. Analyze.

Teacher: Sorry, Marisa. It's A-N-A-L-Y-Z-E. Please sit down. Evan, you're next. Your word is *possibility*. "There is a possibility of snow tonight."

Evan: Possibility. OK. P-O-S-S-I-B-I-L-I-T-Y.

Teacher: Great! OK, it's down to Tony and Evan. First Tony. Your word is *mysterious*. "During the night we heard mysterious noises."

Tony: Um, M-I-S-T-E-R-I-O-U-S. I think.

Teacher: Oh no, that's not correct. It's M-Y-S-T-E-R-I-O-U-S. You almost got it. Well, that leaves Evan. If you spell this word correctly, you'll be the winner today. The last word is *lightning*. "We were scared by the thunder and lightning."

Evan: L-I-G-H-T-N-I-N-G. Lightning.

Teacher: Right! Congratulations, Evan! You're our winner today.

Chapter 8 Tastes and Preferences

Part 1 Conversation: What Do You Like to Do for Fun?

3 Comprehension Questions page 175

4 Listening for Stressed Words page 176

Jeff: Come in!

Dan: Hi.

Jeff: Hey, Dan, how ya doin'?

Dan: Great, thanks. Hey, I burned you some new CDs.

Jeff: Cool.

Dan: Hi. You were at our show last night, right?

Mari: Yeah, I was.

Jeff: Sorry, Mari, this is Dan. Dan, this is Mari.

Mari: It's nice to meet you.

Dan: Nice to meet you, too.

Jeff: Oh, let me get that. I'll be right back.

Dan: OK. So, Mari, did you have a good time at the club last night?

Mari: Yeah, it was pretty wild.

Dan: What did you think of our band?

Mari: Well, your music is great for dancing, but to tell you the truth, it was kind of loud. I guess I really prefer jazz.

Dan: Do you go to concerts much?

Mari: No, not very often. I can't afford them. They're so expensive!

Dan: Yeah, I know what you mean. Well, what do you like to do for fun?

Mari: I love to eat! I love going to different ethnic restaurants and trying new dishes.

Dan: What's your favorite kind of food?

Mari: Well, Japanese, of course. What about you?

Dan: Well, I'm not crazy about sushi or sashimi. But I really like Mexican food.

Mari: Ooh, I can't stand beans, and I don't like cheese. Uh . . . What about Indian food?

Dan: I don't care for it. Too spicy. Um . . . do you like American food? You know, hamburgers, hot dogs, French fries . . .

Mari: Yuck! All that fat and salt and sugar . . . We don't see eye to eye on anything, do we?

Dan: Well, let's see. What's your opinion of modern art? There's a wonderful show at the county museum right now.

Mari: To be honest, I don't get the modern stuff. I prefer 19th century art, you know, Monet, van Gogh, Renoir.

Dan: Hmm. How do you feel about sports? Are you interested in football?

Mari: American football? I hate it!

Dan: Basketball?

Mari: It's OK.

Dan: How about tall musicians with curly hair?

Mari: It depends.

Dan: OK, I got it. How about tall musicians with curly hair who invite you to a movie?

Mari: Science fiction?

Dan: Sounds great!

Mari: Finally we agree on something!

5 Listening for Reductions page 177

1. *A:* Do you like Chinese food?
   B: Not really.
   A: Japanese?

2. *A:* Whew! What a day!
   B: Tired?

3. *A:* Anybody home?
   B: I'm here. I'm in the kitchen.

4. *A:* I guess it's time to go.
   B: Leaving already?

5. *A:* Does he have a wife?
   B: Yes.
   A: Kids?

Part 2   Radio Interview: Generation Y

5 Taking Notes (Part I) page 182

6 Rewriting Your Notes page 182

Host: Dr. Harris, thank you for joining us today.

Dr. Harris: My pleasure.

Host: To begin, could you tell us the meaning of the term "Generation Y"?

Dr. Harris: Sure. Generation Y refers to young Americans who were born between the late 1970s and the early 1990s, uh, that is between 1977 or 1978 and 1993 or 1994. In other words, the youngest ones are still teenagers, and the oldest ones are young adults. And there are more than 70 million of them.

Host: Is that number significant?

Dr. Harris: It is extremely significant. Generation Y is the second-largest generation in U.S. history, and by the year 2020 it will be the largest. So this generation is the future market for almost all consumer brands. Marketers know they have to stay in touch with this generation if they want their products to succeed.

Host: What are some of the most important characteristics of this generation?

Dr. Harris: Well, first let me give you some statistics, OK? One-fourth, that is one in four people in this generation, grew up in single-parent homes. Three-fourths, I mean 75 percent, have mothers who work. And one-third are not Caucasian. To put it another way, this is the most diverse generation in U.S. history.

Host: Would you say they are tolerant?

Dr. Harris: Very tolerant. Also optimistic, confident, independent, and . . . rich!

Host: Rich? Explain that.

Dr. Harris: OK. Here are some more statistics: According to a study by the Harris company, members of Generation Y have total incomes of $211 billion a year. These kids spend an average of $30 on every trip to the mall. And if you have teenagers, you know that this generation practically lives at the mall.

7 Taking Notes (Part II) page 184

Host: Two hundred and eleven billion. That's an incredible amount of money. What do they spend it on?

Dr. Harris: Fashion, fast food, movies, CDs, electronics, concert tickets. Generation Y-ers like to have fun.

Host: Are there special brands that this generation prefers?

Dr. Harris: No, not in the way that their parents preferred Levis jeans or SUVs. Generation Y-ers like anything that's hip or hot at the moment, but that can change very fast.

Host: So what do marketers need to know if they want to sell to this group?

Dr. Harris: I think the main thing to remember is that this is the Internet generation, the generation of Instant Messaging. They have grown up with the media, so they are very smart shoppers. They don't like traditional advertising techniques. And as I said, they are not loyal to specific brands. And they love fads, like right now graphic T-shirts and flip-flops are totally in.

Host: Is Generation Y found only in the U.S. or is it in other countries as well?

Dr. Harris: Generation Y is actually an international phenomenon, although it has different characteristics in different countries. In Eastern Europe, for example, it's the first generation to grow up without communism. And in other countries like, oh, Korea and Greece, this is the first generation to grow up with a high standard of living. These young people want to be modern. I mean they are not interested in the traditional way of life. Also, they identify more closely with the West, and that can cause conflict between them and the generations that came before them.

Host: Dr. Harris, before we conclude, may I ask you a personal question?

Dr. Harris: Go ahead.

Host: What generation are you?

Dr. Harris: I'm a baby boomer, born in 1960. But my daughter, who was born in 1984, is Generation Y. And believe it or not, she loves listening to my old Beatles records.

Host: No kidding. Dr. Harris, this has been very interesting. Thank you for being with us today.

Dr. Harris: You're welcome.

Part 3 Strategies for Better Listening and Speaking

2 Distinguishing Among *Do, Does,* and *Did* page 188

1. Do you have time to eat lunch?
2. Does he play the piano?
3. Did they need help?
4. Do I look like my sister?
5. Did she understand the instructions?
6. Do we sound good?
7. Did they own a house?
8. Do we need to rewrite the composition?

1. Did he decide to take the job?

2. When do we eat?

3. Do I have to rewrite this composition?

4. Where did we park the car?

5. Do they know what to do?

6. Did she miss the bus again?

7. Do you usually walk to school?

8. Did you remember to turn off the light?

Using Context Clues page 189

Conversation 1

Woman: Look at that! Isn't it interesting? I love the colors and shapes.

Man: What's it supposed to be?

Woman: It's not supposed to "be" anything. It's modern. Don't try to analyze it.

Man: Well how much does it cost?

Woman: Let's see. Five thousand dollars. What do you think?

Question 1: What are the speakers talking about?

Man: Five thousand dollars? For *that* painting? I don't think so.

Conversation 2

Woman: Don't wear the brown one.

Man: Why not? What's wrong with it?

Woman: Well, it doesn't go with your suit. Brown and black don't look good together.

Man: Well, what if I wear it with my other suit?

Question 2: What are the man and woman talking about?

Woman: No, you should just wear a different tie. I don't really like brown anyway.

Conversation 3

A: Do you want to try it? It's really fun!

B: No thanks. It's too cold and windy. And honestly, I'm not crazy about the idea of flying down a mountain on one thin piece of wood.

A: But that's the fun part!

Question 3: What sport are the people talking about?

A: I'm sorry, snowboarding isn't for me. I'd rather stay inside by the fire.

Conversation 4

Teen Girl: You colored your hair.

Teen Boy: Yeah, I finally did it. Do you like it?

Girl: Uh, you look so . . . different.

Boy: What do you mean, "different"?

Question 4: How does the girl feel about the boy's hair?

Girl: Uh, I'm not crazy about it. Sorry.

Conversation 5

Teen Girl: You colored your hair!

Teen Boy: Yeah, I finally did it. Do you like it?

Girl: You look so different!

Boy: What do you mean, "different"?

Question 5: How does the girl feel about the boy's hair?

Girl: I love it! It's so cool!

Part 4   Real-World Task: Choosing Someone to Date

2 **Comparing People's Qualities** page 192

I don't know what to do. Katherine and Jean are both wonderful women. So how am I supposed to choose between them? Take Katherine. We went to the same high school and college, and my parents are crazy about her. Also, Katherine is very intelligent, and she's interesting to talk with; we spend hours discussing art and politics and books.

Now Jean is also very smart, but she's much quieter than Katherine. It's not as easy to talk to her. But even though she's quiet, she's crazy about sports, just like me, and she has a great sense of humor; I mean, she tells the funniest jokes, and I love the way she laughs. On the other hand, Katherine is sometimes too sensitive; what I mean is, she doesn't understand that I'm just joking, so she gets offended.

And another thing I don't like about Katherine is that she's not good at managing money. She has a very good job and a good salary, but somehow she never seems to have any money! That's not very responsible, is it? But Jean is great with money. She even insists on sharing the cost of our dates.

On the other hand, I want to have children, but Jean says she's not sure. That could be a problem later on. Katherine loves kids, but sometimes she has a bad temper; she gets angry whenever I'm five minutes late!

I'm really confused. Katherine and Jean—they're so different and I really like them both. But you know, I don't know if either one is serious about me anyway. What do you think I should do?

Chapter 9 New Frontiers

Part 1 Conversation: To Clone or Not to Clone?

3 **Comprehension Questions** Page 199

4 **Listening for Stressed Words** Page 200

Mari: Your dog is so adorable, Nancy. How old is he?

Nancy: Eleven.

Mari: Wow, that's pretty old.

Nancy: Yeah. I just love him so much. I don't know what I'll do when he's gone.

Mari: Well, you can clone him, you know.

Nancy: Clone him? You're joking, right?

Mari: Yeah, of course. But actually, it is possible. Scientists in Korea have cloned a dog, you know; I saw a picture of it in *Time* magazine.

Nancy: Really? I've heard of cloned sheep and mice and rabbits. But not pets like dogs.

Andrew: Oh, yeah. Believe it or not, there is a company in California that offers a pet cloning service. For $15,000, you can have an exact copy of your pet.

Nancy: That's so weird. Actually, it kind of scares me. Pretty soon, they'll start cloning people, and then . . .

Andrew: Nah, I don't think that's going to happen. I think cloning will be used in positive ways.

Nancy: Like what?

Andrew: Like saving endangered species. For example, scientists could save the giant panda and other animals before they become extinct.

Mari: Oh, yeah, and another thing. I heard that scientists will be able to clone body parts. You know, just grow a new heart, or a new tooth.

Andrew: Uh-huh. That's what stem cell research is all about, which is similar to cloning. A lot of medical problems are going to be solved with that for sure.

Nancy: Well, I'm all for that. Especially if it can help us live longer.

Mari: Or if they can help your dog live longer, right?

Nancy: Right!

Part 2 Lecture: Exploring Mars

3 **Listening for Fact and Theory in the Lecture** page 205

1. It's a well-known fact that Mars, just like Earth, has clouds, winds, roughly a 24-hour day, four seasons, volcanoes, canyons, and other familiar features.

2. It's possible that there was some kind of life there thousands of years ago.

3. Scientists know there was water on Mars from analyzing the surface of the rocks where the Mars rovers landed.

4. There's a chance that some form of life existed and perhaps still does exist on Mars.

5. The ability to live on another planet may become necessary in the future.

6. There are possibly more than eight other planets in our solar system.

4 Taking Notes and Outlining (Part I)

page 206

The planet Mars has fascinated people since ancient times, and that fascination has continued to this day. In fact, these days Mars is again receiving a lot of attention. If you watch the news, you probably already know that several countries have announced plans to put humans on Mars. Both the United States space agency—NASA— and the European space agency—ESA—plan to do this by the year 2030. So what's so fascinating about Mars? Why explore Mars and not other planets? After all, there are possibly more than eight other planets in our solar system. What makes Mars so attractive to explore? That's what I want to talk about today.

OK. To begin with, Mars is the second closest planet to Earth. It's our closest neighbor after Venus. And for this reason, it's easy to see in the night sky. Second, Mars is similar to Earth in several ways. It's a well-known fact that Mars, just like Earth, has clouds, winds, a roughly 24-hour day, four seasons, volcanoes, canyons, and other familiar features.

Because of these similarities between Earth and Mars, the obvious question, of course, is "Is there life on Mars?" Well, we don't know. Most scientists think there isn't, but—and this is an important but—it's possible that there was *some kind* of life there thousands of years ago. Why do scientists think so? Well, in 2003, a critical discovery was made. Scientists found some very strong evidence that Mars had water, actually a lot of water, some time in the past. They know this from analyzing the surface of the rocks where the Mars rovers landed. And the surface shows that there most probably was a large body of water there, probably salty seawater.

Now this discovery, that there was water on Mars in the past, is critical because without water life cannot exist. And if there was water on Mars, then there's the possibility of life also. In other words, there's a chance that a long time ago some form of life existed on Mars.

5 Taking Notes and Outlining (Part II)

page 207

Now, while this is an exciting discovery for most of us, some people still ask, "So what? Why should we care? How does this benefit us right here on Earth?" Well, there are lots of ways that we could benefit. First, by exploring Mars, we might be able to find out things about Earth such as why and how life formed here. Second, we might also find that Mars could be a place for people to live in the future. The ability to live on another planet may become necessary in the future—after all, we have limited space, and limited resources here on Earth, right? And finally, we might need someplace else to live in case of a global disaster—you know—a natural disaster or a nuclear war.

So yes, it makes a lot of sense to continue to explore Mars. Not only because human beings have always done that, have always explored new areas, new frontiers of their own knowledge, but also because this specific planet, Mars, seems to be very much like our own earth and therefore holds so many possibilities for the future. As I said earlier, Mars is our neighbor, and it's time we go over and say hello.

Part 3 Strategies for Better Listening and Speaking

Using Context Clues page 210

Passage 1

What is the difference between a discovery and an invention? Well, we discover things that were always there. For example, you often hear that Columbus discovered America. In contrast, people invent things that did not exist before. Long ago someone invented ships, for instance. Discovery and invention are often related because many discoveries are made with the help of inventions. As an example, Columbus used ships to sail to America.

Question 1: What can we infer from this passage?

Passage 2

The ancient Greeks used the energy of the sun to heat their homes. Later, the Romans followed this example and used solar power to heat baths, houses, and greenhouses. The Native Americans were also early users of the sun's energy. Nowadays car manufacturers are developing cars that will run only on solar power.

Question 2: What can we conclude about the use of solar energy?

Passage 3

During the Middle Ages, the people of Europe used the Roman numerals one through ten for basic math such as adding and subtracting. However, the Roman system did not have a number for zero. That made adding and subtracting very hard. Three centuries earlier Arabic people had invented another kind of numbering system, the one we use today, which had a zero. This system was brought to Europe in the 12th century and quickly became popular. Today, Arabic numbers are used universally in mathematics. In contrast, Roman numerals are used only on clock faces—and in outlines!

Question 3: What can we infer about the invention of the number zero?

Passage 4

Shang Yeng was the emperor of China almost 5,000 years ago. For health reasons, he ordered his people to boil their water before drinking it. One day Shang Yeng himself was boiling water outside when some leaves from a bush fell into the large open pot. Before he could remove the leaves, they began to cook. The mixture smelled so good that Shang Yeng decided to taste it. In this way tea was accidentally discovered.

Question 4: What can we conclude about the discovery of tea?

Passage 5

Rubber is an old discovery. When Columbus arrived in the New World, he saw boys playing with balls made from the hardened juice of a tree. Later, in 1736, a Frenchman working in Peru noticed people wearing shoes and clothes made from the same material. In 1770, an English scientist used the material to rub out his writing mistakes. He named the material "rubber."

Question 5: What can we infer from the passage?

3 Distinguishing Among *-ed* Endings
page 213

1. laughed
2. described
3. rented
4. stopped
5. changed
6. ended
7. helped
8. studied
9. invented
10. danced
11. realized
12. crowded
13. worked
14. listened
15. answered

Part 4 Real-World Task: A Game Show

2 Listening to a Game Show page 216

Host: Good evening and welcome to our show! I'm your host, Ronnie Perez. In this game, members of the audience compete with our contestant to answer questions about explorations, inventions, and discoveries. When you hear a question, select your answer from the choices on your answer ballot. Our contestant will do the same. Then we'll see who has the correct answer!

Now let's meet our contestant. He is Roger Johnson from Ottawa, Canada. Roger, as you know, you may continue to play as long as you give correct answers. One wrong answer, however, and the game is over. Are you ready to play?

Roger: I'm ready, Ronnie.

Host: Then here's our first question. For $1,000, what is the name of the computer company that created the first personal computer? Was it

a. Apple,

b. Microsoft, or

c. Intel?

Members of the audience, select your answer. Is it Apple, Microsoft, or Intel?

OK, audience?

Audience: Apple!

Host: Roger, do you agree?

Roger: Yes I do, Ronnie. It's Apple.

Host: You are right! Well done! Let's go to question number 2. For $2,000: George Mallory, Sir Edmund Hillary, and Tensing Norgay all reached the top of which famous mountain? Was it

    a. Mt. Everest in Nepal,

    b. Mt. Fuji in Japan, or

    c. Mt. Whitney in the United States?

Members of the audience, select your answer. Audience?

Audience: Everest!

Host: Roger? Your answer?

Roger: Everest. Absolutely.

Host: And that is correct. Good work so far, but as you know, our questions become more difficult as we continue playing. Here's question number 3. Marco Polo, who traveled throughout China at the end of the 13th century, was a native of which country? For $3,000, was it

    a. Spain,

    b. Portugal, or

    c. Italy?

First let's turn to our audience . . .

And what is your answer, audience?

Audience: Spain! Italy!

Host: Roger, is it Spain or Italy? Which did you pick?

Roger: It's Italy, Ronnie.

Host: You sound very confident. Is it Italy? . . . Yes! You're on a roll now, Roger. Ready for the next question?

Roger: Ready, Ronnie.

Host: Here it is. In which country was gunpowder invented? For $4,000, was it

    a. Italy,

    b. Egypt, or

    c. China?

Choose your answers, please, audience. Gunpowder was invented where?

Audience, what is your answer?

Audience: Egypt! China!

Host: Roger?

Roger: Gosh, this one is difficult. I'm pretty sure it wasn't Italy, but I'm not sure about Egypt or China . . . hmmm . . . OK, I'm going to say China.

Host: Egypt or China? Let's take a look . . . It's China! Well done, Roger! How do you feel now?

Roger: Relieved. I really wasn't sure that time.

Host: Well, let's see if you can do it again, for $5,000 this time. In 1928, Alexander Fleming of England discovered this natural substance, which is still used today to kill bacteria and fight infections. What is the name of the substance? Is it

    a. penicillin,

    b. aspirin, or

    c. ginseng?

Audience members, please choose your answer.

OK, Members of the audience, what do you say? Is it penicillin, aspirin, or ginseng?

Audience: Penicillin!

Host: Do you agree, Roger?

Roger: I sure do, Ronnie. It's penicillin.

Host: Are you right? . . . Yes! The answer is penicillin. Let's see if we can give you something a little more difficult. Are you ready, Roger?

Roger: Yes, sir.

Host: For $6,000, which of the following was *not* invented by the American inventor Thomas Alva Edison. Was it

    a. the motion picture,

    b. the telephone, or

    c. the lightbulb?

Let's give the audience a moment to decide . . .

And what is your answer?

Audience: Telephone! Motion pictures! Lightbulb!

Host: It sounds like the audience is not sure this time. How about you, Roger?

Roger: Oh, I'm very sure. It's the telephone.

Host: Right again! The telephone was invented by Alexander Graham Bell, not Thomas Edison. Now, Roger, so far you have won $21,000, and we've reached the last question of the game. We're going to give you a choice: you can go home right now with $21,000, or you can answer one more question. If you answer it correctly, we'll double your money! Of course if you get it wrong, you go home with nothing. What would you like to do?

Roger: I'll . . . go for the question, Ronnie.

Host: He'll go for the question! Very well. For a chance at taking home $42,000, here it is. Five hundred years ago people believed that the earth was the center of the universe and that the sun revolved around the earth. In the year 1543, a Polish astronomer published a book showing that the opposite is true; that the sun is the center of our solar system, and all the planets go around it. For $42,000, Roger, what was the name of that astronomer? Was it

   a. Isaac Newton,

   b. Galileo Galilei, or

   c. Nicolaus Copernicus?

Members of the audience, what is your answer?

Audience?

Audience: Galileo! Copernicus! Newton!

Host: Hmmm, no agreement there. Roger Johnson, did you pick the right answer? Who is it?

Roger: Well, uh, let me see. Um, Galileo was Italian, and I'm pretty sure Newton was English. So that leaves Copernicus.

Host: Is that your final answer?

Roger: Yes, it is.

Host: Is he right? For $42,000, the correct answer is . . . Copernicus! Roger Johnson, you have won it all! Congratulations! And that concludes our show for this evening. Please join us next week . . .

Chapter 10 Ceremonies

Part 1 Conversation: A Baby Shower

3 Comprehension Questions page 223

4 Listening for Stressed Words page 224

Mari: Hi Jeff. Hi Sharon. Look what I got in the mail.

Jeff: Hey.

Sharon: Hi, Mari.

Jeff: "Join us for a baby shower honoring Nancy Anderson, April 5th, 11 A.M. . . . hosted by Sharon Smith and Carolyn Freeman . . . "

Sharon: Oh good, you got the invitation. So can you make it?

Mari: I think so, but, well, what is a baby shower exactly?

Jeff: You know, it's a party for a woman who's going to have a baby. Um, it's like a welcoming ceremony for the new baby.

Mari: It's a party? Then why do you call it a "shower"?

Jeff: Because the custom is to *shower* the woman with gifts for the baby. Get it?

Mari: I see. Are you invited too, Jeff?

Jeff: No way! No men allowed!

Mari: Really?

Sharon: Well, not exactly. Lots of baby showers include men these days, but traditionally showers are hosted by a woman's girlfriends or female relatives, and they're only for women.

Mari: Hmm. But isn't Nancy and Andrew's baby due at the end of May? And this invitation says April 5th.

Sharon: Well, yes. The custom is to have a shower before the baby is born, when the woman is seven or eight months pregnant.

Mari: Very interesting. And everybody brings a gift?

Sharon: Right. Something for the baby: You know, toys or clothes or something for the baby's room.

Mari: OK. The invitation says it's for lunch, so . . .

Sharon: Yeah, we'll have lunch, and afterwards we'll play games.

Mari: Games? What kind of games?

Jeff: Girl games.

Sharon: Silly games like bingo, or guessing games, or baby trivia games. And the winners get small prizes.

Mari: It sounds like fun.

Sharon: It is. And then, at the end of the party, there's usually a cake with baby decorations, and then the mother-to-be opens her presents.

Mari: While the guests are still there?

Sharon: Sure. That's my favorite part! Everybody gets to see the gifts.

Jeff: And go "oooh, aaah . . ."

Sharon: And see how happy the woman is.

Mari: Wow. That's so different from our custom. In Japan we usually don't open a gift in front of guests.

Sharon: Really? That is different.

Mari: Well what kind of gift do you think I should get for her?

Sharon: She's registered online, so you can see what she's already gotten and what she still needs. Would you like me to write down the Internet address for you?

Mari: Sure, that would be great. Uh, is there anything I can do to help with the party? Maybe do the flower arrangements or something?

Sharon: Oh, thanks, but it's not necessary. Everything is all taken care of. Just come and have fun.

Part 2 Lecture: Water in Traditional Ceremonies

3 Recognizing Digressions page 231

So I thought I'd focus on that today: the role of water in celebrations around the world.

Let's take Thailand as an example. I'll never forget my first time there. It was April, the hottest part of the year. And by the way, Thailand doesn't have four seasons like we do here. Um, depending on which part of the country you're in, there are three seasons, the dry season from November to February, the hot season from March to June, and the rainy season from about July to October. Um, so anyway, back to our topic, I was walking down the street in the small village where I lived and suddenly, two teenagers walked past me and as they did, they threw water on me! I was kind of shocked but didn't really mind because it was so hot. Then I realized that it was the 13th, which is Songkran, the Water Festival in Thailand. On that day, people throw water on each other, and also wash

the hands of their elders with scented water. It's a custom based on the belief that water will wash away bad luck.

4 Taking Notes page 231

5 Outlining the Lecture page 231

Host: And now I'd like to introduce our speaker, Josh Harrison. Josh has just returned from his latest overseas assignment as a Peace Corps volunteer. He's served in at least three different countries and has traveled to many more than that; that's why I thought he'd be the perfect speaker for today's topic: ceremonies and celebrations around the world. Welcome, Josh.

Speaker: Thank you, Diane. And thanks for inviting me. Well, I've thought about the topic and I thought, gosh, how am I going to narrow this down? I mean, I have seen and participated in so many fascinating celebrations in many different cultures. Then I remembered something I noticed just recently: Even though the cultures I experienced were completely different, many of their ceremonies had something interesting in common: the use of water. Yeah, water. Some ceremonies involve drinking the water, some involve pouring it, and some involve dunking or going under water. To me, that was a very interesting discovery. So I thought I'd focus on that today: the role of water in celebrations around the world.

Let's take Thailand as an example. I'll never forget my first time there. It was April, the hottest part of the year. And by the way, Thailand doesn't have four seasons like we do here. Um, depending on which part of the country you're in, there are three seasons, the dry season from November to February, the hot season from March to June, and the rainy season from about July to October. Um, so anyway, back to our topic, I was walking down the street in the small village where I lived and suddenly, two teenagers walked past me and as they did, they threw water on me! I was kind of shocked but didn't really mind because it was so hot. Then I realized that it was the 13th, which is Songkran, the Water Festival in Thailand. On that day, people throw water on each other, and also wash the hands of their elders with scented water. It's a custom based on the belief that water will wash away bad luck.

Now, this idea of washing away bad things, of cleansing or purifying, is also found in Islamic cultures. For example, when I lived in Saudi Arabia, I learned that traditional Muslims pray five times a day, and before they do, they always wash their faces, hands, and feet with water. And the water has to be very clean and pure. This ritual washing symbolizes the removal of sin and disease, in other words, the cleansing of both body and soul, before speaking to God.

All right, now, another religion where water plays an important role is Christianity. And one particular ritual that comes to mind is baptism. Baptism is a ceremony that welcomes a new baby into the Christian religion and the community. Now, since there are many branches of Christianity, there are also many different ways that baptism can be performed. When I lived in Latin America, I attended several Catholic baptisms. And what they do is they bring the baby to the church, where a priest pours or sprinkles some water on the baby's head. This water symbolizes the washing away of sin—somewhat similar to the meaning in Islam. And then, while pouring the water, the priest says a prayer and tells the parents to raise the baby as a good Christian.

So as you can see, water has different symbolic meanings in different cultures. In some cultures it's believed to keep away bad luck, as in Thailand. In Islamic and Christian cultures it's used to purify and wash away sin. Water has rich symbolism in nearly all cultures. So now I'd like to know what you think and see if you can share some of your own traditions. How does water play a part in celebrations in *your* culture?

Part 3 Strategies for Better Listening and Speaking

Using Context Clues page 234

Conversation 1

Man 1: And now, on behalf of our entire staff, I'd like to present this gold watch to Mr. Harry Kim and express our appreciation for 35 years of dedicated service to our company. Congratulations, Mr. Kim!

Mr. Kim: Thank you, Mr. President. All I can say is, it's been a pleasure working with you all these years. This company has been like a second family to me.

Man 1: What are you going to do with your time from now on?

Mr. Kim: I'm going to play a lot of golf, work in my garden, and visit my grandchildren.

Conversation 2

Woman: Well, that was a very moving service. And I've never seen so many flowers. She sure had a lot of friends.

Man: Yep. And the minister spoke beautifully, didn't he? I'm sure it was a comfort to the family.

Woman: I am really going to miss Myra. She was a good neighbor and a good friend.

Man: I can't imagine what Ralph is going to do without her. They were married, what, 40 years?

Woman: Something like that, yes. Poor Ralph.

Conversation 3

Girl: Here they come! Look Mommy, there's Shawna!

Mother: Where?

Girl: She's walking in behind that really tall guy, see?

Mother: Oh yes, yes, I see her. Doesn't she look elegant in her cap and gown, honey? So grown up . . .

Girl: What's going to happen now?

Father: After everyone sits down there'll be speeches, and then they'll give out the diplomas.

Mother: I can't believe that three months from now our little girl is going to be starting college.

Father: I know. Where did the time go?

Conversation 4

Daughter: And now I'd like to propose a toast. To my parents, Lena and Richard: May your next thirty years together be as happy and prosperous as the first thirty have been. Thanks for being an inspiration to us all. Cheers!

All: Cheers! Congratulations!

Father: Thank you, Betsy, and thank you all for coming out to celebrate with us on this happy occasion. You're the best group of friends anyone ever had and we're very grateful. And now *I'd* like to propose a toast: To my wife Lena, who's as beautiful today as she was on our first date more than 30 years ago. To you, darling!

All: Cheers!

Conversation 5

Mother: How are the plans coming?

Daughter: I met with the caterer yesterday and tomorrow we'll order the flowers. We have the rings, and oh, my dress will be ready next Wednesday.

Mother: What about the band for the reception?

Daughter: We hired them months ago. And we ordered the cake too.

Mother: Speaking of cake . . . you and Robert aren't going to shove cake in each other's faces, are you?

Daughter: No, Mom, don't worry.

2 Recognizing the Meaning of Affirmative Tag Questions page 235

1. Alia didn't forget to buy flowers again, did she?

2. That wasn't a very long ceremony, was it?

3. We don't need to bring a present, do we?

4. You're not going to wear that shirt to the party, are you?

5. There aren't many people here, are there?

6. You're not bringing your dog, are you?

7. The wedding hasn't started yet, has it?

8. You didn't like the party, did you?

Part 4 Real-World Task: Making Wedding Plans

2 Taking Notes on Wedding Preferences page 240

Katsu

Consultant: OK, Katsu, to get started, why don't you look at this list for the wedding ceremony, and let me just ask you first of all if there are any items that you have really strong feelings about, like you absolutely must do this or you absolutely refuse to do that . . .

Katsu: Hmm . . . Well, I really don't want a religious service. I think a big, traditional American service would be very strange for my parents. So I'd prefer to get married outdoors, in a garden or something, and have a justice of the peace perform the service.

Consultant: OK. Have you and Sandra discussed a date?

Katsu: Not an exact date but we agree that we'd like to do it in April or May.

Consultant: Got it. What else?

Katsu: I'd like it small, just our families and close friends. And informal. I don't want to wear a tuxedo, and I don't want bridesmaids and all those extra people. I think it would be nice if each of us walked in with our parents and that's it. I really want to honor my parents at my wedding.

Consultant: OK, Katsu, obviously you know that Sandra's family is Christian and they've been in America for generations. So let me ask you, is there anything from that tradition that you really like and would want to include in your ceremony?

Katsu: Let's see . . . Well I'm sure Sandra will want to wear a white dress and that's fine. And, um, well, I don't like organ music, but maybe we could have a flute and a violin, something soft like that.

Consultant: And what about Japanese culture? Is there something you'd like to include from that?

Katsu: Wow. That's a hard question. I've never been to a traditional Japanese wedding. But I know that in Japan purple is, like, the color of love, so maybe Sandra could carry purple flowers.

Sandra

Consultant: OK, Sandra, to start off I'm going to ask you the same question I asked Katsu. Look at this list of items in a typical wedding ceremony and tell me if there's anything you feel very strongly about.

Sandra: Well, I've always dreamed of having a big traditional wedding, you know, in a church, with an organ playing, and bridesmaids and groomsmen, and a beautiful white dress. But that was before I met Katsu. His family isn't

Christian, you know, and my family's not *super* religious either, so maybe we could have a garden wedding instead of a church wedding. But I'd like my family's minister to perform the service, and I definitely want my father to walk me down the aisle, and I want my little cousin to be our flower girl. I guess the most important thing is to be able to include everybody. My family is huge, and I want to invite them all.

Consultant: So you want to wear a white dress.

Sandra: Of course.

Consultant: And what about Katsu?

Sandra: He hates anything formal. It's fine if he wears a suit.

Consultant: OK, Sandra. Tell me, do you like the color purple?

Sandra: Purple? At a wedding?

Consultant: Katsu suggested you could carry purple flowers. He says that in Japanese culture purple is the color of love.

Sandra: Hmmm . . . purple. That could work. I love irises, and maybe the bridesmaids' dresses could be violet.

Consultant: That sounds like a wonderful idea. What about music?

Sandra: Well, if we're outdoors then we can't have an organ, can we; so, hmmm, how about something soft like classical guitar or flute?

Chapter 1

attend
be into
career
cheating
discussion section
experiment
fail a course
get ahead
get kicked out
laboratory ("lab")
lecture
major in
midterm exam
plagiarism
quiz
requirement
sign up
take notes
teaching assistant
term paper

Chapter 2

alarm
break into
break-in
bug
can't miss
come by
deadbolt
decal
device
front/back (of)
get into the habit
license
make it
never lift a finger
prevent
right
slob
(car) theft
timer
valuables
violent

Chapter 3

an arm and a leg
balance (a checkbook)
balance
brilliant idea
broke
budget
earn
enter
found
have (something) in common
hire
identify
income
interest
make ends meet
pay off
quality
raise capital
solution
solve
surf the Internet
take risks
team
tightwad
vision

Chapter 4

automation
bottom line
category
competition
complain
economy
grow by X%
health care
illness
in the mood
job market
labor costs
manufacturing
rank
salary
service

spend time
support
the worst
trend

Chapter 5

benefit
can/can't afford
check up on
cost of living
day care center
flexibility
flexible
homemaker
look into
maternity leave
old-fashioned
opportunity
policy
run out
take off
transfer
volunteer

Chapter 6

appropriate
blog
bow
catch up on
charge
chopstick
comments
download
embarrassing
headset
hug
illustrate
install (software)
insulted
misunderstanding
No sweat.
post (a message or comment)
sound card

stay in touch
title (of a person)
universal
utensils
variation

Chapter 7

category
catch on
dialect
friendliness
friendship
Have a seat.
identical
in the dark
It's hard to say.
majority
make friends
noticeable
sample
standard
two-faced
unique
while
whereas

Chapter 8

brand
can't stand
Caucasian
confident
conflict (noun)
consumer
developed country
dish
diverse
don't/doesn't care for
have a good time
hip (informal)
I'm crazy about it!
identify with
income
loyal
optimistic
phenomenon
see eye to eye
significant
standard of living
tolerant

Chapter 9

all for
analyze
clone
critical
disaster
endangered species
evidence
explore
extinct
fascinate
fascinating
planet
research
resources
scare
solar system
stem cell
telescope
weird

Chapter 10

allowed
cleanse
due
fascinating
focus on
go ooh and ah
host
involve
mother-to-be
narrow (something) down
play a part in
pour
pray
prayer
pregnant
priest
pure
purify
register
ritual
shower
silly
sin
sprinkle
symbol
symbolism
symbolize

Skills Index